Istanbul
Capital of Three Empires

The European with the Asian shore
Sprinkled with palaces; the ocean stream
Here and there studded with a seventy-four;
Sophia's cupola with golden gleam;
The cypress groves; Olympus high and hoar:
The twelve isles, and the more than I could dream,
Far less describe, present the very view
Which charm'd the charming Mary Montagu.

Lord Byron, 1819

Capital of Three Empires

Istanbul

Archaeologist
İlhan Akşit

akşit

AKŞIT KÜLTÜR VE TURİZM YAYINCILIK

Table of Contents

Published by

AKŞİT KÜLTÜR TURİZM YAYINCILIK

Cağaloğlu Yokuşu, Cemal Nadir Sk. 2/4, 34440 Cağaloğlu / ISTANBUL / TURKEY

Fax : (0 212) 527 68 13

Tel : (0 212) 511 53 85 - 511 67 82

www.aksityayincilik.com - mail: aksit@aksityayincilik.com

Copyright © 2007 Akşit Kültür Turizm Yayıncılık

ISBN: 975 7039 - 007

Director of Publishing : Necdet Akşit
Visual Editor : Zafer Emecan
Translations : Stuart Kline
Editing : Sylvia Zeybekoğlu
Photographs : Kadir Kır, Vasken Değirmentaş, Murat Taner,
Erdal Yazıcı, Güngör Özsoy, İzzet Keribar
Color Separation : Figür Grafik Ltd. Şti.
Printed by : Ohan Matbaacılık Ltd. Şti.
Hadımköy Yolu, Çakmaklı Mah.San.1 Bulvarı
4.Bölge 9.Cad. No:143 Büyükçekmece-İSTANBUL
Tel:(0212) 886 70 70

Appointed ambassador to the Ottoman Empire by German Emperor Charles V, Busbecq once remarked, "It is as if Mother Nature created Istanbul to be the capital of the world." Nature really did demonstrate much generosity in making this place the capital of the Roman, Byzantine and Ottoman Empires — thus giving rise to a cultural accumulation that is unmatched anywhere in the world. One needs to look no further than the skyline created by the most important church in Byzantium, Hagia Sophia, and the masterpiece of Ottoman architecture, the Sultan Ahmed Mosque, with its six minarets projecting upwards, just across the square. Along with what remains from the Roman era — still standing erect in the Hippodrome Square, it will be impossible for visitors to keep from taking a trip back through time as he or she encounters the vestiges of three diverse empires standing virtually right next to one other. The intriguing array of mosques, churches and synagogues, all juxtaposed to one another, creates a fascinating picture of tolerance. Istanbul hence holds a unique place in the world, not only as a city home to many civilizations, but also as one that has served to unify many different religions as well.

In taking in the Chora Museum with its precious Byzantine mosaics and wandering about the complexes (consisting, for example, of mosques, medreses (schools of theology), soup kitchens for the poor and hospitals) that reflect the spender of the Ottomans, one cannot help but experience many different feelings. Strolling through the mosques, tombs, palaces, pavilions and other awe-inspiring structures will undoubtedly take up much of your time, but at the end of your spellbinding journey, Istanbul is bound to make you fall in love with it. Tourists visiting Istanbul for even a short time can have an opportunity to become acquainted with this extraordinary city straddling two continents by touring many of its significant sights.

Though I have written several books about Istanbul, I have always felt that I have left out important aspects of the narrative. This is mostly because it is not really possible to squeeze the capital city of three empires into a few hundred pages. Yet, I know that to discover Istanbul is to get to know the distinct pleasure of Istanbul. I took up writing once again to share this pleasure with you and to enrich this work with fresh photographic images. I wish to thank those who have contributed to my efforts to publish this book that I have worked on with such great pleasure.

İlhan Akşit

The Glory of
the Byzantine Empire

A History of Istanbul

"All other cities are mortal, but Istanbul shall exist as long as humanity." Petrus Gyllius, 1547

The straits we call the "Bosphorus" were formed when seawater filled a deep valley during the IV Geologic Epoch. The name is derived from mythology. According to legend, while the God of Gods, Zeus, is making love to Io, the daughter of King Argos, he is caught in the act by his wife, Hera. Zeus then transforms Io into a cow in order to protect her from Hera's vengeance. Nonetheless, Hera learns of this and infests the cow with a swarm of horseflies. Io the Cow swims across the straits in an effort to save herself from the fly infestation. Thus, the name "Bosphorus," which is a corrupt version of "Bovine Passage," must have derived from this tale.

From artifacts uncovered in the Yarımburgaz Cave in Küçükçekmece, on the European side, as well as the tumuli found in Pendik and Fikirtepe, on the Anatolian side, it is clear that both sides of the 32-kilometer-long straits were settled as far back as the Palaeolithic era. It has also been determined that these settlements continued throughout the Chalcolithic era as well. Nonetheless, the timeframe from the Chalcolithic era until the influx from the Aegean Sea region remains relatively obscure.

Of the legends surrounding the foundation of Byzantium, the predecessor of Constantinople and Istanbul, the most commonly accepted goes like this: The Thracian-based Megarians, who lived near Athens, decided to migrate from their lands with Byzas as their leader in 695 B.C. Prior to setting out on their exodus, they consulted the oracles as to where they might settle down. The oracles suggested to them that they establish roots in the land opposite the "Land of the Blind." Not sure of what this implied, the Megarians explored several roads and finally arrived at a hill on the edge of the Bosphorus. They were enchanted by the extraordinary beauty of the Bosphorus and the Sea of Marmara. In reference to the words of the oracle, they thought that those who had abandoned this spectacular site to establish Chalcedon (modern-day Kadıköy) on the Asian side 17 years before must truly have been blind. They proceeded to establish their new city in the area around today's Sarayburnu, naming their new city

"Byzantium" after their leader Byzas. The advent of trading activity did much to contribute to the expansion of the city. It was embellished with magnificent temples, stadiums and gymnasiums and surrounded by a wall measuring five kilometers and reinforced with 27 towers. These walls stretched as far as the site where Hagia Sophia stands and from here they

Mosaic on the dome of the Chora Monastery Church portrays the figure of Christ (Kariye Museum).

Deesis Mosaic of the Virgin Mary, who was known as the Savior of the City. Hagia Sophia.

reached the sea at Ahırkapı. Temples of Aphrodite, Artemis and Dionysus were erected at the acropolis, while those of Athena and Poseidon were put up along the coast. That of Tyche, the Goddess of Luck, was constructed at a higher location. The city's harbor, Neorion, was situated where modern-day Sirkeci stands.

Records show that there used to be a smaller harbor known as the Bosporion Harbor, located where the Sepetciler Summer Palace is today. Nonetheless, it is best to think of these as separate harbors but as a single one.

While the expansion of Byzantium continued, the Phrygians, who had settled in Anatolia in place of the collapsed Hittite Empire, disappeared from the stage as well, to be replaced by the Lydian State in western Anatolia. When the Lydians were defeated by the Persians in 546 B.C., all of Anatolia came under the domination of the Persians. After the Persian Emperor Darius acquired Anatolia, he mobilized against the Iscits in 512 B.C. to counter any threat emerging from the Balkans. It was during this campaign that Byzantium accepted the domination of the Persians. After advancing as far as the Danube, the Persians put the region under their supervision by establishing suzerainty in Thrace.

In 499 B.C., the Ionians initiated a rebellion against the Persians in Western Anatolia. However, the Persians bloodily suppressed this rebellion and then marched on Athens, which had provided the Ionian cities with the impetus to revolt. Nevertheless, the Persians were forced to retreat after being routed at Plataia in 479 B.C. As a consequence, Ionian and Greek cities regained their freedom and in the following year, the Attica-Delos Federation was established in Athens, Greece with 300 Anatolian and Greek cities to defend themselves against further Persian attacks. Federation forces first achieved superiority over the Persians in Thrace and subsequently put the cities of Chalcedon and Byzantium under the control of the Federation. Meanwhile, the Spartan Commander Pausanias captured Byzantium and held it until 477 B.C. After Pausanias, Byzantium passed into the control of the Athenians, who turned it into a naval base for their fleet.

In utilizing the Byzantine harbors, they in turn, began to apply levies on the merchant vessels of other cities. It was because of this pressure that the federation fell apart. Though Byzantium was to remain independent

Mosaic of St. John the Baptist from the Deesis. Hagia Sophia.

A mosaic in one of the domes of the Kariye Museum that depicts Mary holding Christ, surrounded by His descendents.

for a brief period starting in 411 B.C., it was the Athenian Commander Alcibiades who recaptured Byzantium once more just two years later. This situation made the Spartans very concerned and it was up to Commander Lysandrus, who had defeated the Athenians, to retake Byzantium in 405 B.C. Eventually, Athens and Sparta became extremely worn out fighting each other. In contrast, it was the Macedonian Kingdom that developed into a powerful state, with King Phillip II of Macedonia taking advantage of the situation by expanding his territory. After Europe, he entered Thrace in 340 B.C. and besieged Byzantium following his capture of Marmara Ereğlisi. However, it was not he who was to take Byzantium but rather his successor, the young Alexander the Great, who succeeded in entering Anatolia on his way to establishing a global empire. In eliminating the Persian State during the Issus War, which took place near today's Iskenderun in southeastern Turkey, Alexander headed straight for India in 333 B.C. Unfortunately, he died at a young age in Babylon while returning from the Indian subcontinent. The lands he had conquered were subsequently divided up amongst his generals. The task of dividing these lands fell to Lysimachus of Thrace. Though Byzantium occasionally lost its sovereignty during the endless bitter wrangling between the generals over the territory, the city protected its freedom most of the time.

While these struggles continued, the Galatians, who lived in Western Europe, started to invade Byzantine lands in 280 B.C. by coming down the length of the lower Danube. With their third wave, they had entered Thrace. The Galatians did not plunder Byzantium but rather extorted money from the populace on a regular basis. Moreover, in traversing the Bosphorus, they settled between the Sakarya and Kızılırmak rivers.

Phillip V of Macedonia had entered Anatolia by 203 B.C. Around this time, the Pergamon Kingdom, which controlled Western Anatolia, established a league, to which Byzantium belonged, to go up against the Macedonian king. This league was not successful and asked for assistance from Rome. In deciding that it was about time to make its move, Rome declared war on Macedonia. The result of these wars was that Rome was to gain control of the lands of Macedonia, Greece and Anatolia. Rome had become a global empire even as it allowed some cities to remain autonomous. Byzantium continued to exist as a free and federal city-state, which was annexed to Rome from 146 B.C. to 73 A.D.

The Roman Emperor Commodus was assassinated in 192 B.C. The two

A detail of the figure of Jesus on the Zoë mosaic making the sign of blessing with his right hand. This mosaic is one of the most beautiful examples of Byzantine mosaic art.

Jesus holding the Bible in the Zoë Mosaic. He is holding a pearl-decorated Bible on his knees.

candidates to succeed him, Commander of the Syrian Army, Niger, and Commander of the Illyrian Army, Septimius Severus, faced off against each other. Byzantium took the side of Niger, but he suffered a major defeat at the hands of Septimius Severus. It was now time to punish Byzantium, which had supported Niger. As a consequence, Septimius Severus entered Byzantium, plundering and torching it to the ground. After he had appeased his anger by massacring all the people there, he decided to recreate the city from scratch in accordance with the wishes of

Icon of St. Eudoxia. The icon is inlaid with precious, colored stones, and dates from the Byzantine period. Istanbul Archaeological Museum.

his son, Caracalla. Hence, he undertook extensive construction activities. He had a square named Tetrastoon erected next to the city's old agora and extended a porticoed road called the Mese (today's Divanyolu Caddesi), which started off in this square and went out to Çemberlitaş. The city also gained a magnificent Hippodrome and the Zeuxippus Baths. In the meantime, the construction of a theater facing the Golden Horn as well as the temples of Apollo and Aphrodite got underway. The new city the emperor created was given the name "Antonina" and was surrounded with a wall. Thus, the new city, with its dominating Roman architecture, started a new life, the basic tenets of which were based on Roman culture.

How Constantinople became the capital of Rome

It was to be a century after the death of Septimius Severus in 211 before Byzantium achieved a new appearance. Diocletian, who ascended to the throne in 284 and who behaved tyrannically towards the Christians, thought that it was too difficult to administer the entire empire from Rome and considered moving the capital east. Nicomedia, in Izmit, was chosen even though Byzantium was deemed more suitable from a military, economic and political standpoint.

Rome was dragged into a new recession when Diocletian retired from state affairs in 305. Subsequent to the power struggle between Maximianus and Licinius, Byzantium was captured in the winter of 312 by the former. However, Licinius took the city upon defeating his rival in Thrace. As a consequence, a long-running battle between Licinius and Constantine started in 314, with the latter defeating the former in 323 to take control of the city. He thought of turning Byzantium into his capital, a prospect that seemed appropriate in every respect. Constantine, who favored Christianity, said that was "God's command" to make Byzantium the new capital. At first, he had a palace constructed to the east of the Hippodrome. He then tore down the walls that Septimius Severus had constructed and had them rebuilt over a wider area, extending them over the slopes of the city's seven hills. He divided the new city into 14 quarters, which he connected to one another with roads. The square in front of Hagia Sophia was named the "Augusteion" while the Severus Colonnade, which stretched to Çemberlitaş, was renovated. The porticoed road that continued from the forum in Beyazıd Square descended into Aksaray to extend out to Cerrahpaşa. These two-storey porticoes had shops on their lower floors, whereas the second storey, which was accessed by steps, consisted of a promenade. Constantine adorned this new city with large edifices similar to those found in Rome, such as a senate, proterium and hippodrome. While idol worshipping had not been totally abandoned, Christianity was increasing gaining ground.

Therefore, even as ancient temples were being preserved, sanctuaries of Christianity, which was the state religion, were starting to rise in the city. Constantine had the Great Palace constructed and the senate and Hippodrome completed, as well.

The "Dikilitaş" or "Obelisk," which exhorts the victories of Thutmosis III, was brought from Egypt. The Serpent Column was carried from Greece and erected in the center of the Hippodrome. Roman notables who wanted to settle in this new city gave support to the public improvements of the city.

Hence, this city, whose public improvements took five years to complete, was named "Nea Roma," which meant New Rome. Finally, after 40 days of celebrations held in the Constantine Forum, it was named Constantinople after its founder Constantine and was declared the new capital of Rome on 11 May, 330. Constantine earned the title of "Protector of the Christian Church" in 325, at which time bishops were invited to Nicaea (Iznik) to participate in the First Ecumenical Council, which was organized to eliminate the rifts in the religion. The goal of the emperor was to solve the misunderstanding between his bishop and Bishop Arius of Alexandria concerning whether Jesus was of the same essence as his Father. Bishop Arius supported the claim that the Father and the Son were not of the same essence. Though the Ecumenical Council had completely rejected Arius' theory, its tenets managed to spread rapidly amongst the people to the point where it constituted a threat to the Church. Constantine passed away seven years later while his sons contended with one another for the thrown. Finally, Constantine II succeeded in ascending to the throne on his own. The religious dispute flared up because he was a supporter of the Arius Theory. The fact that his successor Julianus was a Paganist and Jovianus an Orthodox, but Valens was also an Ariusist was reason for fueling the flames of perpetual religious turmoil.

Theodosius I, who succeeded Valens, was a true Orthodox. For this reason, he tried to exile paganists and those of other sects. He appointed another true Orthodox, Gregorius from Nazianzos to be Patriarch and tried to create a sense of harmony in the religion by organizing the Second Ecumenical Council in Nicaea in 381. This council ratified the results of the First Nicaea Council and rejected Ariusism once and for all. The Emperor was firmly behind Orthodoxy while fiercely banning Paganism and Ariusism.

Upon the death of Emperor Theodosius in 395, Rome was split into two. The territory in the west was called the Western Roman Empire, while that in the east was called the Eastern Roman Empire. Taking advantage of this awkward situation was the king of the Western Goths, Alaric, who marched on Eastern Rome. The newly crowned emperor of the Eastern Roman Empire, Arcadius, appointed him Commander of the Balkans, thus avoiding a catastrophe at home. However, Western Rome could not put up with this and imploded from Goth pressure. Some time after he appointed St. John Chrysostom as Patriarch of Constantinople in 397 B.C., Arcadius exiled him to Anatolia after the former opposed him, and his wife Eudoxia, in particular. Imposing exile proved to be an unwise move as it angered the people, who ended up tearing down Hagia Sophia.

Bust of the Emperor Arcadius. 4th century A.D. Istanbul Archaeological Museum.

The portraits of Emperor John II Comnenus and his wife Irene with the Virgin Mary in the center. 12th century, Hagia Sophia. (Overleaf)

Theodosius II came to the throne at the age of seven, after the death of Arcadius, with his sister Pulceria being made proxy ruler. It was during this period that the dangerous Hun hordes appeared. The Byzantines slipped out of this danger by paying the Huns off, but once again the decision was made to fortify the city with strong walls.

The commander of the eastern region, Anthemius, was given this task, but once his walls were destroyed by an earthquake in 447, Theodosius II assigned prefect Constantine the task of reconstruction. Not only did he repair the damaged walls, he also added a separate wall as well as a moat. The Third Ecumenical Council gathered at Ephesus in 431 in order to end the religious dissension that had been ongoing since the time of

Theodosius II. After much heated debate, it was decided that the Son of the Virgin Mary was born as the Son of God. However, this time Monophysism, which basically argued that Jesus and God were one and the same, emerged.

When Theodosius II died childless, he was succeeded by his sister's husband, General Marcian, who organized the Fourth Ecumenical Council in Chalcedon in 451 in order to come up with a solution to religious discrimination. At the end of long, drawn out debates at this conference, it was decided to regard the Archbishop of Constantinople to be on equal footing with the Pope. As a consequence, this proved to be the first step towards two separate church sects, that of

Western Catholicism and Eastern Orthodoxy.

With religious dissent running rampant in Constantinople, the Teutonic community appeared out of nowhere to have a strong impact with Aspar as their leader. It was because of him that Marcian was deposed in favor of Emperor Leo I, from Illyria. Later on, the Isaurians, who lived in the upper part of Antalya, were brought in to save the city from Emperor Aspar. It was not long before the commander of the arriving forces dominated the city and declared himself emperor, taking the name "Zeno." After the death of Zeno, his wife married Anastasius, one of the palace guards, and ascended to the throne. Anastasius was a Monophysite, but the people were Orthodox, which upped the tension even further.

Anastasius died without any heirs, which led the palace guards to choose one of their own as a successor to the vacated throne. As a result, Commander Justin, who was a Thracian serf, ascended to the throne in 518. Because the new emperor was Orthodox, he reached an accord with the Pope, thus putting an end to the acrimony between the eastern and western churches. Justin also died childless, leaving his nephew Justinian as heir. Justinian, who was the Council in 521, was a member of the Blues, who represented Orthodoxy and the land barons. This solidarity was the reason for hatred against the Greens, who represented Monophysism, merchants and artisans. In 522, Justinian met a bear trainer, Theodora, and asked for her hand in marriage. As the emperor opposed the wedding,

The death scene of the Virgin Mary, located in the main section (naos) of the Chora Monastery Church (Kariye Museum).

21

Justinian just waited until it was time to succeed to the throne.

When the emperor finally died in 527, Justinian became emperor and Theodora his empress. Justinian undertook great reform by gathering all the laws that had been issued since Hadrian into a 10-volume collection. This restructuring, called "Institutions of Justinian," established a bureaucracy by lifting the duties that had been given to aristocrats. Those maintaining pagan beliefs were killed and schools preaching paganism were closed.

New taxes were imposed as the Emperor put up resistance against the Sasanis on the eastern borders, and the Slavs and Bulgars along the banks of the Danube. This all became reflected in the quarrels between the Green and the Blue factions, with discontent becoming the cause of the bloody uprisings in 532 called the Nike Revolt. Rebels controlled the city for a week, during which time which they looted and burned everything, including sanctuaries such as Hagia Sophia and Hagia Eirene.

The emperor entertained thoughts of fleeing the city but was prevented from doing so by Theodora. Meanwhile, Commander Belisarius, who was returning from the Iranian border, made it back to the city in time to unleash his troops onto the mass of rioters who were holding a protest meeting in the Hippodrome. The rebellion was stamped out, with 30,000 rebels dying as a result.

While the newly emboldened emperor was reconstructing Hagia Sophia and the rest of the burnt out city, he was trying to reunify his empire. For this, he took advantage of the confusion in the Ostrogoth Kingdom in Italy to take Sicily. He went on to capture both Rome and Ravenna in 540, the latter of which was the capital of the Ostrogoths. Nevertheless, it was just a year later that the city was hit by a plague stemming from the Mediterranean, which wiped out the aristocracy, artisans, clergymen and inflicted horrible losses upon the empire.

The suffering resulting from this catastrophe did not have a chance to diminish before the Ostrogoths revolted and the Sasanis declared war on the Byzantine Empire. Empress Theodora, who had always supported Emperor Justinian in these difficult days, passed away in 550. The

Seen above the vestibule, the Mosaic of Justinian holding a modal of the church that he rebuilt. Hagia Sophia

Mosaic of Emperor Constantine presenting a model of the city to the Virgin Mary. Hagia Sophia.

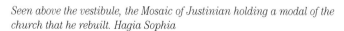

Byzantine Empire succeeded in dominating all of the Mediterranean as a result of these wars. However, both the state treasury and the strength of the Byzantines became depleted from all of this fighting.

The dome of Hagia Sophia collapsed in 559, followed swiftly by a second epidemic. With disasters occurring in quick succession, one of great proportions was about to strike the capital in the form of the Western Huns. In attempting to find a away out of his quandary, the 77-year old emperor left the capital to make peace with the Huns, which, in effect meant paying them a large sum of money. He returned to the city accompanied by victory processions.

The reign of Justinian was the period when the formation of Byzantine culture had reached its zenith. It had been able to discover its true identity, one nourished by plenty of political success. A new style of art had been realized by melting the cultures of ancient Greece, Rome and the East in a Christian pot. The finest example of this was Hagia Sophia. The inspiration for the dome of this structure, which was a Roman basilica, came to the east. It resulted in the church having a synthesis of architectural design reflecting both the east and the west.

Emerging as a result of this cultural amalgamation were its mosaics and icons, which were unique to Byzantine culture. The level of civilization attained during the Justinian period led the way to reversing the relationship that had previously existed between Rome and the Byzantine Empire. The center of arts and culture from that moment on was to be Constantinople and not Rome. The mosaic decorations of Byzantine-period structures in Rome and Ravenna are clear proof of this.

After Justinian came Justin II, Tiberius and Maurice, all of whom struggled against the Lombards, Franks and Slavs, who were approaching from the west, as well as the Sasanis who had arrived from the east. These battles lasted until the year 591.

Mosaic of Empress Zoë. In this detail of the same panel, the Empress Zoë, who was exiled to a nunnery on Büyükada, is seen here in the full regalia of a member of the imperial family. From the Hagia Sophia

Emperor Constantine IX Monomachus. The 10th century mosaic in Hagia Sophia, of which this is a detail, shows Emperor Constantine IX Monomachus in full imperial regalia; all the details of his vestments and crown, with its prominent cross and hanging string of pearls, were carefully copied here.

It was during the era of Phocas, who had ascended to the throne after Maurice, that religious and political skirmishes took place in the capital between the Blues and the Greens. The state attempted to act as a balance by alternately supporting one side and then another. Islam first emerged on the Arabian Peninsula in the first quarter of the 7th century, and it was not long before Islamic zealots had carried their religion beyond the peninsula, thrusting themselves all the way up to the gates of Constantinople by the end of the same century. Though the Byzantine walls had always managed to repulse these attacks, some features of this new religion had gone over the walls to gain favor in the Byzantine Empire.

Leo III (717-41), who halted the Arab raids, was inspired by the banning of pictures in the Islamic religion and subsequently forbade the worshipping of icons and wall depictions of Jesus, the Virgin Mary and the saints. During this century-long period of Iconoclasm, the cross came to replace the exalted figures of Christianity. This decree, which was important from the standpoint of religious culture, was implemented well into the 9th century. During this century, a Macedonian horse groomer named Basil, who was living in Constantinople, strangled the emperor and declared himself emperor in 867. This initiated the era of Macedonian emperors, which was to last until 1081. During this period, new laws that were compatible with the prevailing political conditions were put into practice and published under the name "'Basilica." Moreover, all the merchants and craftsmen on imperial lands were organized in the manner of guilds.

Feudalism began when the noble class was allowed to buy land owned by serfs. This situation brought about the emergence of new problems, resulting in scattered discontent turning into rebellious crowds. Hence, many emperors had to confront some very difficult social and political unrest. While engaged in such strife, the Byzantine Empire also had to come to grips with the Seljuks in the east, the Normans to the west, as well as the Pecheneks, Uz and Kuman groups to the north.

It has been observed that Empress Zoë had a lasting impact on Byzantine history during the final years of the Macedonian dynasty. As there were no male heirs to ascend to the throne when Constantine VIII died in 1028, it remained for one of his three daughters to do so. With his daughter Eudoxia choosing to reside in a nunnery and Zoë preventing her other sister, Theodora, access to the throne, Zoë managed to become empress. She married Romanus III Argyrus, who declared himself emperor. However, some time later, she became rather perturbed with the marriage and had her husband strangled. This, however, was actually done so as to prevent him from learning about her relationship with a son of a Paphlagonian farmer. Upon the death of her husband, she married her lover, who ascended to the throne as Michael IV. He was to die six years later, leaving her to share the throne with their adopted nephew, Michael V. However, it was not long before Michael removed her from the throne and locked her up in a nunnery on Büyükada.

center of the mosaic is Jesus, with the Empress Zoë on one side and her husband on the other side. She was so crafty that she had the head and upper inscription changed every time she remarried. When the empress died before her last husband in 1050, Constantine IX Monomachus had the opportunity to see himself as the emperor depicted on the mosaic.

The figure of Mary with Christ is in the dome of the Paracclesion. Around this are the figures of angels. In the pendentives of the dome are the four hymnographers

One of the depictions of angels in the dome of the Paracclesion

Zoë remained here for some time, but was later able to escape and return to Constantinople. She deposed Michael V, punishing him for what he had done to her by blinding him. After sharing the throne with her sister Theodora for about a year, she married Constantine IX Monomachus, who was 64 years old at the time. This cunning queen commissioned the Zoë Mosaic, which can still be seen in Hagia Sophia today. Depicted in the

center of the mosaic is Jesus, with the Empress Zoë on one side and her husband on the other side. She was so crafty that she had the head and upper inscription changed every time she remarried. When the empress died before her last husband in 1050, Constantine IX Monomachus had the opportunity to see himself as the emperor depicted on the mosaic.

With his death in 1055, Theodora ascended to the throne for a second time, her one-year reign marking the end of the Macedonian line.

The consecutive changes of emperors in the Byzantine Empire could not stem the loss of territory. While the Normans had seized the last of the Byzantine lands in Italy, a major threat had suddenly materialized in the east in the form of the Seljuks. This was due to the fact that the Grand Seljuk State had accepted Islam and declared itself to be the savior of the Islamic Caliphate. It was necessary to capture Anatolia in order to preserve the Caliph. Consequently, the Seljuks seized Iran and began to amass their forces along the borders of the Byzantine Empire. The young and dynamic Seljuk Sultan Alparslan mobilized his army to conquer Anatolia while Emperor Romanus Diogenes mobilized an even larger army to counter Alparslan's movements in the east. The two armies confronted one another in 1071 at Mantzikert, near Lake Van. But it was Alparslan who forced the Byzantine forces into great disarray, taking the emperor prisoner in the process. Although Diogenes was released some time later, his eyes were poked out by his successor when he returned to Constantinople.

The Turks were finally in Anatolia to stay. With the sound of the horse hooves of the Turkish cavalry thundering throughout the land, they established emirates everywhere they were able to gain the upper hand. These emirates ended up being consolidated through the establishment of the Anatolian Seljuk State, with Konya as its capital.

The Kayı Tribe, lead by Ertuğrul Bey, settled along the Byzantine border in Söğüt, Bursa. This led to the Byzantines being squeezed into a very narrow area, with only the capital and the land surrounding it remaining in their possession.

Meanwhile, the dispute over the Byzantine throne continued, with the Comnenus family emerging as the dominating factor. Alexius I Comnenus (1081-1118) halted the onslaught of the Normans and Pecheneks in the Balkans. He also stemmed the advances made by the Seljuks in Anatolia. However, he had neither the strength nor enough money in the treasury to force the Seljuks from Anatolia. In the meantime, the Seljuks continued their momentum, seizing Jerusalem and moving as far south as the Arabian Peninsula.

Mosaics from the Chora Monastery.
Jesus being deceived by Satan (above).
The birth of Jesus (Below).

The Latin Invasion

In reaching an agreement with the Pope, Alexius Comnenus had planned to push back the Seljuks. Consequently, the force that gathered in 1096 was mobilized as the First Crusade and succeeded in halting the Seljuks. Mobilized during the same year, the Second Crusade seized the regions around Antioch (modern-day Antakya) and Jerusalem. Right around this time, Alexius Comnenus died and was succeeded by his son John II Comnenus. This emperor married Irene, the daughter of Hungarian King Ladislaus. Their wedding was immortalized with a mosaic that can be seen in Hagia Sophia. The Virgin Mary is depicted in the center of this mosaic

panel, flanked by the emperor and empress. The purse shown in the emperor's hands symbolizes the donation of the 1,000 gold pieces he made to Hagia Sophia for its upkeep. While the Macedonian dynasty continued to reign over the Byzantine Empire, problems began to emerge in the relationship between the army commanders of the Crusade and the emperors. The pressure that the Crusaders applied upon the local people was reason for much discontent. Meanwhile, a Third Crusade was organized subsequent to Jerusalem's capture by Selahaddin Eyyubi in 1187. While a Fourth Crusade was mobilized in 1203, Alexius IV was deposed from the throne and murdered, which led to the Crusaders

Interior view of Hagia Sophia. Colorful marble plating, brought from a variety of places, placed side-by-side to create decorative motifs.

Different view of Hagia Sophia. First built in 360, Hagia Sophia was burned to the ground in 404, only to be rebuilt and opened for worship again in 415. The building was razed once again by fire in 532. Emperor Justinian had the church rebuilt in its present form, where upon it was reopened for worship in 537.

reversing their direction and heading for Constantinople, where they arrived in the spring of 1204.

The Latins plundered the city, carting off anything they found to be of value, including windows and doors. In short, a millennium of Byzantine wealth was looted. The huge bronze placards on top of the Serpent Column in the Hippodrome were removed and melted down for coins. The statue in the Hippodrome of the four horses was carted off to Venice to be erected in St. Mark Square. Constantinople was looted from top to bottom.

The Latins chose Count Baudoiun of Flanders to be the first Latin Emperor. He, in turn, set aside a quarter of the land belonging to the New Empire and divided up the remainder between the Venetians and the knights of the Crusade. This led to a Latin Empire being established in Constantinople.

This gave rise to the establishment, by the grandsons of Andronicus I, of a state called the Greek Pontus Empire in Trabzon in 1204. In addition, Theodore Lascaris, who had fled Constantinople during the Latin Invasion, set up a government in exile in Nicaea (Iznik). Over time, Constantinople became a Venetian colony. The Latin Invasion came to an end in 1261 after about half a century. The emperor in Iznik, Michael VIII Palaeologus, reached an accord with the Genoese to recapture the city in a sudden attack during a time when the Latin soldiers were on a campaign, which brought the Latin Occupation to an end. With the demise of the Latins, the Palaeologus line came to dominate the Byzantine Empire and was to remain on the throne until the very demise of the Byzantine Empire. When the second emperor of this line, Andronicus II Palaeologus, ascended to the throne in 1282, he saw the state collapsing from within, having become a pawn of the Genoese and Venetians. The Genoese guaranteed their presence in the city by erecting walls around the district of Galata, constructing the Galata Tower as the highest point of their fortifications. Meanwhile, the Catalan leader Toger de Flor arrived in Constantinople to try to reclaim the land in Anatolia that had fallen into Turkish control. He lost his battle and made the Byzantines pay for his losses by looting the city in 1303. Meanwhile, the Ottoman Emirate, which was established in Söğüt and led by Osman Bey, declared its independence in 1299, paving the way towards the founding of a great empire.

While the Anatolian Seljuk State collapsed in 1308, the Ottomans, who had become more independent, began to acquire new land and fortresses from the Byzantines. The cavalry troops, whose ranks had grown from 400 to 20,000 during the sultanate of Orhan Bey, proved to be the decisive force in defeating the Byzantine soldiers practically every time they clashed. Feeling the pressure, the Byzantine emperors appealed to Orhan Bey for his assistance. Emperor Andronicus III Palaeologus facilitated matters when he married off his daughter Asporça to Orhan Bey. At the same time, his people continued to live in poverty and Constantinople was no more than the equivalent of a mass of rubble. The Byzantine historian Nicephorus Gregoras described the poverty of the Byzantines when he recorded his impressions of the coronation ceremony of John Cantacuzenus VI (1347-1354). "... Everyone knew that the precious

stones in the crowns were merely glass, that the gowns were woven with gilded thread and not real gold, that the kitchen utensils were copper, and that everything that gave the impression of magnificent taffeta was nothing other than dyed leather." As it was, John Cantacuzenus VI, who had ascended to the throne amidst all this poverty, married off his daughter to Orhan Bey in a bid to solidify his presence on the throne and try to catch his wind.

While the Ottomans were becoming more and more powerful, the Byzantines were living their final days. So it was that by the turn of the 15th century, the Ottomans had captured most of the Byzantine territory in Europe and Anatolia. The Byzantines had been squeezed into the tight confines of their walls while the Ottomans were off racing their stallions throughout Southern and Central Europe, gaining control of the states there. In the meantime, Constantinople came to look more and more like an irritating abscess in the midst of the vast expanse of Ottoman territory.

Murad, who had ascended to the throne after Orhan Bey, as well as his son Yıldırım Bayezid, thought that it was about time to eliminate the Byzantines once and for all. To this do, Bayezid constructed a fortress on the Anatolia side of the Bosphorus. But the threat of Tamerlane in the east provided the chance for the Byzantines to continue as a state for a bit longer than anticipated. With Yıldırım Bayezid defeating Tamerland, Çelebi Mehmed once again rallied the state. The conquest of the Byzantine Empire once more was put on the agenda. It was his successor, Murad II, who besieged Constantinople in 1422. What was to be a long siege was lifted when he mobilized his forces against Greece. John VIII Palaeologus, who was in power at the time, appealed to the Pope to organize a fresh Crusade campaign in 1425.

The Pope eventually amassed a force of 25,000 Crusaders, who crossed the Danube in 1444 only to be scattered by the Ottoman Army. During the same year, Murad II was succeeded by his son Mehmed II, who was determined to crush the Byzantine Empire for good. Until then, the Byzantines had been able to remain on their feet by means of endless maneuvers and shrewdness. They were to no longer be a problem within the wide lands of the Ottomans.

The young Ottoman sultan decided to conquer them and began preparations to do so. The final emperor of the Byzantines was to be Constantine XI Palaeologus, who ascended to his shaky throne in 1449. It was then that the fate of two emperors was to unfold.

The monogrammed column capitals in the upper and lower galleries of Hagia Sophia, one of the finest examples of Byzantine architecture.

The City Walls

*"It was as though it was naturally created
to be the capital of the entire world." Busbecq*

The walls of Istanbul are rare in that they protected the city they surrounded, keeping out those who wished to capture the city, for an entire millennium. Since the walls were able to deter the largest forces of the Middle Ages – the Huns, the Avar and Arab hordes and Bulgarian attacks, we felt it was appropriate to cover these enormous walls in a separate chapter. The walls that initially surrounded Byzantium were not very broad in scope. It was only after the Roman Emperor Septimius Severius captured Byzantium, which had put up heavy resistance, that the importance of the walls became clear. Because of the resistance, the Romans had destroyed the city and its walls. It was not long, however, before the emperor realized the importance of the city and had it rebuilt – this time surrounding it with a much wider wall.

In grooming the city to be the capital of Rome, Constantine introduced many new architectural edifices and razed the old walls. On 26 November 328, he had erected city walls that encompassed a much more extensive area than was previously the case. Constantinople become the capital of Eastern Rome when Rome split into two in 395; during this period, the city continued to expand to the point where the old walls had became insufficient. Meanwhile, led by Alaric, the Goths captured Rome. This was during the reign of Theodosius II, who, as a small child, had succeeded Arcadius to the throne. It was not long before the Huns, who were terrorizing the east, started to be seen in front of the walls of Constantinople. The Byzantines were only able to stop the Huns from taking the city by paying them large levies. For this reason, the importance of the walls was proven once again. Subsequently, Emperor Theodosius assigned Prefect Anthemius with the task of rebuilding the city walls for a fourth time in 412. It was not long after, in 447, that the walls came down in an earthquake that destroyed 57 of the 96 towers. Shortly thereafter the emperor appointed the new prefect Constantine the job of erecting the walls again. Meantime, it was said that Attila the Hun was getting prepared to march on Constantinople. Thus, the task of repairing the walls was hastened so as to thwart any such move. In addition, a wall two meters thick and 8.5 meters high having 96 towers was constructed in front of the existing one. And a moat 20 meters wide and 10 meters deep was dug in front of the new wall. These walls came to constitute an insurmountable triple defense. Completed as well were the walls around the Golden Horn and the Sea of Marmara. The impact of these strong walls immediately became apparent as Attilla had his armies fall back, commanding them instead to march on the Western Roman Empire and plunder Rome. The walls surrounding the city were comprised of three sections. The first wall, called the Marmara Wall, stretched from the Sea of Marmara around Yedikule to the Mermer Tower. As there was no danger coming from the Sea of Marmara, these walls were of the single-wall variety.

The second wall, which stretched all the way to Tekfur Palace, was made to be quite solid. The third one, called the Golden Horn Wall, stretched from here to the Golden Horn. Today, there are 36 gates of different sizes, as well as 103 bastions and towers, which can be seen from place to place along the Marmara Walls. BegInning with the Marmara Walls, it is possible to examine the interesting as well as aesthetically constructed walls of Istanbul, which have protected the city for centuries.

Belgrad Gate

Shown here is the "Belgrad Kapısı" and section of its walls. The Istanbul city walls and several of the towers are still standing thanks to recent restoration.

The Marmara Walls

These walls start from Sarayburnu and run along the shore 8,260 meters to end at the Mermer Kule (Marble Tower), next to Yedikule. As we mentioned earlier, the walls surrounding the sea were erected during the time of Theodosius. Because of the enormous waves whipped up by the southeasterly winds, the walls have worn out in places, resulting in their collapse. Emperor Theophilus (828-42) was responsible for the construction of the walls that we can see today. The sections around Sarayburnu, which is the starting point of these walls, have remained to the present due to either the expansion of the palace or to the laying of the railroad line in 1871. The St. Barbara (Cannon) gate was once situated here. Advancing down the recently opened shore road, an ancient Byzantine church called Hristos Filantropus is known to have existed inside the walls beyond the statue of Piri Reis. Just beyond this, one can see columns jutting out from the walls as well as an aqueduct. These are ruins of İncili Kiosk, which was one of the outer pavilions of the Great Palace. There is also the Mangana Palace which was constructed by Emperor Basil I. Ahırkapı is located about 500 meters further down the road. It got its name, "Barn Door," from the fact that the palace barns were located here during the Byzantine and Ottoman periods.

Though some sections of the unique Istanbul city walls are in a state of ruin, others have recently been restored.

One can see the Ahırkapı Lighthouse, which was constructed after a maritime accident during the rule of Sultan Osman III. If we pass over the Kalyon Hotel and the seaside restaurants, to continue looking at the walls, we will come across three decorated gates of a balcony located above the walls. This is the balcony section of the Byzantine Bucoleon Palace, which was constructed by Theodosius and expanded by Constantine VII Porphyrogenitus

Phocas Nicephorus II (963-969) later added a villa to the palace and lived there. The palace, which was pillaged and destroyed during the Latin Crusade, subsequently lost its importance and was basically abandoned in favor of the Blachernae Palace in Ayvansaray. A bit further along the way, one comes to the harbor of Bucoleon Palace, which was built by Theodosius II. This once royal harbor, which is just a small indention today, used to be decorated with marble piers and statues. The lion statues that were once there are now in the Archaeological Museum. One passes into the harbor through a gate. As this gate was cracked during an earthquake in the Ottoman Empire, it is called "Çatladıkapı" or the "Cracked Gate." The Small Hagia Sophia Church is located at a spot near this part of the walls. As we are going to describe this church along with all the other churches, it will not be covered at this time.

Just a little way from here is Kadırga. As its name infers in Turkish, this used to be a harbor. It was employed for military purposes and also contained a shipyard. The gate opening into the harbor is called Kadırga Harbor Gate or the Gate of Sophia, who was the wife of Justinian.

A little further down is Kumkapı, where one comes across a harbor, known in antiquity as the "Contoscalion." After Kumkapı, which is famous for its touristic fish restaurants, comes Yenikapı, where there are two churches, which, in relative terms, are not very old. Continuing along the road, we arrive in Samatya, where the walls reemerge. The railroad bridge is helpful in determining the place where the gate to this district is located. From here, one goes into Narlıkapı, where the Byzantine-era Studius Monastery and the St. John Basilica (today's İmrahor Mosque) are found in a place near the gate. Emperors would attend services at this church once a year to commemorate John the Baptist. The Marmara Walls end with the Mermer Kule, which is seen just up the way.

The Territorial Walls

Starting from the Mermer Kule and stretching north for 5,632 meters, the Territorial Walls end at Tekfur Palace. An almost unsurpassable system was created with the walls, which are a product of military genius in and of themselves. They protected Constantinople against swords and small caliber weapons, but were not able to resist the cannons sent in by Sultan Mehmed the Conqueror, which blew holes in the walls, marking the end of the Byzantine Empire. In addition to the ten large gates guarding the territorial walls, there were several service gates. The large gates were erected in pairs in a manner that opened into the inner and outer walls. Combined with the strong towers erected on both sides of the main gates substantial support was provided. Let's move on to Yedikule, which is situated at the beginning of the Territorial Walls and which did not lose any importance during either the Byzantine or Ottoman periods.

Altın Kapı (Golden Gate), the first gate of the walls, is situated 900 meters from the Mermer Kule. Built in 390 by Emperor Theodosius I, it was called "Porta Aure," as it was covered with gold plates. Later on, this gate was merged together with the walls that were put up in 413 during the reign of Theodosius II. Thus, what was first erected as a victory arch became a gate to the walls. On either side of the triple-arched gate, which is 60 meters long, are two towers measuring 17 meters x 18 meters. There were once the statues of Theodosius, Nike and a cart drawn by an elephant positioned over the gate. These were toppled during the earthquakes that struck in 740 and 866. John V Palaeologus had the gate repaired in 1389, having mythological bas-reliefs of Hercules, Venus and Adonis as well as the fall of Phaethon placed over the gate. It is understood that these reliefs were also here when Sultan Mehmed II conquered Istanbul. In fact, 12 sections of these reliefs were still here in 1620, when the English Ambassador Sir Thomas Roe made an unsuccessful bid to ship them off to his country. What became of these reliefs later on is unclear as they simply disappeared. Sultan Mehmed the Conqueror had additional towers erected next to these towers and by surrounding them with walls, transformed them into an Inner fortress where the state treasury was kept. Later on, when the state treasury was transferred to the Great Palace, Yedikule was transformed into the dungeons. As we shall discuss this in the chapter about the castles, we do not wish to go into further detail at this moment.

Beyond Yedikule, it can be seen that within the walls, which have been restored, is the Belgrad Kapısı. After Sultan Süleyman the Magnificent conquered the city of Belgrade in Serbia, he settled the people he brought back with him here in this area, hence the name Belgrad Kapısı. Just a bit inside the wall are ruins of the Panayia Belgrad Church, which was erected for the people who were settled here.

Beyond this location is a gate known in the Byzantine period as "Pege," which is the name of a nearby sacred fountain that was once found in Balıklı. The gate was renamed "Silivri Kapı" during the Ottoman period. About 100 meters from it is a modest work of Mimar Sinan called the İbrahim Pasha

Mosque, along with its adjacent Bala Complex. The gate that comes after Silivri Kapı is Mevlevi Kapı, which gets its name from the fact that there was once a Mevlevi lodge situated there. There is an inscription by Emperor Constantine, who had walls erected over of this gate, which was called 'Region' during the Byzantine period. There is also an inscription mentioning Justinian, his wife Sophia and a Byzantine general named Narses. Once called the Gate of St. Comanus, the gate known as "Topkapı" acquired its present name due to the fact that it was knocked down by Mehmed the Conqueror's cannons ("top" meaning cannon). Until recently, it was in decrepit condition; but restoration has returned it to its former impressive glory. Called "Edirnekapı" because the gate marked the start of the road to Edirne, there is an inscription above it commemorating the victorious soldiers of Sultan Mehmed II who entered through it during the conquest of Constantinople. Right next to the gate is the Mihrimah Mosque, which was constructed by Mimar Sinan for Sultan Süleyman the Magnificent's daughter, Mihrimah Sultan. Near the mosque is a Greek Orthodox church as well as the famous Chora Monastery. Traveling in a northerly direction, one arrives at Tekfur Palace, which was a part of Blachernae Palace. The site where Tekfur Palace is found is also where the Theodosius walls end. Because the walls

Many towers standing over the walls have been restored to their former glorious state.

from here were discovered to be the weakest part of the network, Emperor Manuel Comnenus had them rebuilt and reinforced with towers. The Kırkçeşme Maksemi, where water sluiced in from Belgrad Forest would be diverted to other parts of the city, is located to the south of the Eğrikapı gate, formerly known as "Kaligari," at the center of the walls.

The Comnenus Walls end with the Tower of Isaac II Angelus, which is about 400 meters from Eğrikapı. This tower was built during the reign of Emperor Isaac II Angelus (1185-95). He was dethroned, blinded and ultimately tossed into the Anemas Tower. This tower was named after Anemas, who was a commander from the Arabian Peninsula. Later on, this three-storey tower was used as a dungeon. Although only the top floors are visible today, it is still worthwhile to see the incredible view of the Golden Horn from here.

Situated directly over the Comnenus Walls, the Anemas Tower is still intact.

Adjacent to the Anemas Tower is the comparatively elegant İvaz Efendi Mosque, which Mimar Sinan had erected. Looking out over the Golden Horn from here, you can see the walls that Emperor Leo V and Emperor Heraclius were responsible for building. These were constructed as double walls. Three polygonal towers are found on top of the Inner walls, which were built by Emperor Heraclius in 627 to keep out the Avar hordes. As for the outer walls, they were constructed in 813 by Emperor Leo V to thwart the onslaught of Bulgarian King Krum's forces.

The Territorial Walls turn here to merge with the Walls of the Golden Horn. Construction of the St. Thecla Church, which is located within the walls, was begun by Empress Pulceria and completed by Emperor Leo I. As the shawl of the Blessed Mary was kept in this church, it was considered one of the important sanctuaries after Hagia Sophia. Byzantine emperors frequently attended services at this church until it burned down in 1434, never to be rebuilt. The Tomb of Toklu Dede was subsequently erected over this site.

The Walls of the Golden Horn

While he had the Marmara and Territorial Walls completely renovated, the Prefect Constantine also had the Walls of the Golden Horn put up. He had this done so that they would merge with the Sea Walls, thus ensuring that the entire city was surrounded by walls. As a threatening situation was never expected from the Golden Horn side of the city, it was defended with a single wall. Moreover, security had been greatly increased by means of stretching a heavy iron chain across the Golden Horn. However, this chain proved to be of no value against the Latin Crusaders, who succeeded in capturing the city by getting through the Walls of the Golden Horn and finally in entering the city by overcoming those guarding these walls. As a consequence, the ruined sections of Walls of the Golden Horn were partially restored by the Latins. Nevertheless, they were completely restored after 1261, when the city was retaken by the Byzantines.

Measuring 10 meters high, the Walls of the Golden Horn once stretched five kilometers from Ayvansaray to Sarayburnu and had 110 towers and 14 gates. Not much remains of these walls today. The Ayvansaray Gate of Blachernae Palace was the sea entrance to the city where the emperors would disembark from vessels and mount their steeds to reach the palaces up above. Located near the walls in Ayvansaray, the Atik Mustafa Pasha Mosque was converted from a church, the name of which is not known today. Yet another church was known to have existed over the sacred fountain of Blachernae across from this mosque, on Kuyu Sokak. It was considered one of the most important Byzantine churches until it burned down in 1430. The church there today is the Church of the Blessed Mary. After Ayvansaray comes

Balat, which is the district where the Jews who were rescued from the Spanish Inquisition by Sultan Bayezid II were settled. One can find Balat Kapısı, which was once known as the Gate of St. John the Baptist. There are a number of synagogues located here as well as Greek and Armenian churches. The fact that Mimar Sinan's Ferruh Kethüda Mosque is found here creates an interesting contrast of the world's houses of worship. After Balat, comes the Porta Fenari (Fener Gate) in the district of Fener, which was named in reference to the nearby lighthouse. This district is famous for the Greek Orthodox Patriarchate, which has been located here since 1601. The people of Fener are mostly of Greek origin, which is why the Greek Lyceé (high school), with its red brick structure, is here as well. The Byzantine St. Maria Church is found right next door to the high school. Still in use today, this 13th-century church was constructed in the name of Maria Muhliotissa,

who is more commonly referred to as Mary of the Mongols. We shall cover this building in our chapter on churches, so let's continue to move along the length of the walls. Just a bit further on, we come to a gate in the walls called the Gate of St. Theodosia. It derives its name from the nearby St. Theodosia Church, which was converted to the Gül Mosque after the city was conquered in 1453. Across from the church is the school of Adile Sultan, the sister of Sultan Mahmud II, and across from the apse wall of the church is a bath that was built by Küçük Mustafa Pasha, one of the viziers of Bayezid II. This is one of the oldest hamams in Istanbul. From here, one reaches the neighborhood of Cibali. This is where Cibali Kapısı, known in ancient times as "Porta Pateas," is found. Today, only a single section remains of the Walls of the Golden Horn. From here, the walls once stretched all the way to Yalı Pavilion in Sarayburnu; however, not a single trace remains of this section of the walls.

Tekfur Palace. Located between Edirnekapı and Eğrikapı, this is all that remains of the late-Byzantine Blachernae Palace. It has three storeys and was built upon the order of Manuel Comnenus I (1143-80).

Byzantine Palaces

Palaces with precious floor mosaics stretched from Hippodrome Square all the way to the shores of the Marmara.

As Constantinople was being prepared as the capital of the Roman Empire, great imperial palaces, as well as other structures, were under construction. Before Constantine declared his new city the capital, he had the Great Palace built over land situated between the Hippodrome and Hagia Sophia, stretching all the way down to the sea. This palace, which gradually extended over an enormous area due to the various additions made to it, came to be used by many other emperors over the years.

As the Great Palace expanded to the southeast of the Hippodrome, the Antiochus and Lausus Palaces were erected to the north. The Palace of Philoxenus was also situated over the Binbirdirek Cisterns. In addition, there were several mansions belonging to the nobility along the Mese.

With its polygonal dome and main hall with six semi-circular niches, the Antiochus Palace was transformed later on into the St. Eufemia Church. Just up the way was the Lausus Palace, named after an aristocrat who carried out important tasks during the Arcadius era. This palace was famous for its statues that decorated both its outer walls and its interior. In mentioning the statues of the Lausus Palace, historian Petrus Gyllius wrote in his book "De Topographia Constantinopoleos," "Among all the statues, the most attractive was that of the two-meter high Athena, which was carved from emerald green marble."

A Byzantine recorder of events, Georgios Kedrenos, wrote that the Aphrodite statue of Knidos was also found in this palace and that it was known everywhere to be the famous nude statue of white marble sculpted by Praxiteles. In addition, Lysippus' statue of Hera, which was brought here from the island of Samos, as well as Phidias' statue of Zeus, were placed here. The Lausus Palace burned down in a fire that broke out in the area in 476, at which time the unique statues inside also disappeared.

In essence, Constantine constructed the Great Palace to resemble the one in Rome. This first palace was composed of several elements and situated to the south of the Hippodrome. With the subsequent addition of a number of wings, it was to be called the Great Palace. The first wing added to this palace was constructed for the two wives of Theodosius I. The palaces of Theodosius II (400–50) extend down as far as the

walls he had constructed along the coastline.

The Great Palace was expanded even further during the period of Justinian I, but was put to the torch along with many other surrounding structures during the Nike Revolt of 532. After suppressing the rebellion, Justinian

Detail of two hunters on a tiger hunt. Museum of Great Palace Mosaics

Camel Jockey Mosaic. Museum of Great Palace Mosaics.

had both Hagia Sophia and the Great Palace repaired and expanded, decorating the interior of the latter with mosaics. Today, many of these mosaics have been uncovered in excavations and subsequently restored. They are currently on display at the Museum of Topkapı Mosaics behind the Sultan Ahmed Mosque and are glorious proof of just how rich a collection the palace was once blessed with.

The mosaics were crafted with great expertise, and depict scenes taken from daily life and nature. These include a camel jockey, two hunters stalking a lion with a spear, the life of shepherds, serfs working the fields, children playing games, domesticated and wild animals. The borders surrounding the scenes contribute a distinct beauty to the compositions. In Procopius' book entitled "Structures," he mentions the city and its mosaics in the 6th century. After Justinian, the Great Palace was expanded with other additions on down to the shore until the 11th century. The entrance of the palace was on the side of Hagia Sophia and opened out into the Augusteion Square.

Comprised of rectangular-shaped walls, this entrance was called the "Bronze House" as it was covered on top with bronze. The ceilings of this magnificent entrance were decorated with mosaics depicting Justinian and the victories of Commander Belisarius in Italy and Northern Africa. They also show Belisarius presenting the emperor with booty he captured during his campaigns. Another composition shows the Vandal and Goth kings greeting Emperor Justinian and Empress Theodora.

Emperor Justinian also decorated the entrance of the two-storey tower-shaped palace called Chalce with statues. This highly ornate entrance section was destroyed during the Iconoclastic period of the 8th century.

A section of the large triple border of the floor mosaic of the Great Palace. Museum of Great Palace Mosaics

Directly behind this entrance was the Palace Guard Chamber. From here, one passed into the Daphne Palace, where the private quarters of the emperor were located. Chambers and halls such as the throne chamber, banquet hall and meeting halls were situated here. These quarters facilitated direct passage to the Emperor's loggia, called the "Kathisma," in the Hippodrome. After the renovation of Justinian's palace, Topkapı Palace was repaired and enlarged by Emperors, Justin II, Justinian II, Theophilos, Basil I, Constantine VII Porphyrogenitus. With the additions and new structures, the palace reached all the way down to the Sea of Marmara. Basil I (867-86) constructed the Mangana Palace, which was located in what is today Ahırkapı.

This palace was situated where the Ottoman period İncirli Pavilion stands today. It consisted of a grand hall with an apse on the western edge and side galleries. The hall was decorated with sacred depictions and had a layout not unlike an early-basilica plan church. The palace was repaired by Heracleius, and subsequently transformed into a Byzantine secondary school during the period of Michael III. The palace was also utilized as an imperial courthouse. For instance, the trial of Patriarch Euthymius was held there. Emperors would also make their public addresses from inside the apse of the palace, sitting on their throne flanked by two lions. Theophilus made additions to this palace and set up his famous mechanical toys here.

Basil I also had a church added to the palace. Before Manuel Comnenus I abandoned the Great Palace, he had a very colorful pavilion decorated with

Mosaic depicting a bear killing a bear. Museum of Great Palace Mosaics

gold leaf stalactites made from bricks built there.

At the easternmost edge of the Great Palace complex was the Bucoleon Palace, which was constructed by Theodosius II and later repaired and expanded by Justinian. This palace gained importance over time and was mentioned quite frequently after Emperor Constantine VII Porphyrogenitus expanded it and the adjacent harbor.

Nicephoros Phocas II added a villa to this palace and resided there. Considering that the Great Palace was called the Bucoleon Palace

Border detail with the head of Oceanus. Museum of Great Palace Mosaics

beginning in the 11th century, it is clear that the importance of this palace had increased significantly. The only parts of this palace remaining, however, are three decorated gates and a balcony that appear above the Marmara Walls.

Its name, "Bucoleon," comes from the ancient statue at the harbor entrance next to the palace depicting a lion tearing into a bull. One would pass from the harbor to the palace through a gate once known as "Porta Leonis," in front of which was a statue of two lions. Today, this statue is on display at the Archaeological Museum.

This gate is now called "Çatladı Kapı" because it developed a crack as a result of an earthquake that struck during the Ottoman period. The northwest section of the Bucoleon Palace above the walls consisted of the border of the Great Palace that came down in this direction.

The interior of the palace was decorated with gold leaf mosaics. To the west of Bucoleon Palace was the Hormisdas Palace. Emperor Justinian spent his youth in the latter palace and included it within the Great Palace complex after first having it repaired. Reduced to ruins during the Latin Invasion, the palace remained in this state well into the Ottoman period. For this reason, a new settlement area was established over its remains. The Head Eunuch, Mahmud Ağa, had the Ağa Mosque constructed over a cistern having three sections. The Ahırkapı Lighthouse on the shoreline was constructed during the period of Osman III.

As the Great Palace was left in such a horrific state after the Latin Invasion, subsequent emperors naturally preferred to reside in the Blachernae Palace located over in the western part of the city (today's Ayvansaray). The Sacred Fountain of Blachernae is situated in this neighborhood, which was known as Blachernae.

The sister of Theodosius II, Empress Pulceria had a church erected on top of this fountain. A few years later, two Byzantine citizens brought some relics belonging to the Blessed Mary on their return journey from Jerusalem. Amongst these was her shawl. The importance of this newly built church rose considerably and emperors attended services here after the shawl was presented as an icon for safekeeping. In conjunction with the increased visits to the church, an imperial pavilion was erected next door.

The first structure erected by Leo I (457-74) became the nucleus of Blachernae Palace. Later, Anastasius I (491-518) had new additions built there as well. In subsequent centuries, three more pavilions were added over different terraces. Called "Oceanus," these pavilions were famous for their ornamentation. They consisted of a large hall and various chambers, which were utilized until the Comnenus period. Alexius Comnenus undertook studies to expand the palace. This whole group of structures called the Blachernae Palace once was located where Mimar Sinan's İvaz Efendi Mosque currently stands. The nephew of Alexius Comnenus, Manuel Comnenus I added a reception hall to this palace, which by his time was surrounded by protective walls.

Stretching as far as the two towers of Isaac II Angelus and Anemas, the incredible view from the palace terraces continues to charm those who gaze from this point. The palace and especially its interior became famous for its beautiful medieval-era mosaics. Whoever came to see this palace were left awestruck. One of these was Rabbi Bünyamin, from Tudela, who visited the city in 1161. He called on Emperor Manuel Comnenus at this palace and recorded his thoughts about its splendor: "All the columns and walls are covered with gold. The present emperor, as well as former ones are depicted in the battles they have fought. The imperial throne is crafted from gold and is embellished with precious gems. Connected to chains, the imperial crown is decorated likewise. These diamonds are so brilliant that they reflect enough light into the chamber even if there is no other source of light."

In 1095, Alexius Comnenus I received the nobles who had participated in the campaign of the First Crusade; the European princes were stunned by all this wealth. It was just a little over a century later, in 1204, that they were to plunder all this amazing wealth and burned down all the palaces. The city became unrecognizable after a conflagration lasting two days. It was Michael VIII Palaeologus who drove the Latins out of town only to find ruined palaces looted of all their riches. It was he who repaired Blachernae Palace, with subsequent emperors taking up residence there. The palace was decorated with mosaics depicting the Empire's 1281-82 victory in Berat.

The ascension and consecration ceremonies of the final period of the Palaeologus dynasty were held, and foreign dignitaries were received there as well. During his visit to the city in 1437, the Spaniard Pero Tafur recorded, "The imperial palace must have been splendid once upon a time, but these days, the situation is so depressing as one sees to what extent the disasters that continue to strike the city have affected it adversely."

Today, nothing remains of Blachernae Palace and only a few walls of the Tekfur Palace, which was connected to this palace, remain standing. Situated at the southern edge of Blachernae Palace, this palace was constructed by Manuel Comnenus I (1143-80) and is thought to have been reserved for the Byzantine crown princes. The three-storey palace was constructed from stone and brick, with its entrance to the courtyard made via a pair of twin-vaults on the bottom storey. On the ground floor, there were five windows surrounded in marble, while on the top floor, there were

seven. Moreover, there are the ruins of a balcony on the top floor of the eastern facade. After the Tekfur Palace was left in its abandoned state, Grand Vizier Nevşehirli İbrahim Pasha turned it into a tile furnace during the 18th century.

The palaces, as well as the rest of the city, were extremely dilapidated when Sultan Mehmed the Conqueror took Constantinople. As a consequence, he never considered residing in these palaces, but rather had one constructed in Beyazıt Square, which later proved to be too confining. He then ordered the construction of Topkapı Palace.

A floor mosaic of the Great Palace depicts a tiger ripping apart a deer. Museum of Great Palace Mosaics

Roads, Squares and Monuments

"A capital city with its throne sitting on seven hills."
Von Stürmer 1816

After preparations lasting five years (325-30), the city "Byzantium" underwent a change in name – becoming "Constantinople." At the same time, it was transformed into a city worthy of being the capital of the Roman Empire. Everything necessary was undertaken to make it even more attractive and more beautiful than Rome ever was. The new city found itself with new roads connected to newly constructed forums. Monuments and statues in the squares were brought in from as far away as Egypt, Greece and Rome as well as ancient Anatolian cities such as Pergamon, Ephesus and Antioch.

This mystifying new city carried on as the capital of the Eastern Roman Empire after 395. Byzantine emperors ascending to the throne added to the wealth of the city by embellishing it with new edifices. Like Rome, Constantinople was founded on seven hills. The first hill was the place of the previous city's acropolis over which Hagia Sophia and Hagia Eirene rose. The second hill, in Çemberlitaş, is where Constantine built a forum. The third hill is where Süleymaniye Mosque is today. The fourth and fifth hills are where Fatih and Sultan Selim Mosques stand, respectively. The sixth hill is that closest to Edirnekapı, over which the Mihrimah Sultan Mosque rises. The final hill is that of Cerrahpaşa. Thus, the city of seven hills became decorated like a bride. However, the city was left in ruins during the Latin Invasion between the years 1204-61, when all the bronze works were melted down and all of the beautiful statues were removed from their pedestals and carried away.

Let's now get acquainted with the roads, squares and monuments of Constantinople, the capital of yesteryear. The ceremonial and political life of the city during the Roman and Byzantine periods took place in the Hippodrome and the adjacent Augusteion Square. As we shall focus on the Hippodrome in a separate chapter, let's discuss the Augusteion. Constructed during the reign of Constantine, it was located in an enclosed field in front of the Hippodrome and the Great Palace. Constantine had a column erected in the center of the field and put a statue of his mother Helena at the top of it. This place derives its name from the word "Augusta," which means "Empress." Theodosius I erected a column next to this statue and topped it off with a silver statue of himself. In addition, there were several other statues here such as Eudoxia, the wife of Arcadius as well as one of Leo. These statues were situated on this square, which was essentially the front courtyard of the Great Palace. They were all damaged during the Nike Revolt of 532 but remained in their places until the Iconoclastic period of the 8th century. While renovating the city, Justinian had the 35-meter high statue of Emperor Theodosius standing in the center of the square removed and replaced it with a silver statue of himself on a horse of bronze. Augusteion Square was surrounded by several structures,

Day and night views of the symbol of Istanbul, Leander's Tower. This landmark has undergone transformations since it was first built in 410 B.C. by Athenian Commander Alcibiades.

Constantine's Column in Çemberlitaş. One of Istanbul's oldest monuments, it was erected over the second hill, Çemberlitaş. Damaged during a fire that struck during the Ottoman period, it was reinforced with hoops to prevent its collapse. Its name means "Hooped Stone" in Turkish.

including the Great Palace, which was the largest church in the city, and the Patriarch and Senate buildings. Hagia Eirene was located to east of the Senate building in the area where the Byzantium acropolis was situated. There was also the Column of the Goths, located at a spot inside what is today Gülhane Park. The 15-meter high column made from blue-veined marble was topped with a Corinthian capital upon which there was a relief of an eagle. Set on top of a pedestal with steps, the column had an inscription from which it could be implied that it had been erected to commemorate the victory of Claudius over the Goths in the third century. Representing the begInning of the roads extending west and out to all corners of the empire, the Milion Stone was situated in the corner of this important square, next to the Yerebatan Cistern. It was once in the shape of a domed victory arch rising above a platform upon which the statues of Constantine and Helena with a cross in the center stood. Today, one can see the once-magnificent Milion Stone in the shadow of the Ottoman "water scales" adjacent to the light rail line in the opposite corner of Hagia Sophia.

Comprising the backbone of the city is the Mese, which started from the Milion Stone and extended to the Constantine Forum. The avenue was decorated on both sides with porticoes. Columns lining the avenue were topped with Corinthian or composite capitals. Its statue-lined outer edge, painted ceilings, and shops beneath the roofs all came together to create a picture of harmony. The shops here were all classified according to the merchandise sold. The Halkoprateius Church was situated behind the Yerebatan Cistern, which is directly behind the Milion Stone at the start of the Mese. The Lausus Palace was positioned between the avenue and the Hippodrome while the Antiochus Palace and a church, the name of which is unknown, were also located between this palace and the Hippodrome. Further on down the Mese, one comes to the Forum of Constantine Forum, which is in today's Çemberlitaş.

The oval-shaped Forum of Constantine, a symbolic place where the people would meet, was built over the previous city's necropolis. Ringed with two-storey porticoes, with arched entrances on the southeast and northwest sides, the Forum had statues of horses in the niches between its columns. Ancient sources mention that there was a nymphaeum to the west of the square. To the northeast was the Senate Building and in front of that were the porphyry porticoes, which featured two huge statues of Athena and Tetis. The square itself was decorated with numerous statues that Constantine had erected. The administration of Constantinople was conducted from this forum in particular; the city mayors and prefects would address the people from here. A column commemorating Constantine was erected in the center of this square. Known today as the "Çemberlitaş," the Constantine Column was formed by placing nine pieces of marble on top of each other. Marble laurel wreaths were placed on the column and some holy relics were buried underground during the positioning of this column, which was brought here in 328 from the Temple of Apollo in Rome. A statue of the emperor resembling that of Apollo was positioned at the very top of the 57-meter high monument. The head of this statue was adorned with seven rays with nails representing the suffering of Jesus hammered between them.

This statue was replaced by that of Emperor Julian, then later on with a statue of Theodosius. The latter was toppled in a storm that hit the city in 1105. Emperor Manuel I Comnenus (1143-80) replaced it with a Corinthian capital of marble, which was topped with a cross. This cross was brought down after the Turkish conquest in 1453. Cracks developed in the column as a result of a fire in the 17th century. They were repaired by Sultan Mustafa II, who reinforced its pedestal, wrapping the pillar with copper hoops. It is because of these hoops that the Constantine Column was subsequently named "Çemberlitaş," which means "Hooped Stone" in Turkish.

Continuing down the Mese from the Forum of Constantine, one reaches the Forum of Theodosius in Beyazıt Square. Constructed by Emperor Theodosius, it is identical to the Forum of Traianus in Rome, but on a slightly smaller scale. It was called "Forum Tauri" after Prefect Tauri. There was also a huge statue of a bronze bull in the center of this square. In 386, the Column of Theodosius I was erected in the northern part of this forum. Reliefs symbolizing the victories of the emperor were placed close to the top. At the very top of this column was a statue of the emperor sitting on a silver horse. Though this statue came down in an earthquake that struck in 480, the column remained standing for many years. Angiolello recorded that he had seen the column during his visit to the city in 1477, which implies that the column had remained erect until at least this date.

To the north of the Mese was the Capitol, which was one of the ancient pagan temples. Theodosius II converted this building into a university where courses such as Greek, Latin, philosophy and law were taught.

The Philadephieum was not so much a square as a junction decorated with many statues. Although its location is not precisely known, it is thought to have been in the place where Laleli Mosque stands today. There were once statues here of the three sons of Constantine, hugging each other. These statues were carried off by the Latins, who subsequently erected them in front of the Church of St. Marco in Venice. Today, this group of statues is known as the Tetrarchia Group. A second road that broke off from the Philadephieum passed next to the Church of the Apostoleion, traversed the Aetius open-air cistern, and then over to Edirnekapı. As for the Mese, it passed on to the Forum of Bovis to reach Amastrianun Square, which was situated between Beyazıt and Aksaray. Embellished with statues of Zeus, Heracles and Hermes, this square had a sports arena as well as an area of heavy commercial activity. There was also a theater located in the immediate vicinity. Famous as a place where death sentences were carried out as well as a center of soothsaying activities, this square, as well as the nearby theater, was destroyed during the latter part of the 8th century. It was replaced with a palace known as Eleuterius, built for Empress Irene. From here, the Mese reached the Forum of Bovis, which was

known to have been situated in today's Aksaray on the plain where the Mese and Lycus Stream converged. The name of the forum was derived from a huge bronze kettle wrought in the shape of an ox.

This kettle, which was brought here from Pergamon, was used as an oven during votive ceremonies. Like the city's other squares, this one was decorated with porticoes and statues. In the middle of the square once stood statues depicting Constantine and Helena holding silver crosses. All these statues disappeared in a fire that struck in 562. From here, Mese turned up to the

The "Kıztaşı" (Maiden's Monument) was constructed by Prefect Tatian on behalf of Emperor Marcian in the year 452.

The Galata Tower was reconstructed many times after it was first erected in 1348. Its commanding silhouette over the other buildings creates a stunning panoramic view from the sea.

seventh hill at Cerrahpaşa. Dating back to 403, the Forum of Emperor Arcadius was the last forum to have been built in Constantinople. Emperor Arcadius erected a column, decorated with reliefs symbolizing victories won over the Goths, in the center of the forum. His son, Theodosius II had a statue placed atop the column of Arcadius riding a horse.

This statue was toppled in an earthquake in 740, while the column itself was brought down intentionally in 1715 as it posed a threat to the surrounding area. However, before it was torn down, the reliefs decorating it were all drawn, and published in Paris in 1702. The pedestal, 8-9 meters of which still survives, can been seen in a garden of a home found on Haseki Kadın Sokağı in Cerrahpaşa. Another monument is that of "Kıztaşı" (Maiden's Monument), which is situated

in Sarıgüzel, Fatih. It was erected by Prefect Tatian in 452 to commemorate Emperor Marcian. Measuring 17 meters in height, the granite column was positioned on top of a marble pedestal.

The statue of Marcian that once topped it was brought down by the Latins. Its name was derived from the reliefs of a pair of angels on its pedestal. The Mese continues west from the Forum of Arcadius to reach the city gate in the walls of Constantine. From here, the avenue makes a sharp turn and heads south to reach Porto Aurea, also known as "Altın Kapı" in the walls of Theodosius II. Byzantine emperors returning from their victorious campaigns would enter the city through this gate and retreat to their palaces, saluting their people who lined the length of the Mese. Now, let's take the time to mention something

about Leander's Tower and Galata Tower, two landmarks that have graced the city skyline since the Byzantine period.

Galata Tower

An important site that continues to attract much attention in Istanbul today is the Galata Tower. Situated between Karaköy and Tünel, the tower offers a magnificent panoramic view of Karaköy. It was constructed as the principle tower of the surrounding protective walls in 1348 by the Genoese, who had a colony in the Galata District. First named the "Tower of Jesus," it remained within the newly constructed walls; both the tower and walls were raised a bit higher in 1448. All but 13 meters of the tower collapsed in an earthquake that struck in 1509. It was reconstructed by the Ottomans, who used it as a dungeon

in the 16th century to keep prisoners of war who worked in the Kasımpaşa Shipyard. The tower was rebuilt once again in 1794, after a devastating fire that engulfed the district, with an additional storey with windows extending on four sides and topped with a conical roof. It was subsequently used as a fire tower, only to be repaired in 1875 after it was once more gutted by fire.

The 68-meter high tower, which had 12 stories including the basement floor, was completely renovated and opened as a tourist attraction in 1967. The tower is famous as the site where, during the reign of Sultan Murad IV in 1632, Hezarfen Ahmed Çelebi leapt from the top of the tower in a pair of homemade wings. Çelebi is known to have landed in Doğancılar Square in Üsküdar, on the Asian side of the Bosphorus.

Leander's Tower

Situated on a group of submerged rocks just off the shore from Üsküdar and regarded as the symbol of Istanbul, Leander's Tower was first erected in 410 B.C. by the Athenian Commander Alcibiades to observe maritime vessels sailing in from the Black Sea.

It was used as an observation tower throughout the Byzantine period. Emperor Manuel I Comnenus (1143-80) converted the tower into a fortress. Ancient sources mention that he wanted to prevent enemy ships from getting through the Bosphorus by tying one end of an immense chain from the nearby Damalis Hill and stretching the other end over to the Mermer Tower in the Mangana district of Sarayburnu.

After conquering the city, Sultan Mehmed II converted the tower into an observation tower. It was destroyed in an earthquake that struck in 1509 and was subsequently rebuilt using timber planks. The wooden tower was to be repaired several times, but it was in 1725-26 that the Grand Vizier Damat İbrahim Pasha had it replaced with a stone block tower after being destroyed in a fire. Sultan Mahmud II ordered it to be completely renovated in 1832. Turned over to the Lighthouse Administration in 1857, it was recently restored and given a totally new appearance. It is currently

operated as a tourist attraction. The Leander's Tower is the source of a number of legends, one of the most enduring of which surrounds the tale of a young maiden named Hero and her lover Leander.

For some reason, Hero is locked up in this tower and, guided by a torch held in her hands, Leander would swim across the Bosphorus every night to be at her side. However, as fate would have it, the torch was blown out by the wind, and poor Leander lost his way, perishing in the stormy waters of the Bosphorus. It is because of this tale that western sources refer to the Leander's Tower as the Maiden's Tower. However, this story is actually in reference to Leander of Abidos and Hero of Sestos who lived along the shores of the Strait of Dardanelles. Over time, this story became erroneously identified with Leander's Tower.

Another legend concerning the tower dates back to the Byzantine Empire. According to the legend, soothsayers prophesied that the daughter of a Byzantine emperor was to die from a snakebite. The emperor had his daughter kept in this tower to protect her from any such dangerous snakes. However, the girl's lover sends her a basket of figs and alas, a serpent slithers out of the basket to bite her with his poisonous fangs. Fate has coupled this everlasting tale as the one most suitable for the Leander's Tower.

The Hippodrome

The Hippodrome has reverberated with people's screams for thousands of years.

As a place where yesterday's chariot races were held, the cries of victory resounded, and endless exuberance was experienced. Today, the Hippodrome stretches through Sultanahmet Square in comparatively deep silence, in the shadows of obelisks of the past. Nevertheless, it was once a place for social gatherings, where political conflicts occurred, and where thousands of voices rose in unison during both the Roman and Byzantine eras. The grounds where excited shouts cheered on chariots jockeying for position echoed later became the place where the people would express their dissatisfaction. Contests in which the "Blues," representing the sky, the "Greens," representing the earth, the "Whites," representing water and the "Reds," representing fire, were previously held here. Later the "Whites" and "Reds" diminished and ultimately disappeared, leaving only the "Blues" and "Greens," groups representing two separate political ideologies.

The silk awning of the imperial loggia was the harbinger of contests to take place the following day. The "Blues," who represented Orthodoxy and the large land barons would cheer on their chariot jockeys competing against those of the "Greens," who represented merchants, artisans and Monophysists. Over time, the fervor of these races became transformed into a rebellion against the emperor; the Greens and Blues, with their differing ideologies, staged a joint riot against the emperor. What was to be called the Nike Revolt led to the burning to the ground of the Hippodrome, Hagia Sophia and the Augusteion in 532.

The construction of the rectangular-shaped Hippodrome, which stretched in an east-west direction, was started by Septimius Severus and completed by Constantine around 330. The Hippodrome measured 440 meters x 117 meters. Its entrance, where a statue by Lysippus of a chariot drawn by four horses was situated, was from Hagia Sophia Square. In a semi-circular shape facing East-West, the section across the entrance was known as "Sphendone." It rose up via galleries, as the ground here was inclined. Wild beasts used to be kept in the galleries, but they were later used as a cistern. When Petrus Gyllius passed through here in 1544, he acknowledged that the gallery, surrounded by 17 columns, was still intact. This section remains as the back end of Marmara University. The gallery walls can be seen to the right of the road sloping down to the shore. There is also a cistern located across these walls. As the Great Palace was once situated on the site where the Sultan Ahmed Mosque is today, the imperial loggia, called the "Kathisma Palace," faced this direction as well. The loggia was reached from the palace via a winding staircase. Placed over a platform supported by four marble columns, the loggia had a marble throne for the emperor to sit on as well as armchairs for his entourage. There were undoubtedly other chambers found

Compared to today's relative calm, the Hippodrome once resonated with frenzied chariot races.

The Egyptian Obelisk and minarets of the Sultan Ahmed Mosque racing each other to the sky.

adjacent to the loggia. For instance, the guards' chamber was beneath the loggia. The grandstands of the Hippodrome were at first made of wood, but because they all burned down during the Nike Revolt, Justinian had them made of marble.

The section for women at the Hippodrome consisted of a gallery with bars posited over 37 columns that were connected with vaults. The center of the Hippodrome where chariots raced was called the Spina and was decorated with a number of monuments. These included the Serpent Column, which Constantine had brought from Delphi, the Obelisk of Egyptian Pharoah Thutmosis III, which was shipped here from Egypt but erected many years later, as well as the Column of Constantine VII Porphyrogenitus, which was erected here by the emperor of the same name in the Late Byzantine period and which once had bronze placards attached to it. Ancient sources tell us that there were seven other columns besides these obelisks, with a statue of dolphins at one end of the Spina and egg-shaped emblems of the gods Neptune, Castor and Pollux at the other end. In addition, there were statues – one of which had been sculpted by Diocletian – that had been brought here from the previous capital, Nicomedia, positioned in front of the imperial loggia. There were up to 60 statues on top of the walls of the Hippodrome, which reflected the splendor of this structure.

Among the most popular forms of entertainment held in this place, where the emperor and his subjects carried on with their daily activities, were the chariot races. Commencing at the gate, seven laps would be run around the Spina. Chariot jockeys who won these races would gain the great admiration of the people and become famous. There were statues of several jockeys in the Hippodrome. These include the one of Porphyrius, a famous rider during the reign of Anastasius I.

During the Ottoman period, the Hippodrome was the scene of javelin throwing on horseback, which is why it is called "At Meydanı" in Turkish. In addition to other sporting events, this is where the weddings of Ottoman crown princes were held. Cut blocks of stone where removed from the foundation of the Hippodrome to build the İbrahim Pasha Palace, known

Views of both the Serpent Column and Egyptian Obelisk. The hieroglyphics inscribed on the latter tells of the victories of Pharaoh Thutmosis III, whereas the former was presented as a votive at the Temple at Delphi by the Greek cities for their victory over the Persians in 479 B.C.

today as the Museum of Turkish and Islamic Art. The construction of this palace spelled the end of the magnificent Hippodrome of the Byzantines. However, the statues here had disappeared well before the Ottomans came into the picture. The work of Athena with a lance was destroyed by the Christians, and the Latin Duke Henricus Dandolo carted off the statue of Lysippus' chariot pulled by four horses and had it erected it at the entrance of the Church of St. Marco in Venice.

In the northern part of the Hippodrome is the German Fountain, which was presented by Kaiser Wilhelm II as a gift to Ottoman Sultan Abdülhamid II. Cast in 1898 by the German architect M. Spitta, it was placed in this site in 1901 and given the name "Alman Çeşmesi." Supported by columns, the dome of the fountain is decorated with golden mosaics on its interior and tiles on its exterior.

Now, let's try to imagine the old days in the splendid Hippodrome as we get acquainted with the monuments remaining today.

The Egyptian Obelisk

Two monuments can be seen right next to each other in Sultanahmet Square today. The one containing Egyptian hieroglyphics was brought from the Temple of Karnak in Egypt by Constantine, but it was not immediately put up due to technical reasons. It was erected by Theodosius I in 390, when it was commemorated with his name. Including its pedestal, it stands 24.87 meters high. It sits on a pink granite pedestal weighing 200 tons and has reliefs that depict the life of Emperor Theodosius. On its northern face are the Byzantine Arcadius and his wife Eudoxia sitting in their Hippodrome loggia. Its western face shows Emperor Theodosius on his throne with his wife and children sitting with Arcadius and Honorius, with defeated enemies in front of them. On its eastern face is a depiction of Emperor Theodosius watching a chariot race with his two sons on one side and Valentinian II on the other. Brought from Egypt, this obelisk was transported here from the shore over a specially made road. From the inscription of the pedestal, it took Prefect Proclus 32 days, putting up scaffolding all around it. The hieroglyphics on this single-piece obelisk, which was erected at the Temple of Karnak in Lower Egypt by Pharoah Thutmosis III in 1547 B.C., describes his victories. The east face of the obelisk, from which a section of the lower part has broken off, has the words, "Thutmosis III of the 18th dynasty, master

The sequence of reliefs on the plinth of the Egyptian Obelisk constitute a record of the daily life of the Byzantine Emperor Theodosius. It was erected over a period of 32 days during the year 390.

of Upper and Lower Egypt, on the 30th anniversary of his reign, as conqueror of the seas and rivers, has set up this obelisk for the countless anniversaries to come." The inscription on its southern side, states, "Thutmosis, the all-powerful and all-just son of the Sun, ruler of Upper and Lower Egypt, has penetrated as far as Mesopotamia, at the head of his armies, has shown his might on the Mediterranean, and has fought great battles."

The western face reads, "Thutmosis, son of the Sun, who bears the crowns of Upper and Lower Egypt on his brow through the strength, might and wealth of Horos, after paying tribute to the god Amona, built this work for his father, the god Amon-Ra, that it may spread light like the rays of the sun to Mankind." The northern side is inscribed with the pictorial symbols, "Thutmosis paid tribute to the god Amon-Ra, and then, with the might and power of Horus he determined to take the borders of his country as far as Mesopotamia."

Column of Constantine Porphyrogenitus

Situated at the back of Sultanahmet Square, the Serpent Column was most likely made towards the end of the 4th century, during the reign of Arcadius. It was repaired later on by Constantine VII Porphyrogenitus (913-59), who also had it bronze-plated. This is why it is commonly referred to by his name. This ancient monument is a roughly built pillar of stone 32 meters high. The bronze plates depicted the victories of Constantine VII Porphyrogenitus and his grandfather Basil I (867-86). It is unfortunate that the Latins removed these plates to mint coinage during their occupation of Constantinople.

The Serpent Column

Situated in a gap between two monuments, the Serpent Column was placed here by Constantine the Great, who had it brought from the Temple of Apollo at Delphi. Dating from the Hellenistic period, this trophy was dedicated to Apollo as a token of gratitude by the 31 Greek cities that had defeated the Persians in the battle of Plataea (479 B.C.). According to tradition, the bronze serpents were cast from the shields of the fallen Persian warriors and a gold kettle was positioned on top. The Latins removed this kettle from its place during the occupation of Constantinople and melted it down as well.

Column of Constantinople VII Porphyrogenitus. It has lost its brilliance as the plates covering it were removed during the Latin Invasion.

Byzantine Cisterns

Reflections of the cistern columns on the water transport visitors into a dream world.

Having ruled the city for about a millennium, the Byzantines were besieged several times, but could not be defeated. Forces surrounding the walls would cut off the water supply to leave the Byzantines without water and wait for the city to surrender.

It was the Romans who brought water to the city with aqueducts, which came in from western Thrace. Constructed in 368, the Valens Aqueduct, known as the Bozdoğan Aqueduct today, was 20 meters high and 971 meters long. A large section of the two-storey aqueduct is seen at the top of Saraçhane. The Byzantines constructed huge cisterns to store water and to meet the city's water needs whenever enemies attacking the city cut off the water supply. Thus, with these cisterns, they were able to hold out for months against the Ottoman efforts to take the city. As the Ottomans did not regard stagnant water very highly, they did nothing with the cisterns, but rather repaired the Byzantine Mazul and Valens Aqueducts. They also constructed new works, such as those of Mağlova, Uzunkemer and Güzelce, to bring the city water, which was piped throughout the city so as to flow copiously from its numerous fountains.

Until now, while 40 cisterns have been positively identified in Istanbul, ancient sources describe the existence of about 24 others, the locations of which have not been determined. In addition to meeting the demand for water, cisterns also formed the terraces of structures such as palaces, churches and monasteries. For instance, those found in the Mangana Palace and the Great Palace situated on the slope of Topkapı Palace overlooking the sea, were of this form. Moreover, a number of cisterns such as those of the Studius Cistern, Pantocrator Cistern, Yerebatan Cistern and Binbirdirek Cistern were monumental in scope.

The largest and most splendid of these cisterns, called Yerebatan Palace, was situated near Hagia Sophia. The second largest was that of Binbirdirek Cistern, situated behind today's Courthouse Building in Sultanahmet. It was constructed for Philoxenus, one of the senators who had come from Rome to Byzantium with Emperor Constantine. This cistern measures 64 meters x 54 meters and is comprised of 224 columns in rows of 14 x 16. Together with its columns with plain capitals, the Binbirdirek once reached a height of 20 meters. As the columns were not tall enough, this height was attained by stacking two columns on top of each other. Not far from this cistern is one called the Theodosius Cistern, which is situated under the Eminönü Municipality Building on Piyer Loti Caddesi. There are many more cisterns beneath Istanbul. For instance, the remains of a large cistern were discovered in the garden of Topkapı Palace during the construction of an additional wing of the Archaeological Museum. Cisterns have also been found on Soğukçeşme Sokak behind Hagia Sophia, beneath the Istanbul High School, as well as under the Merzifonlu Kara Mustafa Pasha Complex in Çemberlitaş. There is also a cistern in Çarşamba, of indeterminate date and name, which has seven columns. Other cisterns include the one that is on the site of a former church under the At Pazarı Square in Fatih, one uncovered during the construction of the Istanbul University parking lot in Beyazıt, another one belonging to Topkapı Palace in front of Sultan Ahmed Mosque, as well as one to the east of the Hippodrome, to the left of the Shore Road. There is also an interesting rectangular-planned cistern with 28 columns next to the Kasım Ağa Mosque in

Yerebatan Cistern (left). Situated opposite Hagia Sophia, this was the largest and most magnificent cistern constructed by the Byzantines. It is supported by 336 columns in rows of 12.
The second largest after Yerebatan Cistern was Binbirdirek Cistern, which has 224 columns measuring 64 meters x 54 meters (below).

Karagümrük and a series of cisterns beneath the Zeyrek Church Mosque. The niches of this cistern can be seen on the perimeter of Atatürk Boulevard. There are also those cisterns beneath Istanbul that met the water needs of palaces, monasteries, baths and private buildings. Besides these enclosed cisterns, there are a number of large open-air ones. The best preserved of these is the Hebdomon Cistern, also called "Fil Damı," which is situated behind the Veliefendi Race Track in Bakırköy. Measuring 127 meters x 76 meters x 11 meters, this cistern is surrounded by walls four meters thick. This cistern was built to meet the water needs of the Byzantine soldiers gathered here and to provide water to the nearby district called Hebdomon. Subsequent to looting by the Latins in 1204, this district diminished in importance, eventually emerging as a small fishing village.

It is for this reason that this open cistern, which had met the water needs in the area, also lost its importance. When the conquering Turks found this cistern in ruins along with a number of other structures, they housed the palace elephants here, which is why it was named "Fildamı" ("fil" meaning elephant). Beneath the Karagümrük Stadium was another open-air cistern, which measured 244 meters x 85 meters. It was constructed by Aethius, an important commander during the Valentinian period. Yet another large Byzantine open-air cistern, which covered 170 meters x 140 meters (23,800 m2), was that of

Left over from an earlier period, these Medusa column heads were placed under the short pillars of the Yerebatan Cistern as support.

the St. Mocius Cistern, constructed by Emperor Anastasius (491-518). This cistern is also known as "Altımermer - Çukurbostanı." Its name is derived from the nearby St. Mocius Church. Another cistern is the Aspar Cistern beneath the Selim the Grim Complex in Yavuzselim. Constructed by Commander Aspar in 460, the cistern encompasses an area of 23,104 m2. This cistern is also known as "Çukurbostan" as it was utilized as a vegetable garden ("bostan" meaning garden) during the Ottoman period. Because of a prophecy that he was to drown in water, Emperor Heracleius (610-41) had some of these cisterns filled in. Though they were dug out by Basil I of Macedonia (867-86) and utilized once again, the cisterns were never completed filled to capacity. In fact, they all filled up with mud and silt over time. Prior to the Ottoman period, these cisterns were turned into vineyards and gardens during the Byzantine period.

Yerebatan Cistern

Situated across from Hagia Sophia, this cistern was constructed to meet the water needs of Topkapı Palace and other edifices. It was called the "Yerebatan Saray," which means, "Sunken Palace," during the Ottoman period. It is also called the "Basilica" or "Justinian" Cistern. Prior to being turned into a cistern, it was a basilica that had served as a cultural center during the reign of Constantine. The basilica is understood to have had a terrace overlooking the harbors and the Bosphorus. One had to climb 72 steps on the north side to reach the top. It is also known that Constantine II had a 120,000-volume capacity library put inside. When the library was lost in a fire in 476, it was

capitals was placed sideways while the other was positioned upside down. The bricks, vaults and domes above the columns bolster the ceiling. Although it may appear that the distance between the columns is the same, they do vary. For instance, the eight naves in the southwest are 4.7 meters in width, while the four naves in the east are 5.10 meters wide. Following the conquering of Istanbul, the water from this cistern was used to water the gardens of Topkapı Palace. The cistern was then neglected and its existence forgotten about for decades.

In visiting the city between 1544-47, the wealthy Frenchman Petrus Gyllius recorded that he saw some folks in the homes across from Hagia Sophia hang buckets down through holes in their homes to draw water. Wondering where the water was being drawn from, he went down the steps that the residents showed him and saw the incredible cistern. Under the reflection of a torch, the homeowner peered into the cistern, showing the burbling waters and explained that fish were netted there as well.

It was to be hundreds of years before the cistern was dredged. Between 1986-88, fifty tons of mud were removed, after which the cistern was opened to tourism. Illumination of the 800 meters of concrete paths has enabled tours to be made there. The illuminated forest of columns and their reflection in the water provides the cistern with an impressive ambience.

Two different scenes of the Yerebatan Cistern. It has recently been cleaned and opened for visits. Reflections on the water emanating from the forest of pillars are quite striking.

rebuilt by an individual named Illus, who lived during the rule of Emperor Zeno. Beautifully decorated, the vaulted ceilings of the basilica were painted with gold leaf. There were also several statues, sculpted during different periods, in the courtyard. They were all destroyed during the Iconoclastic period.

The basilica was never mentioned after the 10th century, when it was most probably utilized as a marketplace. As with many other structures, this basilica was badly damaged during the Nike Revolt. It was Justinian I who restored places that had been destroyed by fire. In repairing the basilica in 542, he had the gold leaf carved out and subsequently had the cistern constructed. The historian Procopius had this to say about the basilica: "This basilica, which has a very large courtyard and is surrounded on four sides with pavilions, was a structure which sat upon a rock foundation. This was where lawyers and judges held their trials. It was also where Emperor Justinian, digging under the courtyard and southern pavilions, had water storage areas built that would be beneficial during the summer months."

Measuring 138 meters x 64.6 meters, the perimeters of the cistern were surrounded by brick walls. A total of 336 columns were laid out in 12 rows of 28 in order to bolster the basilica above. With columns measuring 9-10 meters high, the cistern was calculated to hold 75,000 m3 of water. Some marble columns brought in from Marmara Island that were too short were shored up with other material. For example, Medusa-head capitals, which were of an earlier period, were placed under one of the short columns. One of these

Churches and Monasteries

God cooperated with Man and Mother Nature collaborated with art to create this incomparable and magnificent piece of nature.

A. Lamartine

There are numerous Byzantine churches in Istanbul today. Out of the nearly 50 churches and monasteries that existed in the city during the final period of the Byzantine Empire, about 40 were converted into mosques between the period of Sultan Mehmed II until that of Murad IV. Twenty-five of the churches continue to exist, albeit with new names. The oldest of these is Hagia Eirene. It, along with Hagia Sophia, was damaged by fire during the Nike Revolt of 532 and was rebuilt by Emperor Justinian. It was second only to Hagia Sophia in size. In addition to these very large and important churches, there is also the Kariye Museum, also known as the Chora Monastery, which is world-famous for its mosaics.

Located at the top of Saraçhane, the Church of St. Polyectus was one of the large, magnificent churches in the Byzantine Empire; it was plundered during the Latin Invasion. Another church, which still has mosaics decorating its interior, is the Church of St. Mary Pammakaristos Church, also known today as the Fethiye Mosque. Overlooking the Golden Horn on a hill in the district of Çarşamba, the church was dedicated to Mary. Murad III, who converted this church into a mosque, named it the "Fethiye Mosque" to commemorate his conquests in Azerbaijan and Georgia in 1591 ("Fetih," meaning conquest). A section of the structure is still used as a mosque, while one can also stroll through the "parecclesion" section, which is a museum.

The Small Hagia Sophia (Church of St. Sergius and St. Bacchus), which has a floor plan resembling that of Hagia Sophia, is located at a spot near Çatladı Kapı, along the shore of the Sea of Marmara. The church was built by Emperor Justinian and his wife Theodora between the years 527-36 and is dedicated to St. Sergius and St. Bacchus. It was said that Justinian plotted the assassination of Emperor Anastasius before he ascended to the throne. Justinian was saved from certain death when these two saints appeared to the emperor in a dream and informed him that Justinian was Innocent. Justinian had this church built in a place near the palace when he himself became emperor as a debt of gratitude to the saints.

The interior of the church is round and covered with a broad and shallow dome on top, positioned over eight pillars. There is an inscription winding completely around the structure's walls, which are decorated with very meticulous stone craftsmanship. This inscription contains the names of Emperor Justinian and his famous wife Theodora. In addition, the column capitals, which are themselves masterpieces of craftsmanship, also have the emperor's monogram etched into them. One of the principal centrally

(left) A close-up view of the inner Parecclesion Dome of the St. Mary Pammakaristos Church (Fethiye Museum).

(below) Interior view of the Parecclesion of the St. Mary Pammakaristos Church.

planned structures of the Early Byzantine period, it was converted into a mosque around the year 1500 by Darussaade Ağası Hüseyin Ağa. The Tomb of Hüseyin Ağa, with its single-balcony minaret and five-domed main prayer hall, was added in later years.

Situated in Laleli on Sait Efendi Street, the Bodrum Mosque was once known as the Myrelaion Monastery. It was constructed by Emperor Romanus Lecapenus (920-44) and his co-emperor Constantine VII Porphyrogenitus next to the private palace. The ruins of a round structure 30 meters in diameter, dating back to the Roman period, was found next to a church with a plan in the form of a cross. When the monastery and church were built, this structure was transformed into a cistern to meet the water needs of the monastery. Romanus Lecapenus I, who was born the son of a peasant and had ascended to the throne through sheer luck, was buried in this church upon his death in 948. His wife and children,

Christopher and Constantine VII Porphyrogenitus (946), were also buried here. The church was converted into a mosque, to be called the Bodrum Mosque, around the year 1500 by Mesih Pasha, who was the Grand Vizier and of Palaeologus descent.

Another Byzantine church that has managed to remain intact to the present is the Kalenderhane Mosque, at the bottom of the Bozdoğan Aqueduct in the vicinity of Şehzadebaşı. It is believed that the church, the name of which was not quite clear, was the church of the Acaleptus Monastery, constructed in the 11th century during the period of the Comnenus. Proceeding the conquest of Istanbul, the four-armed church with a cross plan was converted into a mosque by Sultan Mehmed the Conqueror and handed over to a group of dervishes in the army who were called "kalender." It is for this reason that it was called Kalenderhane Mosque. In recent years, a group of American researchers conducting

St. Mary Pammakaristos Church. Built in the 11th century, this church was converted into the Fethiye Mosque by Murad III in 1591. Now open as a museum, visitors can view the numerous mosaics of Jesus Christ covering the walls.

The mosaic of Jesus Christ found in the "parecclesion" (Fethiye Museum) apse of St. Mary Pammakaristos Church (Fethiye Mosque).

studies at the mosque uncovered an inscription in Latin mentioning the name of St. Siscus. From this inscription, it is understood that the church was utilized as a Catholic church during the Latin Invasion of Byzantine between 1204-61.

The oldest Byzantine church in the city is located between Yedikule and Samatya. The St. John the Baptist Church, or the İmrahor İlyas Bey Mosque as it is known today, was built in 461. Returning victorious from the battlefront, the emperor would enter this church to pray after entering the city through the victory arch called the "Golden Gate." This church was among those looted during the Latin Invasion of 1204. After the city was conquered by the Ottomans, the church was converted into the İmrahor İlyas Bey mosque and dervish lodge during the Bayezid II period. Representing a fine example of the basilicas of the Early Christian era, this church is divided into three naves by rows of columns. The floor mosaics here are stunningly beautiful. The Studius Monastery, which made up part of this church, was one of the largest monasteries. A sad incident took place in the church in 1057. The young Emperor Michael V had taken refuge there, only to be hauled out by an angry mob, which drove a shaft into his eyes. A huge cellar that was once the monastery's cistern was left partially in ruins in a fire a few years ago while it was being used as a workshop.

Located in the Inner part of the Walls of the Golden Horn at Ayvansaray, the Atik Mustafa Pasha Mosque was originally a church that was constructed in the 9th-10th centuries to dedicate St. Thecla. The cross-planned church was converted into a mosque by Atik Mustafa Pasha, who was a Grand Vizier during the reign of Sultan Bayezid II. The dome of the church was repaired at a later date. The baptismal fount, which was once situated in front of the structure, is currently on display in the Istanbul Archaeological Museum.

Also located on the banks of the Golden Horn, in the district of Cibali, is the Gül (Rose) Mosque, which was once a Byzantine church. The church was constructed in the 9th century and later called the St. Theodosia Church. It was converted into a mosque in the final decade of the 15th century.

The reason the church came to be called the Gül Mosque was that the day of St. Rose happens to fall on the same day Istanbul was conquered, e.g., the 29th of May. This church was found decorated with roses after

Mosaics of some church priests are exhibited alongside those of Jesus Christ in the Fethiye Museum.

Istanbul was captured and it was because of this that it bears her name.

The upper sections and dome of this church, which was a tall structure built on a cross-plan, were configured in their current state during the Turkish period. The Fenari İsa Mosque, which was the Constantine Lips Monastery during the Byzantine period, is situated at the corner of Halıcılar Caddesi, just off Vatan Caddesi.

The church of this monastery was dedicated to Mother Mary and built in 907 by Constantine Lips, who was a naval commander during the period of Leo VI. This church was expanded in later years when Empress Theodora, the wife of Michael Palaeologus VIII (1259-1282), added a second church in the name of John the Baptist.

This is also the burial ground of the Palaeologus dynasty. Because the graves of the emperors in the Church of the Aposotleion and Pantocrator Monastery Church in Fatih were ransacked during the Latin invasion, the new graves of the Palaeologus lineage are thought to be here. Andronicus Palaeologus II as well as a number of persons from the imperial family of that period were buried here. Located in the close vicinity of these churches was also the Lips Covent and a hospital connected to it. Subsequent to the Istanbul conquest, these churches built on a cross plan were converted into a dervish lodge and mosque by Fenarizade Alaeddin Ali Efendi during the period of Bayezid II. Sheikh İsa turned this into a dervish lodge during the period of Murad IV; this is why the complex assumed the name, the Fenari İsa Mosque.

A structure consisting of two adjacent wings added to the west and south of these two churches burned down in 1633. This structure underwent a number of changes during the renovation, which included the addition of large vaults to the interior of both churches, carried out by Vaultram Pasha in 1638. Having distinctive masonry, the structure was reduced to rubble in a fire in 1918. It was repaired and reopened for religious services in 1960.

The Vefa Church Mosque is located on Molla Şemsettin Gürani Street in the Vefa district. Though its name is not known for certain, this church must have been constructed in the name of St. Theodore in either the 11th or 12th century. This church bears the features of two different periods. An outer hall with three domes and five sections was added to the western side of the church at the end of the 13th century. It was converted to a mosque in the post-conquest period and named for Molla Gürani, a famous theologist of the period who lived in this district and was highly revered by his followers. Mosaics depicting Pentateuch prophets were discovered within the southern domes of the outer narthex during archaeological studies of the mosque in 1936. In the center of these mosaics is Mary, who is holding the Christ Child in her bosom, and is surrounded by eight prophets. The Koca Mustafa Pasha Mosque in the Koca Mustafa Pasha district is also an ancient Byzantine church. It is the church of the St. Andreas Monastery, which was founded in the 13th century after the Latin Invasion.

This church was converted into a mosque by Koca Mustafa Pasha, a Grand Vizier, during the rule of Sultan Bayezid II. A dervish lodge was built next door by Sheikh Sümbül Sinan. As the exterior of the mosque was changed during the Turkish period, traces of Byzantine architecture may only be seen on the inside.

The Ahmed Pasha Mescid in the Çarşamba district of Fatih was once the St. John the Baptist Church, which was converted into a mosque during the Murad III period. The Kefeli Mosque, in the vicinity of the Chora Museum, was an old Byzantine monastery. Today's Kefeli Mosque is believed to have been the St. Nicholas Church. It was converted into a mosque during the reign of Selim I, at which time the minber was constructed by Hekimoğlu Ali Pasha.

Overlooking Atatürk Bulvarı in the Zeyrek quarter of Fatih is the Pantocrator Monastery Church, which was one of the largest and most important structures of the Byzantine Empire. The church was constructed by the architect Nicephorus upon the orders of Emperor John Comnenus II (1118-43) and his wife Irene, both of whose pictures are found in Hagia Sophia. There are a number of buildings, including a monastery, hospital and geriatric home. The monastery was plundered during the Latin Invasion. Of these structures, only three churches remained standing after the Byzantine Empire was rescued from the Latins.

The three churches that are still intact today are the Christ the Pantocrator, in the south, the Blessed Mary Church, in the north, and a church in the middle, the name of which is unknown, where tombs of prominent members of the Comnenus dynasty are found. This church continued to provide cemetery functions until the end of the Byzantine Empire. The floor of the southernmost of these churches, which are among the most important in the Byzantine Empire, is covered with mosaics. After his conquest, Sultan Mehmed the Conqueror turned this church into a medrese (a Muslim school of theology) and appointed Molla Zeyrek Mehmed Efendi to be its Head Teacher. Later on, the medrese was named Zeyrek Mosque to commemorate its first teacher. Today, only the Church of Christ the Pantocrator in the south is used as a mosque.

Another mosque in Istanbul that was converted from a church is the Arap Mosque. This mosque was erected over a church that existed when Karaköy was dominated by the Genoese. The Gothic style St. Domenico Church, which was constructed by members of the Dominican sect, was converted into a mosque after the conquest of Istanbul. Moors who were forced to flee Andulusia in Spain settled here and named the mosque "Arap Camisi." Nevertheless, it is widely believed that this mosque was built during the Arab siege of Byzantine. Restored in 1911-12, the mosque is in use today.

While large churches were converted into mosques, the smaller ones were used as mescids. Examples of these are the Monastery Mescid in Topkapı,

Interior view of the Parecclesion Dome of the St. Mary Pammakaristos Church. (Fethiye Museum).

the İbrahim Pasha Mescid, which is situated within the grounds of Cerrahpaşa Hospital, the Sheikh Süleyman Mescid in Zeyrek, the Balaban Ağa Mescid in Laleli and the Sheikh Murad Mescid along the shore of the Golden Horn. Just as several churches were converted into mosques, many of them continue to serve as churches. For instance, one of these which still holds services is the Panhagia Mouchliotissa Church in Fener. Constructed over a late-Roman period tomb site, this church is also known as St. Mary of the Mongols. Her story is quite intriguing.

Maria was the illegitimate daughter of Michael Palaeologus. At the beginning of the 13th century, Mary embarked on a trip to Mongolia; her objective was to become the bride of Hulagu Khan, who resided in the great Mongolian Palace. On the way, she learned that Hulagu had passed away, but she continued on her way, determined to marry his son, Abaka Khan instead. While Mary was expending tremendous effort to spread Christianity amongst the Mongolians, Abaca was killed in 1281 by his brother Ahmed, who sent Mary back to Constantinople. She in turn chose to be a nun and had this church built. It is for this reason that the church is called St. Mary of the Mongols. Hanging on its walls are copies of Sultan Mehmed the Conqueror's decree for preserving this site as a church. It continues to conduct religious services.

Also located in Fener, the Greek Orthodox Patriarchate is an historical building. The Patriarchate was situated next to Hagia Sophia when Istanbul was conquered by Sultan Mehmed II and later transferred to the Church of the Apostoleion in Fatih. Gennadius, who was brought to the Patriarchate, continued his duties here. However, a decision was made to tear down the church, which was already in ruins, and to construct the Fatih Mosque. Subsequently, the Patriarchate was transferred to the St. Mary Pammakaristos Church and from there, over to

The Eski İmaret Mosque in the north of the Fatih district was first erected as the church of Pantepoptes Monastery upon the orders of Anna Dalassena in 1087.

Interior view of the "Small" Hagia Sophia Church built under the orders of Emperor Justinian and Empress Theodora between 527-36.

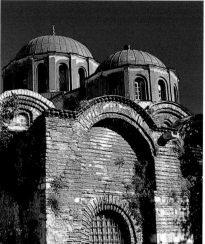

Two views of the churches of the Pantocrator Monastery in Zeyrek. Comprised of three separate chapels that were ordered by Emperor John II and his wife Irene. The center structure was constructed as a "grave chapel."

the St. Demetrius Kanabu Church in 1597 and finally to its current site in 1601. Constructed in the 1720s and repaired in 1830, the St. George Church is situated within the Patriarchate. In recent years, it has been renovated and has since reopened to hold services. Besides the religious relics preserved here, there are also the coffins of three saints. Also within the church is the Patriarch Throne, a masterpiece of wood craftsmanship, Bible stands, and the absolutely stunning Blessed Mary Icon mosaic, which was transported here from the St. Mary Pammakaristos Church. When the Bulgarians did not wish to remain loyal to the Patriarchate, they went ahead and constructed the Bulgarian Church on the shores of the Golden Horn in 1898. The iron works were wrought in the Waagner Foundry in Vienna were brought to their present location and put into place. The Peribleptos Monastery Church situated in Samatya was donated to the Armenian constituency after the conquest of Istanbul.

The Surp Kevork Church was constructed on the site of this church in 1870. Moreover, there are also several Catholic Armenian churches and Jewish synagogues located in various parts of Istanbul.

Thus, one can see the places of worship of all religions in Istanbul. Besides all these, the skyline is filled with minarets of mosques, possessing great beauty as well as great significance. This is evidence of just how tolerant Turks have been of different religions over the years.

Hagia Sophia

"Let's Praise the Lord for providing me the opportunity to construct such a wondrous place of worship."

Justinian, 27 December 537

After the proclamation of Christianity as the official state religion, the Emperor Constantine laid the foundations of Hagia Sophia. In doing so, he began outfitting Rome's new capital with new buildings. The construction of this church, which is in the shape of a basilica with a wooden roof, took quite a long time. It was completed during the reign of Constintine's son, Constantinus II, with an inaugural ceremony taking place on 15 February 360. After remaining erect for 44 years, this first structure was burned to the ground during a rebellion that occurred in 404. It was subsequently repaired during the reign of Theodosius II and reinaugurated in 415. After remaining intact for just over a century, it was razed to the ground as a result of the Nike Revolt, which took place in 532.

One of the leading landmarks of world art history, Hagia Sophia was first called "Megale Ecclesia," which means "Great Church." It began to be known as Hagia Sophia from the 5th century onwards. Turks call this church "Ayasofya." To refute a popular misconception, this church was not presented to a saint named Sophia but rather dedicated to "Theia Sophia," e.g., the Sacred Wisdom, known as the second element of the Christian Trinity. Not wasting any time, Emperor Justinian undertook to replace the charred embers of the church by assigning the task to two architects, named Isidoros of Miletos and Anthemius of Tralles, ordering construction materials to be transported in from the far corners of the empire. In addition to bringing in valuable columns from one of the Seven Wonders of the World, the Temple of Artemis in Ephesus, from the Temple of Zeus in Kyzicus, as well as from Egypt, they also had marble from the most important quarries transported to the site. It took 7,000 workers five years and ten months to complete the work and when it was finished, it became the unofficial Eighth Wonder of the World. Clasping hands with the patriarch at the opening ceremony on 27 December 537, the emperor expressed his amazement by saying, "Praise the Lord for giving me the opportunity to construct such a wondrous place of worship."

The structure was not entirely finished, though, with the interior mosaic decoration work continuing through the reign of Justin II (565-78). While the interior decorations were just beautiful, the size of its dome impressive and its architecture Innovative, the dome was statically imperfect. Both the large dome and the semi-dome on the eastern side had cracked and collapsed as a result of earthquakes which struck in 557 and 558. Repairs were made at once as the reigning Emperor Justinian appointed Isidoros the Younger, the nephew of Isidoros, the task of repairing the structure. He came up with a stronger dome by raising it by seven meters and utilizing

Aerial and interior views of Hagia Sophia. As one of the world's largest churches, it has remained intact for almost 1500 years.

lighter materials. Upon the completion of the repair work, the church was once again inaugurated – on 23 December 562. All the pictures in Hagia Sophia were removed and were replaced with crosses during the Iconoclastic period, which lasted between 726-842. When the Iconoclastic period ended, Emperor Michael III began the process of decorating the church with mosaics again. However, this work was interrupted by a fire that broke out in 859. An earthquake striking 10 years later caused the greatest damage – resulting in the collapse of one of the semi-domes on the western side. Emperor Basil I had the necessary repairs carried out, even taking care of the damage that had been caused by the earthquake of 869.

There were to be other earthquakes such as the one that came on the night of 26 October 989, which caused a section of the main dome to collapse. Subsequently, Basil II commissioned an architect named Tiridat to repair the church. He replaced the 16 supportive frames of the church, which did not reopen to services until 13 May 994. The interior décor of the church was finally completed during the reign of Romanus III (1028-34).

While the Fourth Crusade was heading towards Jerusalem, they changed their route quite abruptly and came to occupy Byzantine. Hagia Sophia, as well as the rest of the city, was plundered. The occupiers carted off all the sacred relics and other valuables they could find. The church was subsequently organized along the lines of Latin culture.

The church resumed its Orthodox traditions after the Latins were expelled in 1261. In order to support the burned out church, Andronicus II had flying buttresses constructed on the eastern and northern sides in 1317. Nonetheless, tremors struck yet again in 1343 and 1346, causing part of the dome, the eastern arch and other sections of the church to collapse.

Funds to repair the church had depleted so it had to remain closed for some time until a special tax was collected for the work. It was eventually reopened but some travelers passing through Istanbul in the 15th century wrote that Hagia Sophia was in rundown condition and that the gates were falling off their hinges. While Sultan Mehmed the Conqueror found Hagia Sophia in a dilapidated state, he ensured its continued existence by transforming it into a mosque. Subsequent Ottoman sultans also assisted in its upkeep and renovation.

A minaret added to Hagia Sophia in 1481 was accompanied by another minaret during the Bayezid period. In renovating the worn-out Hagia Sophia, Selim II had Mimar Sinan put in auxiliary support buttresses. Repair work continued during the period of Murad III and it was during his reign that two more minarets were added. Moreover, tombs were erected in the

garden of Hagia Sophia for Ottoman sultans who had passed away. These include Selim II, Murad III and Mehmed III. The church's baptismal chamber was turned into the Tombs of Sultan Mustafa I and İbrahim. Having had repairs made to it throughout the entire Ottoman period, it underwent extensive restoration during the reign of Sultan Abdülmecid by the Swiss architect Fossati. The previously whitewashed mosaics inside were cleaned while repair work was done on the structure. The decision to transform Hagia Sophia into a museum was made during the Republican period, on 24 November 24 1934. It was officially opened to the public as a museum the following year.

After having summarized its history, let's now go inside Hagia Sophia and examine this magnificent structure up close. There is an ablution fountain

Interior view of Hagia Sophia.

Plan of Hagia Sophia.

1. The remains of the previous Hagia Sophia; 2. Exonarthex; 3. Narthex; 4. Fountain; 5. South Gate; 6. Baptistery; 7. Imperial Gate; 8. Gallery Ramps; 9. Marble Urns brought from Pergamon; 10. Library of Mahmud I; 11. Mutatorion; 12. Omphalos; 13. Sultan's Lodge; 14. Minber; 15. Apse - Mihrab; 16. Ottoman-era Structures; 17. Treasury

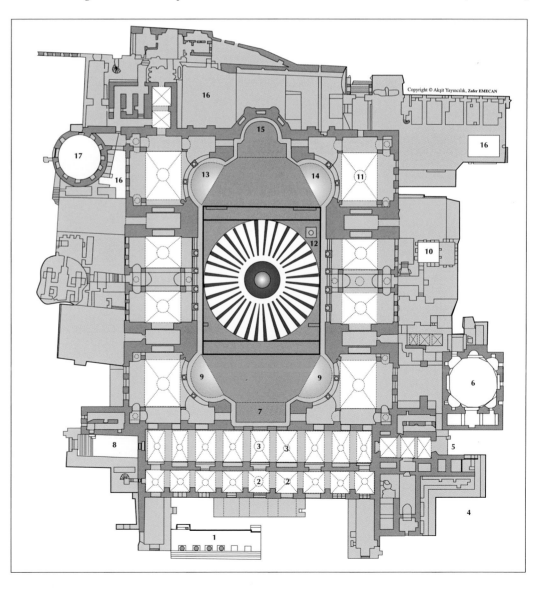

belonging to the Ottoman period in the garden. Right in front of it is a primary school that was constructed during the reign of Mahmud I. The ruins next to the entrance of Hagia Sophia are those of a church built during the period of Emperor Theodosius. One enters the outer narthex of Hagia Sophia through three gates. This 5.75-meter-wide space is comprised of nine sections, none of which bearing any significant architectural features. One passes from the outer narthex into the 9.55-meter-wide inner narthex through one of five gates, which were carved from oak logs and covered with bronze. The ceiling decorations here reflect the old splendor of Hagia Sophia. The museum's exit gate, which is in the southern part of the inner narthex, was brought from a temple in Tarsus in 838 and assembled here. There were once Hellenistic gold leaf tablets above this gate but they were carted off during the Latin Invasion of 1204. In this section one can see a mosaic panel with three figures above the gate that opens into the inner narthex. This remarkably well-preserved mosaic panel has a gold leaf background in the center of which is the Blessed Mary, with Emperor Constantine to her right and Justinian to her left. The Blessed Mary, who is in a dark blue dress, is holding the child Jesus in her lap. On both sides of her head are monograms that state that she is the Mother of God. Emperor Constantine is presenting the Blessed Mary with a model of his city, Constantinople. There is an inscription to the side of the emperor which reads, "Emperor Constantine the greatest amongst the saints." Constantine is not wearing the costume of the period he lived in, but rather that of the 10th century, when the mosaic was made. To the right of the Blessed Mary is Emperor Justinian (527-65), who is presenting her with a model of Hagia Sophia. The Blessed Mary became the "Savior of the City" after the Avars brought great suffering upon the Byzantine Empire in 626. This is why models of the city and Hagia Sophia are being presented to her by the emperors in this mosaic, which was made by Basil II while he was having repairs carried out on Hagia Sophia.

One passes into the main area of Hagia Sophia through one of nine gates in the inner narthex. The bronze covered gate located in the center of these gates was reserved for the use of the emperors. The mosaic above it shows Emperor Leo VI genuflecting in front of Jesus. Over a gold leaf background, one can see Jesus, depicted as the ruler of the universe, Pantocrator, sitting

Mosaic of Empress Zoë. Emperor Constantine IX Monomachus and his wife Empress Zoë seated beside Christ the Pantocrator. 11th century.

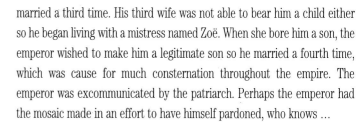

on a throne and holding a Bible in his hand. The words "Peace be with you, I am the light of the World" are written in Greek on the book. Jesus is making a sign of blessing with his other hand. The Blessed Mary and the archangel Gabriel are seen inside medallions on both sides. Kneeling on the ground, can be seen Emperor Leo VI (886-912), who is famous for his scandalous marriages. He remained childless from his first and second wives and

married a third time. His third wife was not able to bear him a child either so he began living with a mistress named Zoë. When she bore him a son, the emperor wished to make him a legitimate son so he married a fourth time, which was cause for much consternation throughout the empire. The emperor was excommunicated by the patriarch. Perhaps the emperor had the mosaic made in an effort to have himself pardoned, who knows ...

In passing through this gate, one enters the main hall of Hagia Sophia, called the "Naos," which is covered by a 55-meter-high dome. Having been repaired several times, it has taken on an elliptical shape, some 31 meters in diameter. There was once a cross inside the dome, but it was replaced by a mosaic of Jesus in 842. Today, one sees only an inscription here as the Jesus mosaic was ruined in 989 and had fallen off completely by 1346. John Palaologus had a mosaic of Pantocrator Jesus within a medallion measuring 11 meters across made in 1355. It is not known whether this mosaic is beneath the inscription seen there today.

Four huge pillars support this dome. Pendentives consisting of large arches that connect the pillars to one another facilitate passage to the dome. The place in the center is supported by gallery floors having four large green marble columns on the northern and southern perimeters. The six green columns in the galleries on the top floor bear the large arches that hold up the dome. Along with the naves on the sides, the dimensions of the main space are 60.30 meters x 69.50 meters.

There are two angel figures in the bema vault of Hagia Sophia. Though the one of Gabriel on the right is in good condition, only the wingtips and feet of Michael, on the left, are visible. Above the pendentives, which provide passage to the main dome, are four angels. Of these, the ones in the east are original while it is not certain if those in the west are also original.

In Hagia Sophia's north tympaneum niches are figures of patriarchs that were made in the 10th century. Those that have survived until the present are the Patriarchs of Constantinople, St. Ignatius the Younger and St. John Chrysostom, as well as the Antioch Patriarch St. Ignatius Theophorus. There is also a mosaic of the Blessed Mary in the semi-dome of the apse. This mosaic was made here to replace the previous cross that had been put in place during the Iconoclastic period. Therefore, this 9th-century mosaic of the Blessed Mary is the oldest mosaic in Hagia Sophia. The gold leaf background next to the Blessed Mary is even older, dating back to the 6th century.

Here, the Blessed Mary is sitting on a throne and is holding the child Jesus in her lap. There are four pillars situated to the left and right of the naos of

9th-century mosaic of the Virgin Mary holding the child Jesus in her lap. One of the oldest mosaics in Hagia Sophia, it is found in the semi-dome of the apse.

Found in the Hagia Sophia, the Deesis Mosaic is one of the finest in the world. 12th century.

Hagia Sophia. Hence, there is a total of 107 columns inside Hagia Sophia, 40 on the bottom floor and 67 in the upper galleries. Collected from ancient temples, the capitals of these columns possess the finest examples of Byzantine stone workmanship. The monograms of Emperor Justinian and Empress Theodora are seen on these column capitals, which date back to the 6th century. The eight columns of green porphyry on the lower floor were shipped in from the Temple of Artemis in Ephesus, while the burgundy ones were brought from Egypt. The walls are covered with Tesalya marble. They were made even more attractive by positioning colorful marble

Imperial Gate. Emperor Leo VI is depicted genuflecting before Christ in a mosaic above this gate, which opens into the naos from the inner narthex.

between the columns that had been brought in from other regions. The panels on the Inner walls were made from colorful marble. One of them is situated next to the imperial gate. There is the so called "Perspiring Column" in the northern nave of the naos, which possesses legendary powers. Visitors stick their thumbs in the hole and make a wish while rotating their thumb inside the hole 360°.

As for the two Hellenistic-period marble cubes at the entrance, they were brought in from Pergamon. A number of additions were made to Hagia Sophia after it was converted into a mosque in the Ottoman period. The Library of Mahmud I is situated between two buttresses on the northern side. The mihrab in the apse section, the imam's quarter, minber and inscribed placards are all works remaining from this period.

The spot with the varicolored marble circles in front of the stand from which the call to prayer is made is called the "Omphalos." This was where the coronation of the Byzantine emperors was held. One goes up to the upper galleries via the passage on the northern side of the inner narthex. The first section of the upper floor is a place that stretches over the inner narthex. It is covered on top with cradle vaults. This space, which belonged to the women, used to be called the "Gynekaion." Right in the center, there is a place that looks like a loggia, consisting of marbles and a green column, which belonged to the empress. There used to be chambers, called the "priest's chambers," on the southern side of this gallery. One passes from here into the southern gallery through a marble gate. Passing through this imitation bronze gate, called "Heaven and Hell," one sees the famous Deesis (Yakarış) mosaic on the right.

In the center of this mosaic is Jesus, flanked on his right by the Blessed Mary and on his left by John the Baptist. The Blessed Mary and John the Baptist are begging for intercession for people from Jesus on Judgment Day. This trio composition is known as the Deesis.

The bottom parts of this panel measuring 6 meters x 4.68 meters are no longer extant. What is still in the panel is a symbol of the cross in the halo around the head of Jesus, upon a gold leaf background. Only half of the body of Jesus, who is making the sign of blessing with his right hand while holding a Bible in his left hand, is visible. A blue cape is draped over his left shoulder. Only the head and right shoulder of the Blessed Mary remain visible. To the left of Jesus is John the Baptist, who is bowing slightly, an indication that he is begging for intercession. On the same level as the heads are monograms indicating their names in abbreviated form. The surprisingly fine quality in the picture of this wonderful mosaic made between the 12th-14th centuries is the biggest factor that gives credence to the claims it was made during the

Palaeologus Renaissance at the beginning of the 14th century.

The tomb of Dandolo of Venice, one of the leading names of the Latin Invasion, is found on the floor across from the Deesis Mosaic and just beyond it is the magnificent Comnenus Mosaic. In this mosaic panel, Mary is depicted holding the Christ Child on her lap. To one side of Mary is Emperor John Comnenus II (1118-43) while on the other is Empress Irene. Seen from the front, the emperor has a dignified expression. The purse in his hand must be a symbol of his donation to Hagia Sophia of 1000 gold pieces.

To the left of Mary is Empress Irene, who was the daughter of Hungarian King Ladislas and was famous for her religious piety. She is wearing a ceremonial costume with a crown on her head and a scroll in her hand.

There are the words "Pious Augusta Irene" next to the head of the empress. Along side this trio composition is a portrait of their 17-year old son Alexsius, who shared in the administration of the empire. The Comnenus Mosaic was made in 1122 and is an example of the realism in the portrait art of the time; people are portrayed the way they actually looked rather than conforming to some idealized form. The best example of this is the way the prince, who died of tuberculosis shortly after this mosaic as made, was portrayed with a pale, sickly expression on his face.

In addition to the Deesis and Comnenus mosaics in this upper gallery of Hagia Sophia, there is also one of Zoë. Measuring 2.40 meters x 2.44 meters, a 35-cm section of the lower part of this panel is missing. Jesus the Pantocrator is portrayed in the center, sitting on a throne in a dark blue gown. He is making a sign of blessing with his right hand and is holding the Holy Bible in his left hand. On either side of this head, there are the abbreviations, "IC" and "XC," which are shortened forms of his name. To his left is Empress Zoë, who is standing up. Famous in Byzantine history for her many marriages, she would change the head of the emperor to the right of Jesus everytime she got married. It is for this reason that one sees her final husband Constantine IX Monomachus (1042-55) portrayed here. These 11th century mosaics provide us with meaningful information about Byzantine imperial costumes and the realism exhibited in the portrait art of the time.

Passing from the southern to the northern gallery, one can see a mosaic of Emperor Alexander on the eastern side of the two pillars. Alexander was the brother of Leo VI, who is seen above the Imperial Gate genuflecting in front of Jesus. Famed for being fond of debauchery and his colorful lifestyle when he was young, Alexander became emperor in 912 after the death of Leo. As it was, he continued with this lifestyle after becoming the emperor. He had this mosaic made within a year of his coronation. There are four medallions

here with the words "Dear God, please help your loyal Orthodox servant Emperor Alexander." One also sees a depiction of a galleon with sails that was etched into the marble railing placards along the edge of this pillar. There are some etched inscriptions above the other marble railing placards. In addition, there is a Viking inscription etched into the marble railing placard in the southern gallery.

Thus, we have become acquainted with every aspect of the history, architecture and mosaics of this world-renown structure that has succeed in remaining intact for more than 1500 years

The southern entrance gate opens into the inner narthex. In the mosaic over the gate, the Virgin Mary is portrayed holding the child Jesus in the center. To her right, is Emperor Constantine I, who is presenting her with a model of the city, while Emperor Justinian who is on her left, offering her a model of Hagia Sophia.

Hagia Eirene

The 1600-year old Hagia Eirene is one of the oldest churches in the world.

Situated in the outer courtyard of Topkapı Palace, the Church of Hagia Eirene, the oldest church in Istanbul, was constructed during the reign of Constantine the Great (307-37). Together with several other structures, this church was burned to the ground during the Nike Revolt of 532. It was reconstructed in 548 only to be heavily damaged as a result of earthquakes that struck in the 8th century. Emperor Constantine V had the church completely renovated and its interior decorated with mosaics and frescoes. It is known that the church was expanded during the 11th-12th centuries. After the conquest of Constantinople in 1453, it was drawn into the Sultan's Walls and subsequently used as an armory and a warehouse where war booty was kept. For this reason, the church bore the name "Cebehane" and converted into a sort of weapons museum during the reign of Sultan Ahmed III (1703-30). It was repaired in 1846 by Topkapı Field Marshall Ahmed Fethi Pasha, who turned it into the first Turkish museum, called "Müze-i Hümayun," in 1869. The structure was used as the Military Museum starting in 1908, and finally it was turned over to the Ministry of Culture in 1978.

After Hagia Sophia, Hagia Eirene is the largest church in Istanbul. Measuring 100 meters x 32 meters, it consists of three naves and has a basilica-like appearance. It is comprised of a naos, a narthex, upper and lower galleries and an atrium. The naos is divided into three naves with columns and pillars and is covered with domes and vaults. The main dome, which has 20 windows, is 15 meters wide and 35 meters high.

There is a depiction of a cross in the apse. Moreover, one can see an inscription of two lines taken from the Pentateuch there. One passes from the naos into the narthex through one of five doors and from the narthex into the atrium through one of another five doors.

This is the only Byzantine church in Istanbul to have survived with its atrium intact. Ringed with porticoes and vaulted arches, it was made narrower during the Ottoman period with the addition of another row of porticoes. Constructed during the reign of Justinian I, it is believed that the interior decoration of the church was quite ornate. However, the mosaic and frescoes have long since disappeared as a result of damage caused by earthquakes and other disasters. Currently open to the public as a monument/museum, Hagia Eirene is also a venue where various fine arts and cultural events are held.

Interior and exterior views of the Church of Hagia Eirene.

The Chora Monastery (Kariye Museum)

The lives of Jesus Christ and the Blessed Mary are reflected perfectly on the mosaics of this church.

Open to visitors as the Kariye Museum, the Chora Monastery was constructed on the site of an old church by the mother-in-law of Alexius I Comnenus, Maria Dukaina. The church of this monastery was dedicated to Jesus. The damage which struck the right side of the church was repaired by the younger brother of John II (1118-43), Isaac Comnenus. It is quite possible that the mosaics were made at this time. The portrait of Comnenus found in the corner of the Blessed Mary and Jesus mosaic must have been put here as gratitude for his contribution.

This church suffered the same fate as the other churches in the city during the Latin Invasion. One of the most important personalities of the age, Grand Logethete Theodore Metochites, became one of Emperor Andronicus Palaeologus II's most trusted advisors, serving as Treasury Minister between 1310-20. He was also a diplomat, scientist, philosopher, astronomer and poet.

Metochites repaired the church and had a cemetery chapel erected there as well. The emperor subsequently appointed him Head Treasurer, the highest position in Byzantium. However, when the grandson of Andronicus deposed the emperor in 1328 and took over the throne, this favorite figure of the ex-emperor was sent into exile and all his possessions were confiscated. After remaining in exile for two years, Theodore Metochites returned to the church he repaired as a destitute Christian monk. Living here under the name of Theoleptus, he passed away on 13 March 1332 and was buried in the cemetery chapel next to the church. This famous church was converted into a mosque in 1511 by the Grand Vizier of Bayezid II, Hadım Atik Ali Pasha, who had the mosaics covered with whitewash and added a minaret on the outside.

The church and its mosaics were repaired between 1948-58 by the American Byzantine Institute and subsequently opened as a museum. The building, which measures 27 meters x 27.50 meters, is comprised of an inner and outer narthex to the west, a cemetery chapel to the south and a gallery to the north. The actual building and walls of the inner narthex are covered with marble. The naos is covered by a large dome that is surrounded by five smaller ones. While this section is completely covered with mosaics, the cemetery chapel, or "parecclesion," is decorated with frescoes. The subjects found on the inner and outer narthex of the church follow each other in sequential order. The 18 scenes explaining the life story of the Blessed Mary in the northern wing of the inner narthex are of indescribable beauty. Those on the northern side of the outer narthex show important events in the life of the Holy family as well as the birth of Jesus and his baptism. As for the

Theodore Metochites presents Jesus with a small model of the Chora Monastery Church that he built (left).

(Below) The interior of the naos of the Chora Monastery Church. (Kariye Museum)

Plan of the Chora Monastery Church (Kariye Museum).

The Census Registration Mosaic. Prefect Cyrenius is seated on his throne with a guard standing behind him. Census officials in the center register The Virgin Mary while Joseph and his children stand behind her.

miracles of Jesus and the Lord announcing his Bible, these are found in the southern wings of both narthexes. However, some of the important mosaics were irreparably damaged as a result of the plaster that once covered them during the Ottoman period.

The short text on the mosaics consists of text or symbols explaining that particular mosaic. All of the scenes contain subjects taken from the Bible. Before we start to trace them chronologically, let us start from the left side of the entrance and examine the mosaics according to the plan we have provided. Passing through the museum's entrance gate, one arrives in the outer narthex. There are three scenes in mosaic no. 1 in the section we have marked out in our plan as "A." One of these is of Mary and her fiancé Joseph under a tree. Feeling uneasy about her pregnancy, and unaware of the divine secret, she falls asleep under a tree while trying to think of a way to break off the engagement with Joseph. In her dream, an angel breaks the news that her child is from God and that she should name her newborn child Jesus. Just beyond this scene, Mary is speaking to Elizabeth, the wife of Zachariah. On her right, Joseph has accepted what the angel has said and is taking Mary from Nazareth to Bethlehem, which is the place where she would give birth to Jesus.

A census count is depicted in mosaic no. 2, in the northern part of section A. Emperor Augustus has decreed that a census count be conducted in all of the Roman provinces. This scene shows Mary and Joseph registering in the presence of Prefect Cyrenius, who is seated in an armchair with an armed guard behind him. In the center, the census clerk is registering Mary while Joseph is looking on from behind with his three sons.

Mosaic no. 3, in the southern part of section A, shows Jesus Christ, Mary, Joseph and his sons going to Jerusalem for Passover. Mosaic no. 4 shows Jesus Christ in the midst of some doctors at the temple. Tarachus and Andronicus are shown in mosaic no. 5 in the vault between sections A and B. These two individuals were made saints because they were tortured on the same day during the rule of Emperor Diocletian. Tarachus, from Cilicia, is shown to be an old soldier while Andronicus of Ephesus is depicted as a youth.

The birth of Jesus is the subject of the mosaic no. 6 in section B. This is indicated by the inscription in the center. At the extreme left, one sees a woman pouring water and opposite her is a woman seen holding the newborn Jesus. Behind them is Mary lying in a bed after having given birth. A holy light has descended from above upon a swaddled Jesus. To the right are three shepherds to whom an angel has descended to say something. Joseph is sitting in the lower corner.

Mosaic no.7 in section B in the outer wall of the church depicts the holy family returning from Egypt. Joseph dreams that an angel informs him that King Herod is looking for Jesus to have him killed. He is advised to take Mary and Jesus to Egypt and stay there until the danger passes. While in Egypt, Joseph has another visitation with an angel who informs him that the danger has passed, the king had been killed and that they could return to Nazareth. This subject has been depicted on this mosaic very harmoniously. The depictions of Saints Philemun, Lucius, Callinicus, Tirsus and Apollinus

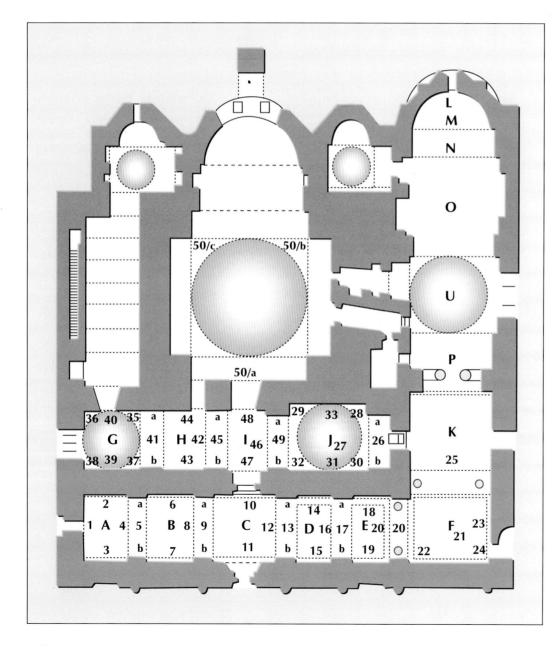

appear above an arched vault. The theme of Satan tempting Jesus has been taken up on the ceiling in section B. The subjects are developed in the center around a medallion. John the Baptist is baptizing Jesus in one corner of the dome, while the Holy Ghost is putting Jesus to the test. Satan is also trying to deceive him.

One can see the depictions of St. George and St. Demetrius in the vault between sections B and C of the outer narthex. Seen in No. 9a is the father of St. George, who was from Cappadocia. He was an early Christian executed for his beliefs in 296. Mosaic No. 9b shows St. Demetrius, who was from Thessaloniki. When Roman Emperor Maximianus came to Thessaloniki, seeing Demetrius amongst the Christians, had him imprisoned for life. These two saints are pictured in the vault facing each other.

The mosaic of Christ the Pantocrator is found above the gate that opens into the inner narthex just opposite the entry gate of the museum. Here, he is shown holding in his left hand a Bible ornamented with precious stones, and making a sign of blessing in his right hand. In the magnificent mosaic indicated in our plan as C10, the abbreviations "IC-XC" appear around the head of Jesus.

A splendid mosaic showing Mary praying is seen in C11 above the entrance gate of the museum. There are angels on either side of Mary and the inscription on the panel reads, "The Mother of God, the dwelling-place of the uncontainable." There are fragments of scenes of saints in the vault between sections C and D. The miraculous scene of turning water into wine is found on the ceiling of the museum entrance gate. Jesus Christ, the Blessed Mary and the apostles are invited to a wedding in the town of Kana on the Sea of Galilee. As the night wore on, they ran out of wine at the wedding. Having water poured into goblets, he performed a miracle whereby the water turns into wine. Other miraculous scenes are depicted, such as the multiplication of bread and the sacrificing of a bull.

In the section to the right of the entrance gate, one sees three oracles in the presence of King Herod on the inner narthex wall. As for the mosaic seen on our plan as D 14, the three oracles from the east inform the king, who is sitting

The Anastasis (Harrowing of Hell) Fresco is found on the apse of the Chora Monastery Church parecclesion. It shows Jesus descending into Hell to save the sinners.

A mosaic found in the south section of the Chora Monastery Church shows Christ healing a cripple while another mosaic depicting King Herodus giving the death order for the murder of innocent infants. *(Kariye Museum)*

in an armchair, of the birth of Jesus and that he was going to be deposed by him. The king then ordered the oracles to "Go and find that child and I shall genuflect in front of him." However, the king does not keep his word. Behind this scene, the oracles are shown on their way to Jerusalem. To the right of the entrance gate, on the panel of the inner side of the outer wall, Elizabeth and John are seen fleeing from soldiers. Elizabeth is a relative of Mary, the wife of Zachariah and the mother of John. The mosaics on the domes have

fallen off in this section. Saints are depicted in No. 17, between sections D and E, right next to this and above the vault. Unfortunately, the mosaics in the vaults in the middle and on the perimeter have disappeared. In the scene, the "Interrogation of King Herod," which is on the panel shown as E 18, only himself and a single guard have remained. Across from this is a mosaic of women mourning. Panel F 24, above the east wall of the museum's outer narthex, shows King Herod giving the order for the deaths of Innocent people. King Herod sent the three oracles to Bethlehem to seek out Jesus and they did find him. He tells them in a dream to go back to the king. They abide by going back to their country without informing the king. Consequently, the king gives the order to have all children in and around Bethlehem up to the age of two years put to death.

Above this scene is one of Jesus Christ healing a cripple. Just across from it is another like it. In panel no. F 23, a woman from Samaria is standing at the edge of a well. Jesus encounters her while passing through Samaria. However, this mosaic of Jesus is in very poor condition. There is a decorative medallion in the middle of the dome of this section. Let's continue to stroll about the museum by passing from section F, in the southernmost part, over to section K.

Unfortunately there are not many mosaics remaining here. Nonetheless, while not in very good condition, on the southern wall there is the scene of the flight to Egypt, and on the arch of the column, a scene in which the oracles are presenting gifts. From here, one passes into a section of the inner narthex marked J, which contains depictions of the forbearers of Jesus Christ. Miraculous scenes of Jesus Christ healing a youth with a diseased arm as well as the healing of a leper are seen on the arch between sections J and K.

In the center of the dome, shown on our plan as J 27, ancestors of Jesus are gathered around him. Twenty-four forefathers, ranging from the Prophets Adam to Jacob appear here, with the 15 children of Jacob depicted below as the second generation.

The mosaic shown in the plan as J 28 is of a female hemophiliac who is being healed while in the other corner, there is scene of Jesus healing the mother-in-law of the Apostle Peter. Across from these, are the miracles of two blind and mute souls being healed. On a large panel below these is a scene depicting Jesus Christ healing some sick people in a village.

There are also mosaics of Mary and Jesus on the large panel on the dome where Jesus and his forefathers are found. Though the lower part of this panel, shown as J 33, has fallen off over time, it has lost none of its

magnificence. Isaac Comnenus is in a state of collapse under Mary, who is shown praying. The youngest son of Alexius Comnenus, Isaac, was the person who had the eastern side of this church repaired. This is perhaps why this picture was placed here. The nun Melane is next to Jesus. It is thought that Melane, the daughter of Michael Palaeologus, was given a place on this panel for her services as a bride who had traveled to Mongolia and then became a nun upon her return. In the inner narthex of the Chora Monastery, Mary is seen seated in the second dome, which is marked as G 34 in our plan, holding the child Jesus in her lap. Positioned in 16 partitions around her are her ancestors, consisting of the Prophet David and 16 prophet-king figures.

In the panel under this dome, indicated as G 35, Joachim is shown wishing for a child while wandering through the mountains. Joachim and Anna, who are the parents of Mary, are descendents of David. This elderly husband and wife had no children. For this reason, Joachim is treated with contempt at the temple. Deeply saddened, Joachim ascends up into the mountains and spends his days with the shepherds. He stays up there to pray for 40 consecutive days and nights, when finally, Gabriel visits Anna to give her the good news that she is expecting a child. Anna greets her husband at the town gate and gives him the good news. Finally, Anna gives birth to a girl named Mary. G 35, G 37 and H 44 on our plan are all concerned with the Nativity scene.

On the panel, indicated as H 42, which is on the ceiling to the left of the inner narthex, Mary, Anna and Joachim are being blessed by priests, who are standing between their arms. These mosaics, which are very well preserved and colorful, are the most striking mosaics in the Chora. In the nearby vault, one can see Mary as a child taking her first seven steps when she was six months old.

Before Mary was born, her father had promised that he would leave his child in a temple if he had one. Keeping his promise, he leaves Mary in the care of temple. She stayed in the temple for 10 years until she was 14-15 years old, at which time the nuns told her that she was old enough to marry. Around this time, the High Priest Zachariah called all the widowers together and had them place their rods on the altar, praying for a sign showing to whom she should be given. They all gathered at the temple one night. When morning came, the rod of Joseph, a carpenter from Nazareth, began to sprout green leaves. The Virgin Mary was subsequently awarded to him. One can see this subject dealt with on panel H 43.

On panel G 39 Joseph is taking leave of Mary; next to him is Mary and the Head Priest Zachariah. Mosaic No. 40 shows Anna receiving the good news that Mary is going to give birth, as well as the scene of Joseph taking Mary home. Mosaics of St. Peter and St. Paul are found on either side of the gate through which the naos is reached from the inner narthex. To the right of the gate, St. Paul is depicted wearing a blue tunic. He is holding a book in his left hand and has his right hand in the air. St. Paul from Tarsus has joined Jesus' Apostles here. He was taken into custody during the period of the Roman Emperor Nero (54 – 68 A.D.) and subsequently sent to Rome, where he was

The presentation of the Virgin Mary at the temple. The child Mary is seen seated between her parents, Anne and Joachim. In the other section, Joachim is seen taking Mary to the temple. (Kariye Museum)

killed. To the left of the gate is St. Peter, who once earned his livelihood as a fisherman. Jesus approached him one day while he was mending his net. Amazed by what he witnessed, Peter dropped what he was doing to become a devoted Apostle. St. Peter is depicted in the mosaic holding in his right hand the scroll of a letter he has written, and in his left hand, he appears to be holding the key to Heaven. Above the gate that opens out into the nave is a panel that shows the builder of the church, Theodore Metochites, as he gives Jesus a model of the church. Above this panel, which is shown as I 48, Mary is being presented in the church as well. Also above the gate through which the inner narthex is reached from the outer narthex is a scene of Mary buying some wool to knit a cloth cover for the temple.

Both the natural appearance and actions of the people, and the harmonious mix of colors on this panel indicate that the artist who painted it was extremely skilled at what he was doing. To the right of the door through which the main hall is reached (I-J 49), angels are feeding Mary, who had been left at the temple in accordance with her father's promise. Above these scenes, at the bottom of the dome, there is a procession of Virgins.

The scene of Mary's death is on the inside of the gate that passes into the naos of the church. In this scene, indicated as no. 50 A on our plan, Mary is at rest in a catafalque, with Apostles, clergymen and soothsayers on both sides of her. Jesus Christ is holding Mary's soul, which has the form of an infant. The scene, including the facial expressions, curves in the garments worn and the stances of the people are depicted in a fine, realistic manner.

On the right, on the front side of the apse pillar in the naos of church, Mary is holding Jesus on her lap. On the northern wall of the apse pillar is a mosaic of Jesus. Though the mosaic is in very poor shape, one can still make out Jesus holding in his hand the Gospels, in which are written the words, "Come unto me, all ye that labor and are heavy laden, and I will give you rest." After having viewed all of these mosaics, let's now pass from here into the parecclesion to see the frescoes.

One reaches this section, which stretches the length of the church, by passing between two narrow columns. There are four tombs, including that of the builder of this church, Theodore Metochites, at the top left, located in the "paracclesion," or cemetery chapel. Subjects dealing with Judgment Day are taken up in the frescoes in this section.

The most striking fresco in this part is that of the splendid Anastasis Fresco found in the apse semi-dome. This scene, called "Anastasis" (Resurrection) in Greek, is known in English as the "Harrowing of Hell." Christ has broken down the gates of Hell, which lie beneath his feet. Satan, bound, lies before

Mosaic of St. George (below).

One of the impressive domes of Kariye Museum depicts a mosaic of Jesus and his 24 descendents.

him. With his right hand, he pulls Adam out of his grave; behind Adam stand St. John the Baptist, David, Solomon and other righteous kings. With his left hand, he pulls Eve out of her grave; standing in it is Abel and behind him another group of righteous souls.

Below the fresco of Anastasis are the pictures of six church priests. On the bema section of the walls on either side of the apse are scenes of two of the miracles of Jesus. On the southern wall of the apse, there is a fresco of Mary affectionally hugging the child Jesus. Behind this is a depiction of St. George.

After the Anastasis Fresco, comes that of the Last Judgment, which occupies the whole vault. It contains one of the richest scenes in Byzantine art. Jesus is seen sitting on a throne in the exact center of the panel. The Blessed Mary and John the Baptist are begging Jesus for intercession on behalf of humanity. The 12 Apostles are sitting in rows on either side. Above them is an angel who is carrying a snail, the symbol of Heaven. On the bottom, we see Adam and Eve genuflecting in front of the throne.

"Sinners Burning in Hell" occupy the scene on the right side of the vault. The other sections of the vault are made up of groups, such as the "Choir of the Select," the "Rich Man Burns in Hell" and other figures. On the left, there is the figure of St. Peter accompanying those selected on their way to Paradise, followed by angels. After that there is a depiction of the half-naked Good Thief with a cross in his hand. There is also one of the Blessed Mary who is sitting in Paradise amongst trees and angels. In addition, one finds the figure of the Rich Man in the pendentive as well as a fresco of Lazarus the Beggar on the opposite side. On the western side of the vault, there are angels in flight playing pipes, as well as other figures of children and angels.

The dome of the parecclesion is decorated with the Blessed Mary surrounded by 12 angels. There are also four Biblical poets shown in the pendentives of the dome. One can see Jacob's ladder on the arches and wall under the dome, and beneath it, Jacob, who is dreaming, with the Blessed Mary and the child Jesus above. There is also the scene of "Moses Burning in the Bushes" as well as the scene of the transporting of the "Ark of the Covenant."

Scenes of the "Prophet Solomon and the Israelites" appear to the left of the window with three apertures with scenes of an "Angel in Front of Jerusalem" and the "Ordeal of the Assyrians" found to the right. One can also see frescoes of battle scenes here. Thus, we have seen and become acquainted with the most important mosaics and frescoes of Late Byzantine art, in particular those of the Palaeologus Renaissance.

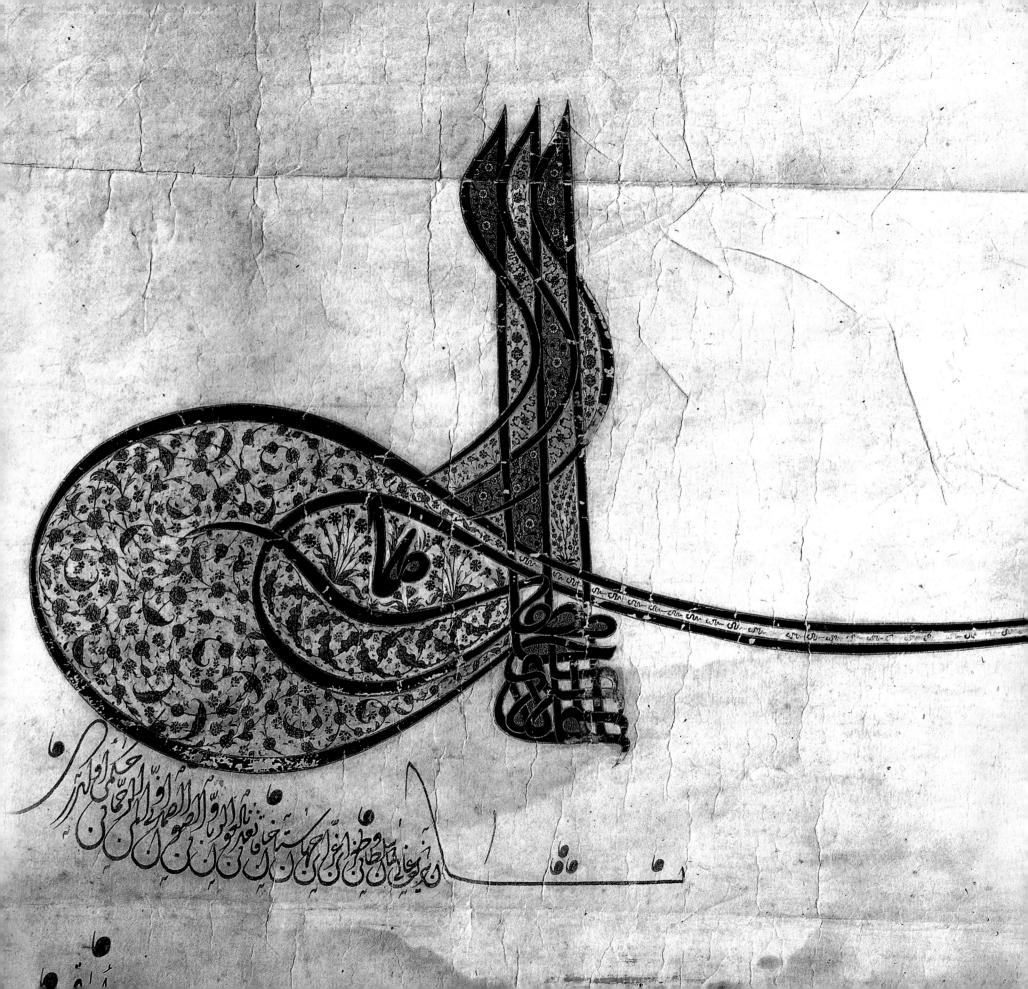

The Splendor of the Ottoman Empire

"First Constantinople conquered my heart, then I conquered Constantinople."

Sultan Mehmed the Conqueror

The Magnificence of the Ottomans

Having defeated the Byzantines at the battle of Malazgirt, the Seljuks founded the Anatolian Seljuk State and declared Konya as their capital. It was with this Seljuk success that Anatolia rapidly started to submit to Turkish rule. The Mongols forced the Kayı Tribe, who were led by Ertuğrul Bey, to leave their motherland in Central Asia. The Kayı migrated further west and made Söğüt in Anatolia their home, with the Byzantine Empire as their neighbor. Upon the death of his father Ertuğrul Bey, Osman Bey started to rule the emirate, declaring its independence in 1299. Orhan Bey, who succeeded Osman Bey, invaded Bursa and made it his capital. From a community of just 400 tents, he soon created a cavalry division of 20,000 men. Murad I ascended to the Ottoman throne after Orhan Bey and started to move into the heart of Europe on horseback. Turning their face towards Europe, the Ottomans chose Edirne as their capital and it was not long before they were strong enough to devastate the Byzantine Empire, which was squeezed in the middle of the Empire. While Murad I was victorious in Kosova, he was killed on the battlefield by a Serb. Upon his death, Yıldırım Bayezid ascended to the Ottoman throne. Nevertheless, he had to postpone invading Constantinople until later, as the threat of Tamerlane had grown in the East. The Byzantines breathed a collective sigh of relief when Tamerlane defeated Yıldırım Bayezid in the ensuing battle. After Yıldırım Bayezid, it took Çelebi Mehmed quite a while to recoup the losses suffered by the State. In the meantime, Constantinople struggled to exist. Çelebi Mehmed, who had to wrangle with family members over the throne from 1412 to 1420, was finally able to put the State on firm footing. His son Murad II was the next to ascend to the Ottoman throne, and because of his courageous heart, Ottoman armies appeared in Europe once more. Murad's son, Mehmed, was born on a cold March day in 1432 in Edirne. Mehmed would acquire the title "Conqueror" in later years. This boy was appointed to the post of Regional Governor to Manisa at the tender age of 10. While having received a proper education, he was trained to be familiar with the running state affairs as well. In the meantime, his brother who was the governor of Amasya died, leaving his father Murad II in great sorrow. So deeply affected was he by his son's death, Murad II abdicated in favor of his 12-year old son Mehmed. This child sitting on the Ottoman throne in Edirne became the unwitting root of riots and rebellions throughout the Empire as well as in Europe. The Pope, who

(Previous overleaf) Aerial view of Istanbul with the Sultan Ahmed Mosque in the foreground and the Hagia Sophia Museum in the background.

(Facing page) A monogram of Sultan Süleyman the Magnificent, dated 1558.

(Below) A portrait of Osman Gazi, the founder of the Ottoman Empire.

A portrait of Sultan Mehmed the Conqueror. Painted by Gentile Bellini in 1480. The National Gallery - London.

A painting by Zonaro showing Sultan Mehmet II leading his troops who are lowering vessels into the Golden Horn during the conquest of Constantinople. Dolmabahçe Palace.

had been plotting to expel the Ottoman armies from Europe, gathered the Crusaders and received the support of the Byzantines and the Karamanoğul Emirate to start the Crusade. Having realized that such an attack was imminent, Çandarlı Halil Pasha asked the former Emperor Murad II, who was then in Bursa, to proceed to Edirne immediately and take over as the Commander of the Ottoman Army. After Murad II defeated the Crusaders in November 1444, he went to reside in Manisa, leaving the throne to his son once again. But this time around, the Janissaries rebelled in Edirne and the sultanate of the young emperor was threatened. His father ran back once more to assist his son. Mehmed II was appointed to Manisa after his father

regained the throne for the last time. Four years later, in December 1450, Mehmed II married the daughter of Süleyman Bey of the Dulkadiroğul Emirate, Sitti Hatun. Just after he got married and had returned to Manisa, he received news of his father's death and rushed to Edirne. He thus ascended to the Ottoman throne for a third and final time, at the age of 19. His temporary ascensions to the throne on two previous occasions had already matured him. Now, he had the capacity to resolve many state affairs, including the one regarding Constantinople. After making peace with various factions in Anatolia, he began to prepare for the invasion of Constantinople from Edirne. In the meantime, the debate over the unification of Western and Eastern Churches, which the Byzantines opposed, was continuing. Lucas Notaras, who had the second-highest position after the emperor, and Gennadius Scholarius, who was appointed as patriarch by Sultan Mehmed in later years, were also against this unification. Notaras was quoted as saying, "Seeing the Turkish turban is much better than seeing the Latin cap." Both this dispute over religion and the poverty of the local people weakened the Byzantine Empire. In the meantime, in Edirne, Mehmed II decided that his primary objective in conquering Constantinople was to seize control of the Bosphorus, so he gave the command to have the Rumeli Fortress constructed opposite the Anadolu Fortress, built earlier by Yıldırım Bayezid. The Hungarian cannon maker Urbana fled Constantinople and started to prepare artillery pieces that would devastate the Byzantine city walls, which had not been penetrated for 1,000 years. After all the plans and preparations had been made, Sultan Mehmed set off from Edirne and, in reaching the outskirts of Constantinople on 05 April 1453, imposed a blockade on the city the following day. Positioning his army of 150,000-200,000 strong and their cannons against the walls from Ayvansaray to Altın Kapı, he established his headquarters in Topkapı. Rumeli Beylerbeyi Karaca Pasha was to command the forces on the left flank from Ayvansaray to Edirnekapı, while he himself stayed in the middle flank from Edirnekapı to Topkapı. The right flank, which extended from Topkapı to Yedikule, was commanded by İshak Pasha and Mahmud Pasha, while the Ottoman fleet was under command of Baltaoğlu Süleyman. Sultan Mehmed II sent envoys to the Byzantine Emperor with an ultimatum to surrender. This was rejected, whereupon those meticulously made cannons started to pound the city walls of Constantinople with tremendous force. However, the naval forces did not obtain the results it initially expected and were forced to retreat towards the shore. Upon seeing the greatly upset Sultan Mehmed II ride his horse into the sea, the naval officers pulled themselves together and started to make progress. As the days passed, the devastated wall sections were patched up and it seemed as

Previous overleaf. Ottoman mosques constructed on the hills above the Golden Horn altered the silhouette of Istanbul. The Bosphorus and a minaret of one of those mosques overlooking the Golden Horn are pictured.

A miniature showing the Bayram ceremony of Sultan Süleyman the Magnificent in front of the Gate of Felicity. Süleymanname 1558.

though Constantinople would never fall. Finally, all the ships of the Ottoman Navy were pulled overland to the Golden Horn. It was this action that proved inevitably to be the decisive blow in the campaign against the Byzantines. After a fierce battle on 29 May 1453, Ottoman soldiers scrambled through the gaping holes in the walls. Constantinople fell, with the emperor dying along with his soldiers. Sultan Mehmed the Conqueror, who started a new era by invading Constantinople, went straight to Hagia Sophia, where he was met by the Patriarch and the local people, who prostrated themselves with fear in their hearts. Sultan Mehmed II declared to the Patriarch "Rise to your feet, I am telling you that neither you nor your people must be afraid of your lives or your freedom from now on." He ordered his men to have the city rebuilt and treat the local populace well. In a bid to increase the population of the city, he brought in thousands of people from Anatolia and Rumeli into the city. Meanwhile, he converted Hagia Sophia into a mosque and held his first Friday Prayers there. Sultan Mehmed II started the task of reconstructing the city by bringing in many skilled craftsmen from all corners of the Empire. He had a palace built in Bayezid Square, but as soon as palace population increased, he ordered a new palace to be built in 1465. This palace was to later be called, "Topkapı Palace." In addition, he had the Fatih Complex constructed over the site of the Church of the Apostoleion. Sultan Mehmed II was not the only person to work hard at rebuilding the city; viziers and pashas were involved, too. Grand Vizier Mahmud Pasha had a complex built with additional compounds consisting of a mosque, a bath and a mausoleum. Murad Pasha had a complex in Aksaray built while Rum Mehmed Pasha had another one constructed in Üsküdar at the time.

The face of the city was changing as the Ottomans rapidly rebuilt the city according to Islamic beliefs and style of art. Minarets that touched the sky were erected. As for the city's commercial life, many markets were built, along with hamams, complexes and mausoleums. In mobilizing his forces into the most remote corners of Anatolia, Sultan Mehmed II wanted absolute sovereignty over this land. He first attacked the Karamanoğul Emirate. He then defeated Uzun Hasan, the ruler of the Akkoyuns in Otlukbeli, thus eliminating an important rival. He went on to conquer the Crimea, and with his invasion of the Trabzon Pontus Empire in the eastern Black Sea region on 15 August 1461, he sealed his bid to possess all the lands in Anatolia. He then shifted his attention towards Italy. His ambition was to expand the Ottoman Empire on both continents, just as the previous Roman emperors had done. For this reason, he rode into Anatolia to gather his forces in 1481. While he was waiting for his army to gather in Gebze, he became ill and died on 03 May 1481, at the young age of 49. As he still had much to accomplish, his untimely death shocked everybody. He was buried in the tomb of the Fatih Complex he had had ordered to be built for himself. His son, Crown Prince Bayezid was to be the successor to the Ottoman throne. However, Bayezid's brother Crown Prince Cem, who was the Governor of Konya at the time, also staked a claim to the throne. Cem put up a valiant fight, but lost against Bayezid, who forced him to flee the country. Cem took refuge in various lands but was finally tracked down and poisoned to death in 1495. Sultan Bayezid II, who ruled the empire for 31 years, had a much milder personality than his father. He was a scientist, a poet and very fond of religion. He preferred to wage peace, not war. He put an end to the tradition of marrying Ottoman princes with the daughters of the surrounding emirates and initiated the establishment of a Harem in the palace. As a consequence, concubines began to be brought up in the Harem as prospective marriage candidates for the sultans. During his era, the last Islamic province of Spain was in dire straits as the Spanish were forcing them, along with the Jews, to convert to Catholicism during the Inquisition. Sultan Bayezid II ordered one of his top admirals, Kemal Reis to sail there and free the Arabs and Jews. They came to be resettled in Ottoman territory in and around Istanbul. This event went down in history as Sultan Bayezid II's greatest contribution to humanity. He had eight sons but only three of them, Ahmed, Korkud and Selim survived to adulthood. As the Regional Governor of Trabzon, Selim was in a position to monitor the Iranian Shah Ismail's efforts to expand Shiism into Anatolia. The fact that his father did not pay the necessary attention to this steadily worsening situation drove Selim mad. In 1512, he rallied the Janissaries behind his cause to depose his father, who was rather old at the time, and ascended to the Ottoman throne. In the meantime, Shah Ismail had eliminated the Akkoyun State to establish the Safevi State in its place, thus gaining a solid foothold in Anatolia. Having resolved the problems amongst his sons, Sultan Selim (the Grim) proceeded to attack Shah Ismail at Çaldıran, north of Van Province. After wiping out the Iranian forces, Selim pressed south with his campaign, defeating the Memluks of Egypt, remaining in the region for eight months. Thus, he brought the title of Caliphate into the Ottoman fold. Having spent most of his brief eight-year reign on horseback, Sultan Selim died on his way to Edirne in 1520 as a result of an infected boil on his backside. Contrary to his nasty looks, he had a rather benevolent nature and was known for his poetry. He had great respect for scientists. He was such a kind person that one day, when his tutor's horse splashed mud on his caftan along the road to Egypt, everyone in the entourage expected the tutor to be punished. However, Selim merely told his instructor, "Safekeep this caftan until I die and place it on my tomb. Mud splashed by the horse of a scientist's horse can never stain us." His only son, the well-educated and mature Sultan Süleyman the Magnificent, ascended to the Ottoman throne upon his death. Though he had become sultan at an early age, he ruled the country with great success. He was on the side of the righteous and the law, never forgiving any actions against the state and punished harshly those who committed crimes. He introduced a new constitution based upon the laws of Sultan Mehmed the Conqueror, hence his other moniker, the "Lawgiver." His quote, "There is nothing as honorable as the state for my public, but no state on Earth is more important than any one of my citizens..." clearly showed his political state of mind. He was an excellent statesman as well as a well-known poet, using the pseudonym "Muhibbi" in all his poems. He was only 25 years old when he ascended to the Ottoman throne on 30 September 1520. As he was gaining recognition around the world, the whole of Europe was gathering behind the leadership of the young and dynamic emperor of Germany and Spain, Charles V. Now, it was time for two rivals to face off against each other. While making successful raids into Central Europe, Süleyman the Magnificent did not neglect the east, taking the Ottomans to the zenith of

Sultan Süleyman the Magnificent is shown seated on his throne and receiving the tributes of his viziers. Palace servants are also seen in the background. Arifi, "Süleymanname." 1558.

their power through his conquests. Under the command of Admirals Barbaros Hayreddin Pasha, Sokollu Mehmed Pasha and Sinan Pasha, the Ottoman Navy turned the Mediterranean into a Turkish lake. During his reign, the Ottoman Empire expanded over three continents – Asia, Africa and Europe, with eight million km2 of land and 120 million inhabitants. 38 countries were placed under the administration of the Ottomans. Süleyman the Magnificent married Mahidevran Sultan while he was Regional Governor of Manisa. She bore him a boy named Mustafa. After ascending to the throne, he married his second wife, Hürrem Sultan who would bear him four more sons – Mehmed, Selim, Bayezid and Cihangir. Süleyman was deeply in love

Otherwise known as Roxelana, Hürrem Sultan was the daughter of a Russian priest who married Sultan Süleyman the Magnificent. She played a pivotal role in the course of Ottoman history.

with Hürrem and would do anything she asked him to do. They both took great inspiration from poetry. He would read her poems when they were separated to forget about his loneliness. As her children were growing up, Hürrem Sultan plotted to prevent Crown Prince Mustafa from ascending to the throne after his father, Süleyman the Magnificent. The crown prince was obviously from another woman but was greatly admired by the army. She was trying to do her best to pave the way for one of her sons to ascend to the throne, eliminating the Grand Vizier, İbrahim Pasha, who had the capability of preventing her offspring from ascending to the throne. She made her daughter marry Rüstem Pasha so as to create a balance of power in the palace. Letting her ambitions go too far, she finally persuaded Süleyman that his son Crown Prince Mustafa had betrayed and rebelled against him. This led to the needless death of Mustafa. But it was not long before Hürrem's two sons Selim and Bayezid began to fiercely struggle over the throne. This rivalry exhausted Hürrem and her heart could not face the strain. She passed away at the age of 54 in 1558, resulting in the loss of Süleyman's best friend and greatest supporter. With Hürrem's death, Süleyman's daughter Mihrimah was to become his closest confidant. Meanwhile, Bayezid had rebelled against the state but his fate was ultimately linked to that of Crown Prince Mustafa – for Süleyman the Magnificent had ordered his death as well. The death of Crown Prince Mustafa was the cause of Süleyman's last son Cihangir dying at an early age. So, having lost his four sons, the overly fatigued sultan duly submitted himself to religion. He had Mimar Sinan, who was the most famous architect of the time, build the famous Süleymaniye Mosque. The skyline of Istanbul was changed forever with the addition of several mosques commissioned by Süleyman the Magnificent as well as his daughter and son-in-law.

Exhausted in both heart and mind, the elderly Süleyman the Magnificent died during a raid on Zigetvar, Hungary on 06 September 1566 at the age of 72. His Grand Vizier, Sokollu Mehmed Pasha kept his death a secret from the Ottoman Army and waited for his son Selim II to arrive. After Selim ascended to the throne, he transported Süleyman's coffin to Istanbul to be buried in a tomb prepared for him. So, the era of Süleyman the Magnificent came to a close and his son, the only heir left to the throne, Selim II, became the sultan. The state, however, was administered by Sokollu Mehmed Pasha during Selim's eight-year reign. In comparison to his father, Selim II exhibited a milder character and never led a military campaign during his entire rule. He used the pseudonym "Selimi" in all his poetry and commissioned the architect Sinan to construct the famous Selimiye Mosque in Edirne. With it the country gained a great work of art.

The end of the Era of Ascension, and the beginning of the Era of Stagnation

Upon the death of Selim II in 1574, his son Murad III ascended to the throne. Selim II was buried in the courtyard of Hagia Sophia in a tomb constructed by Mimar Sinan. The Celali Riots began in Anatolia during the reign of Mehmed III, who succeeded his father Murad III in 1595 and remained on the throne until 1603. The rebellions continued on and off for 17 years, weakening the economy and social order of the country. The splendor of the Ottomans came to an end with the initiation of the Era of Stagnation, which began towards the end of the 16th century, persisting for about 100 years. The Ottoman sultans who followed Sultan Süleyman the Magnificent left all state affairs to their grand viziers and never lead their armies in military campaigns. During this era, high offices in the palace were appointed to those close to the sultans, eunuchs, and dowager sultans. Those who deserved these positions because of their talent and capacity were excluded. This explains why state authority steadily became weaker. As a result of this irregularity in the palace, regional revolts broke out in the empire.

These caused disorder and social breakdown in the country. Previously, the crown princes were appointed to provinces as regional governors, but this tradition changed as they started to live in the Harem with their families. So, another important custom went by the wayside. As they started to live in the Harem, crown princes isolated themselves from public life, becoming pathetically untalented and cruel. They knew nothing of the people they ruled or how the state functioned. Thus, once they ascended to the throne, they had a hard time administering state affairs.

In addition, certain geographical discoveries had made the Ottoman trade routes less important, resulting in a sharp drop in the amount of customs duties collected by the Ottomans. Thus, they began to weaken economically as well. The wars against Austria and Iran during the 17th century put a heavy strain on the Ottoman Treasury since expenditures exceeded income. Moreover, compromises made with France during the reign of Süleyman the Magnificent gradually piled up against the best interests of the empire. These capitulations, as they came to be known, finally became the most important factor causing the Ottoman economy to weaken. While experiencing such economic difficulties, corruption began to run rampant in the Ottoman Army. Training and discipline became too lax and as a result, the Janissaries took to rebelling from time to time, claiming that they were unable to make a decent living for their families. Under these circumstances, achieving any new victories became more and more unlikely. Also, the

women's stronghold in the Harem resulted in a great amount of chaos in the running of state affairs. The sultans ascending to the Ottoman throne at an early age found it impossible to rid themselves of their mothers' influence. All authority the sultans had at the time was diminishing. The Ottomans found themselves lagging behind the scientific and technological developments that had been taking place in Europe. During the first years of the era, these developments had seemed trivial, but it was not long before the Ottomans suddenly found themselves trailing Europe.

This era started with Mehmed III. Upon his death in 1603, his son Ahmed I ascended to the throne. The Sultan Ahmed Mosque he had commissioned

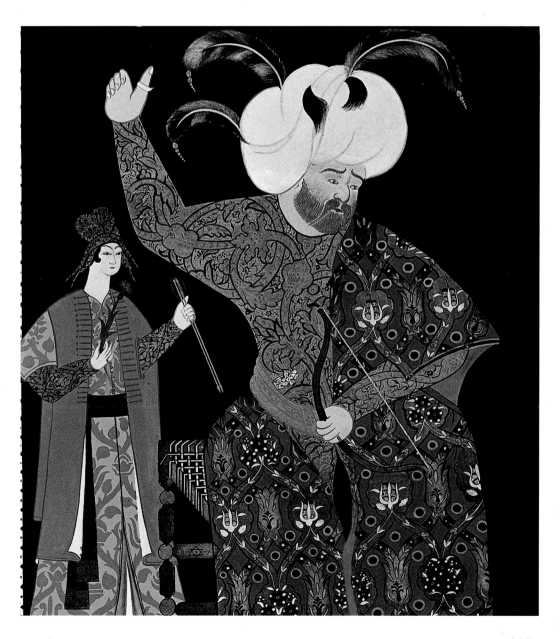

Portrait of Sultan Selim II (1570). A miniature by artist Nigari, this scene depicts Selim II, who ascended to the throne through the tremendous effort of his mother Hürrem Sultan. A palace servant standing behind the sultan has a mace in his left hand and a carnation in his right hand, while Selim is shown here honing his archery skills.

made the already shaky Ottoman economy even worse. Sultan Ahmed I died at an early age in 1617 and was succeeded by his son Mustafa I. As Mustafa I's health worsened, his young son Genç Osman ascended to the throne three months later at the age of 14. Osman strived to bring back some sense of order both in the palace and the empire, but factions led by Kösem Sultan thought the petty self-interests they had worked into the system would be lost. As a consequence, Genç Osman was strangled to death by their supporters. Kösem Sultan was Ahmed I's wife. Upon Ahmed I's death, Mustafa was allowed to ascend to the throne, as her children were still too young. But, when the son of another woman, Genç Osman, ascended to the throne, Kösem Sultan threatened officials and army commanders, saying that heads would roll if they failed to depose him. In receiving their orders, they ended up strangling Genç Osman at Yedikule, whereupon Kösem Sultan had her 11-year-old son Murad IV take the throne in 1623. He ruled the country under his mother's tutelage until the age of 20. With Murad IV's untimely death in 1640, İbrahim ascended to the throne with his mother Kösem Sultan taking the reins of the state once again. But as İbrahim behaved rather irrationally, she had him replaced with her six-year-old grandson Mehmed IV. Thus, armed with the assumption that she would continue to rule the country, a dispute rose between Mehmed IV's mother, Hatice Turhan Sultan and herself. This time around, it was Kösem Sultan's

A portrait of Sultan Bayezid II (1481-1512), This canvas oil painting measures 83 x 57 cm. (below)

A portrait of Yavuz Sultan Selim (1512-20) Oil. (right)

A portrait of Murad III (1574-95) Oil. (upper right)

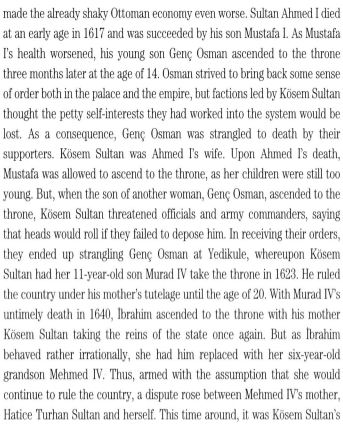

time to be strangled, thus ending her long-lasting sultanate. The dowager Sultan Hatice Turhan, who was a clever woman, then appointed Köprülü Mehmed Pasha as Grand Vizier to put an end to the domination of women in the empire. When Mehmed IV, otherwise known as 'the Hunter,' died in Edirne in 1687, he was succeeded by Süleyman II, Ahmed II and Mustafa II, respectively. A third military expedition was undertaken against Austria during Mustafa II's reign, but it ended up in ignominious defeat at Zenta, a town in the outskirts of Vienna in 1689. As a result of this defeat, Ottomans gave up a great portion of their lands in Europe. The signing of the Carlowitz Treaty in 1699 marked the end of the Era of Stagnation and the beginning of the Era of Decline, which was to last 150 years. Throughou' this period, while Europe was getting much stronger, the Ottoman Empire weakened by the day and the distinction between Europe and the Ottoman Empire was becoming quite apparent. Ahmed III's reign coincided with the peaceful Tulip era, one that brought peace and tranquility for the Ottomans from 1718-30. As a result, though fine arts and entertainment life flourished in the country, there were some parts of society that were rather discontent. French military experts brought here to teach the Ottoman Army some new methods and techniques were not made very welcome by the officer corps. Meanwhile, the once-brilliant Janissaries had begun to disregard their duties, preferring to get involved with trade instead. The defeat on the

and Romania from invasion. He signed a peace accord with Iran and put an end to Nadir Shah's demands over Anatolia. The construction of public works projects started all over the empire and reforms were carried out in the Ottoman Army as well. Mahmud I died in 1754, to be succeeded by Mustafa III, who was to rule for 20 years. Abdülhamid I acscended to the throne in 1774. During his reign, the first Russian-Ottoman war broke out even as the war against Austria continued. Sultan Abdülhamid I was incapacitated with paralysis when the empire suffered a major rout by Russia, dying soon afterwards. Better known for his music composition and poetry, Selim III ascended to the Ottoman throne in 1789, afterwhich inconclusive wars were ended with treaties and relations with France subsequently improved. However, the French Revolution broke out during this period, which had a heavy impact throughout the rest of Europe. Having also been influenced by that movement, Selim III initiated a set of wide-ranging reforms that created tension among certain factions. The Janissaries were rivals bent on eliminating the newly established "Nizam-i Cedid" Army. The people accused Selim of being an atheist. Certain statesmen with their many self-interests at stake were the underlying force against Selim's reforms. As a result, a rebellion led by Kabakçı Mustafa soon broke out and marched on the palace to depose Selim, who did not order his newly organized Nizam cedid Army against the rebels as he was against bloodshed.

Portrait of Murad IV (1623-40), who ascended to the throne at a young age. (left).

Portrait of Ahmed III (1703-30), whose sultanate coincided with the peaceful Tulip era (lower left).

Portrait of Abdülmecid (1839-61), who moved the Ottoman dynasty out of Topkapı Palace and into Dolmabahçe Palace (above).

Iranian front gave those wanting to revolt a great opportunity to go ahead with their plans and it was not long before for a rebellion broke out. It was an Albanian bath attendant, Patrona Halil, who gathered all the innumerable unemployed and wayward citizens together in 1730 to commence the rebellion. This action spread like wildfire throughout the country with even some of the Janissaries joining up with the rebels. In the end, many statesmen lost their lives, Ahmed III was deposed and his nephew Mahmud I was installed on the throne by the rebels. Patrona Halil and his supporters dominated all the crucial posts, choosing officials from among his supporters. Thoroughly corrupt, they sold available state positions to the highest bidder. A Greek butcher who was appointed as Governor of Boğdan was a tragic example of that practice. These tyrants attended all the meetings held at the Council of State and had all favorable decisions passed by ruthless means. Thus, the rebellion ended the glorious Tulip era. The people of the empire were becoming increasingly full of animosity towards what was happening in the palace. Mahmud I could foresee the future and he was very intelligent, too. He was able to reassume authority by breaking the rebels influence over the state, thereby regaining the confidence of the people. He had been brought up very well, had a decent educational background and was known as a composer and a poet. During his era, he defeated Austria, occupied Belgrade once again and saved Serbia, Walachia,

Portrait of Sultan Selim III (1789-1807). Painted by Konstantin Kapıdağlı in 1803. This oil canvas measures 110 cm x 89 cm.

Another work of Konstantin Kapıdağlı depicts the Coronation Ceremony of Selim III in front of the Gate of Felicity. Selim is seated on the throne, receiving the tributes of all the palace officials while his Grand Vizier, the Grand Vizier's Chief Magistrate and clergymen standing to his right with Harem Eunuchs and other palace officials standing behind him.

Just as Mustafa IV ascended to the throne after Selim III, Ruscuk Senator Alemdar Mustafa Pasha mustered 20,000 men to attack the palace in a last-ditch effort to save Selim III. His army camped right outside the palace while he ordered his soldiers to imprison Mustafa and to reinstate Selim III. In the meantime, Mustafa's advisors had convinced him to execute both Selim III and Crown Prince Mahmud II immediately if he wanted to continue being the sultan. However, Selim III was viciously murdered in cold blood while he blowing on his reed flute. His murderers then proceeded to hunt down Crown Prince Mahmud II, who was able to save his skin just as Alemdar Mustafa Pasha's soldiers arrived on the scene. In punishing all those who had been involved in execution of Selim III, Alemdar deposed Mustafa IV, leaving Crown Prince Mahmud II to ascend to the throne. Under the influence of his mother, Nakşidil Sultan, who was originally from the French colony of Martinique, Mahmud II tended to lean towards Europe. He had received a very good education, thanks in part to his uncle, Selim III. He was a poet and a calligrapher. He initiated reforms in all levels of the state, as he wanted the Ottoman Empire to integrate with Europe and the West. He did not reside in Topkapı Palace, preferring instead to stay in smaller wooden palaces along the Bosphorus, which he had restored. When he passed away in 1839, his eldest son Abdülmecid ascended to the throne. Like his father, Abdülmecid was open-minded and had a tendency to lean towards Europe as well. He went even further than his father by moving the Ottoman family completely out of Topkapı Palace and into Dolmabahçe Palace after its construction was finished in 1853. Upon his death in 1861, his brother Abdülaziz ascended to the throne. His work was also the continuation of the previous two sultans. This included the construction of public works all over the country and improving relations with Europe. Istanbul acquired many pavilions and works of art through his efforts. He had the Beylerbeyi and Çırağan Palaces built. Murad V succeeded to the throne after he was deposed in 1876. He was able to stay on the throne for only 93 days but as his bad health kept him from performing state affairs, he was allowed to live in the Çırağan Palace after he was deposed. Abdülhamid II ascended to the throne, moving his sultanate into the Yıldız Palace. His authoritarian ways caused dissent among the people, whose freedoms were restricted. Abdülhamid II's rule continued for 33 years during which time many advances in public works, construction and education were made. He declared a Second Constitutional Monarchy in 1908 to counter the turmoil that had begun to break out all over the empire. Fundamentalists staged a rebellion, but this was suppressed by the Mobilization Army, brought in from Macedonia. The Commander-in chief of this army was Mustafa Kemal, the future founder of the Turkish Republic. After the Revolt of 31 March 1909, Abdülhamid II was deposed and succeeded by Mehmed Reşad V, who was quite elderly. He died in 1918 after ruling for nine years, whereupon the last Ottoman Sultan, Mehmed Vahideddin ascended to the throne. He was forced to flee the country for his own safety in 1922. The Ottoman Empire entered World War I on the side of Axis Powers. However, as Germany was on the losing side, the Ottomans were considered defeated, as well. As a result, large expanses of Ottoman territory were divided up by the Allies. Under the leadership of Gazi Mustafa Kemal Pasha, the Turks won all battles fought during the War of Independence. He then founded the Republic of Turkey in the ashes of the Ottoman Empire. With Ankara chosen as the capital of the new republic, Istanbul completed its 500-year mission as the Ottoman capital, becoming a world city with an accumulation of cultural heritage.

classrooms still exists. One of the most outstanding deeds of Sultan Mehmed the Conqueror was to have his own complex constructed. Built between 1463-70 by the architect Sinan-i Atik over the site of the Church of the Apostoleion, the Fatih Complex consisted of a mosque in the center, the "Mediterranean" and "Black Sea" medreses, a small hospital, a caravanserai, a small charitable soup kitchen, a kindergarten, a hospice, a bath and a library on both sides. One of the viziers of Sultan Mehmed the Conqueror's era, Rum Mehmed Pasha, had a complex consisting of a mosque, tomb, school and a bath constructed in Üsküdar in 1472. Around the same year, Murad Pasha had another complex built in Aksaray. In 1476, the Sheikh Vefa Complex was constructed in Vefa and a tomb was later added upon death of the sheikh in 1480. Bayezid II, who ascended to the throne after Sultan Mehmed the Conqueror, had his own complex constructed in one the most outstanding squares of Istanbul. As one of the first examples of Classical-era architecture, this complex was constructed by the architect Yakup Sheikh Bin Sultan Sheikh between 1501-06. It consists of a mosque, medrese, bath, soup kitchen and a tomb.

During the era of Bayezid II, Grand Vizier Davud Pasha had a complex constructed in 1485 in Cerrahpaşa. That public work was comprised of a mosque, medrese, fountain and a soup kitchen, the latter of which no longer exists. The mosque in the complex was constructed on a square plan and had a single dome. The inscription of the mosque was written by Sheikh Hamdullah.

Another dazzling complex was constructed by Atik Ali Pasha, who was promoted to the rank of Grand Vizier from the pool of eunuchs during the reign of Bayezid II. Built in 1496, this complex consists of a large mosque, the roof of which is covered with a semi-dome. The main prayer hall is covered with five small domes. The central dome measures 12.5 meters in diameter and has authentic inscriptions. Atik Ali Pasha had another complex constructed in Karagümrük, Fatih.

Sultan Selim the Grim, who reigned after Bayezid II for a period of eight years, was always out on the battlefront. Situated on top of the fifth hill of Istanbul, his mosque was built by his son Sultan Süleyman the Magnificent in 1522. Acem Ali was the architect of this mosque, which was the third Selatin type of its kind in Istanbul. The dome of the mosque measures 24 meters in diameter and is 33 meters high. The mosque, medrese, bath, a soup kitchen, tomb and hospice of that complex no longer exist. With a magnificent view, this complex situated on the slopes of the Golden Horn

Constructed by Mimar Sinan for Grand Vizier Rüstem Pasha in 1560, the Rüstem Pasha Mosque is essentially a tile museum.

114

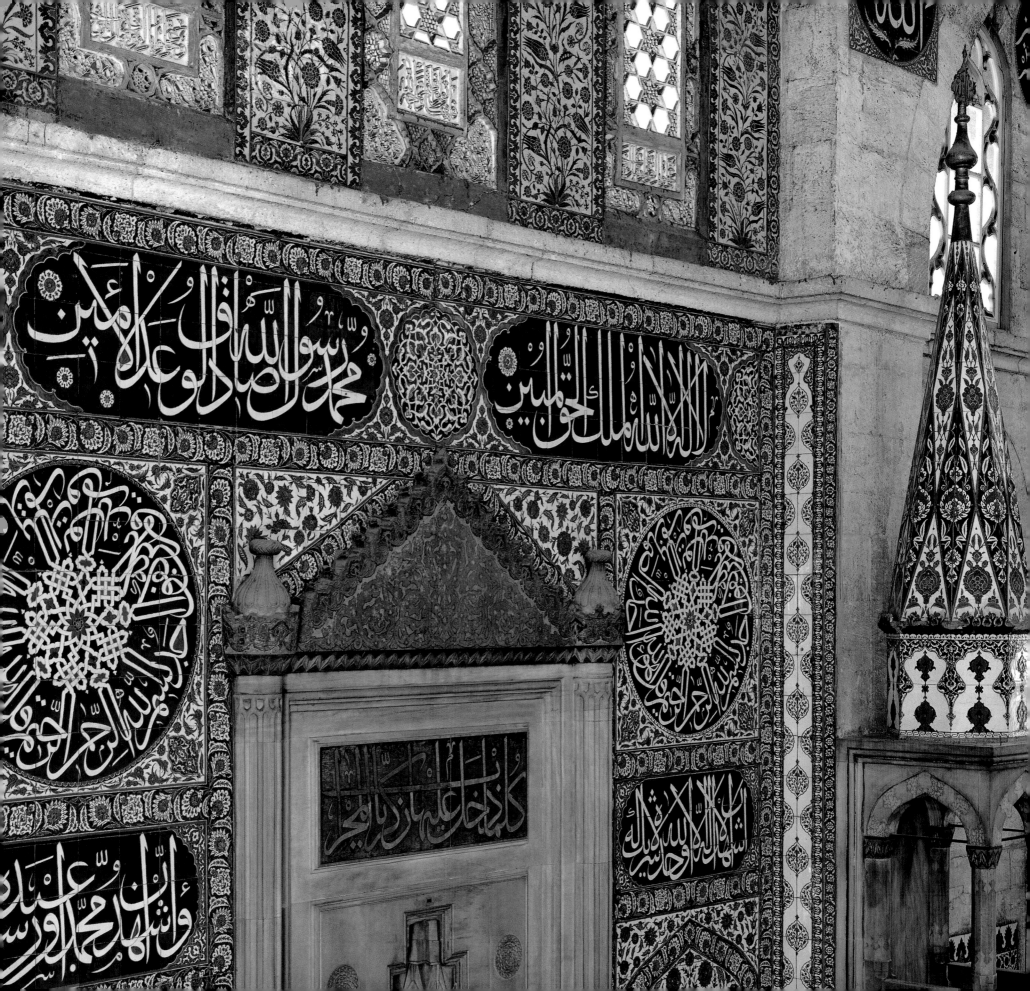

Classical-Era Mosques

"I honestly hope that as long as this world turns, people looking at my works of art will take the seriousness of my efforts into fair consideration and always remember me in their prayers." Mimar Sinan

The most beautiful works of art of Istanbul are of course her mosques with their skyscraping minarets, poised as if to touch God. Mosques commissioned by the Ottoman sultans hold distinguished places in Turkish society. Their interior décor as well as exterior architecture are unique. These mosques are called "Selatin," which is the plural of the word "Sultan." Besides their overall magnificence, their many minarets make them particularly striking.

After his conquest of Constantinople, Sultan Mehmed the Conqueror initiated a number of public works throughout the empire. The appearance of Istanbul started to change rapidly with many complexes that the dowager sultans and pashas ordered built. These were multi-functional structures consisting of a mosque in the center generally surrounded by a school, soup kitchen, small hospital, charity and a caravanserai. People would make use of complexes by sending their children to the schools, praying in its mosque, dining in its charitable soup kitchens and receiving hospital care when they were taken ill. Complexes were essentially social communities built for the use of the common folk. Beside the mosques built within the complexes, there used to be other small single mosques around them, too. Today, Istanbul has a total of 989 historical mosques dating from the time of Sultan Mehmed the Conqueror up until the late-Ottoman period. They were built according to various stylistic periods, e.g., Classical, Baroque, Rococo and Empiric. We will try to describe these splendid complexes and their mosques along with other single grand mosques.

Sultan Mehmed the Conqueror had a complex built to commemorate the site where Ebu Eyyüb-el-Ensari died. He was the flag bearer for the Prophet Mohammed during the siege of Constantinople in the 7th century. The mosque of that complex collapsed during the 18th century and was rebuilt by Selim III in 1798. This mosque is covered with a central main dome surrounded by eight other smaller domes. Its interior hall is enclosed by 13 vaults with domes on 12 columns. Classrooms of the medrese are adjacent to the hall. The soup kitchen is found to the southeast of this complex. The Tomb of Eyüp Sultan, which fills up with visitors everyday, stands directly across from the mosque. Sultan Mehmed the Conqueror appointed his

pashas and viziers to rebuild Istanbul over again. Grand Vizier Mahmud Pasha ordered a complex with a mosque in the middle surrounded by a school, soup kitchen, small hospital and a caravanserai to be built near the Grand Bazaar in 1462. The part consisting of the mosque, tomb and

Sokollu Mosque. Mimar Sinan constructed a complex with a mosque for Sokollu Mehmed Pasha in 1577. Shown here is the niche decorated with splendid Iznik tiles.

classrooms still exists. One of the most outstanding deeds of Sultan Mehmed the Conqueror was to have his own complex constructed. Built between 1463-70 by the architect Sinan-i Atik over the site of the Church of the Apostoleion, the Fatih Complex consisted of a mosque in the center, the "Mediterranean" and "Black Sea" medreses, a small hospital, a caravanserai, a small charitable soup kitchen, a kindergarten, a hospice, a bath and a library on both sides. One of the viziers of Sultan Mehmed the Conqueror's era, Rum Mehmed Pasha, had a complex consisting of a mosque, tomb, school and a bath constructed in Üsküdar in 1472. Around the same year, Murad Pasha had another complex built in Aksaray. In 1476, the Sheikh Vefa Complex was constructed in Vefa and a tomb was later added upon death of the sheikh in 1480. Bayezid II, who ascended to the throne after Sultan Mehmed the Conqueror, had his own complex constructed in one the most outstanding squares of Istanbul. As one of the first examples of Classical-era architecture, this complex was constructed by the architect Yakup Sheikh Bin Sultan Sheikh between 1501-06. It consists of a mosque, medrese, bath, soup kitchen and a tomb.

During the era of Bayezid II, Grand Vizier Davud Pasha had a complex constructed in 1485 in Cerrahpaşa. That public work was comprised of a mosque, medrese, fountain and a soup kitchen, the latter of which no longer exists. The mosque in the complex was constructed on a square plan and had a single dome. The inscription of the mosque was written by Sheikh Hamdullah.

Another dazzling complex was constructed by Atik Ali Pasha, who was promoted to the rank of Grand Vizier from the pool of eunuchs during the reign of Bayezid II. Built in 1496, this complex consists of a large mosque, the roof of which is covered with a semi-dome. The main prayer hall is covered with five small domes. The central dome measures 12.5 meters in diameter and has authentic inscriptions. Atik Ali Pasha had another complex constructed in Karagümrük, Fatih.

Sultan Selim the Grim, who reigned after Bayezid II for a period of eight years, was always out on the battlefront. Situated on top of the fifth hill of Istanbul, his mosque was built by his son Sultan Süleyman the Magnificent in 1522. Acem Ali was the architect of this mosque, which was the third Selatin type of its kind in Istanbul. The dome of the mosque measures 24 meters in diameter and is 33 meters high. The mosque, medrese, bath, a soup kitchen, tomb and hospice of that complex no longer exist. With a magnificent view, this complex situated on the slopes of the Golden Horn

Constructed by Mimar Sinan for Grand Vizier Rüstem Pasha in 1560, the Rüstem Pasha Mosque is essentially a tile museum.

The Atik Valide Complex (1577-83). The mother of Sultan Murad III, Dowager Sultan Nurbanu commissioned Mimar Sinan to construct it in Toptaşı, Üsküdar. The mosque of this complex is adorned with 16th-century Iznik tiles seen around the niche (facing page) as well as the close-up view (below).

changed the panorama of Istanbul. There are no columns inside the rather plain mosque. The section above the windows is adorned with tiles and interior domes with authentic inscriptions. Its hall is surrounded by 20 domed-vaults. The Ottoman Empire, which had reached its zenith during the mid-16th century, displayed its power and wealth in many ways, which included the splendid public works built during the era. Mimar Sinan

prospered then to his full capacity and fame. He was born in the small village of Ağırnas in Kayseri in 1490. He was raised in the Boy's Apprenticeship School, where he received a good education. As we have learned from the books of poet and author Sai Mustafa Çelebi, Sinan accompanied Sultan Selim the Grim on his military expedition to Egypt and Iran where he was able to observe architectural styles in those lands. Afterwards, he joined the Janissary Corps as a member of the military expedition to Belgrade in 1521. Through subsequent travels through other lands such as the Balkans, Hungary and Austria he amassed an impressive accumulation of architectural knowledge. He was extremely successful on the military expedition to Moldova and Iran and he attracted Sultan Süleyman the Magnificent's attention by building bridges over the Prut and Danube rivers.

Once a fortification officer in the Ottoman Army, he completed engineering and architecture training, and was appointed the post of Palace Architect upon the death of the architect Acem Ali. During his glorious career, Mimar Sinan constructed a total of 477 works of art: 107 mosques, 74 medreses (schools of theology), 56 hamams (baths), 52 mescids (small mosques), 45 tombs, 31 caravanserais, nine bridges and palaces as well as several pavilions. In studying all other works that were built before his time, he established a whole new era in Ottoman architecture. Though 345 of his works of art were erected in Istanbul and its environs, 100 of them no longer exist.

Mimar Sinan's first work was commissioned by Sultan Süleyman the Magnificent in 1539 in Istanbul for his wife, Hürrem Sultan. The Haseki Complex consisted of a mosque, medrese, boy's school, soup kitchen, fountain and a small hospital. The main feature of this complex, which bore all the architectural features of the early-16th century, was that its mosque was constructed outside the complex. Devoting herself completely to religion in the latter part of her life, Hürrem Sultan had ordered the construction of many charities, hospitals, complexes and fountains. One of them was the Haseki Complex. The square-planned, single-dome mosque structure of the complex marked Sinan's transition to multi-domed mosques. The mosque has a niche in Baroque style, a marble pulpit and a wooden podium. The medrese is adorned with colorful tiles in the classical-Ottoman style. One of the tile panels from that school is exhibited in the Çinili Pavilion today. The mosque of that complex standing at the corner of the street was restored with some additions by Sedefkar Mehmed Ağa in 1612.

The Şehzade Complex is Mimar Sinan's splendid and monumental work of art. Sultan Süleyman the Magnificent ordered it to be built in the name of his son Crown Prince Mehmed, who had died at the age of 21. Completed in

1548, the complex consisted of a mosque, medrese, bath, soup kitchen, hospice, school, caravanserai, and a tomb. Sinan would call it a work from his apprenticeship days. But, in fact, he surpassed the schemes of Hagia Sophia and the Bayezid Mosque, by constructing a complex with four semi-domes for the first time, creating his own architectural style. While completing the construction of the Şehzade Mosque, Mimar Sinan began work on another complex for Mihrimah Sultan, the daughter of Sultan Süleyman the Magnificent and Hürrem Sultan, and wife of Rüstem Pasha. Mimar Sinan was

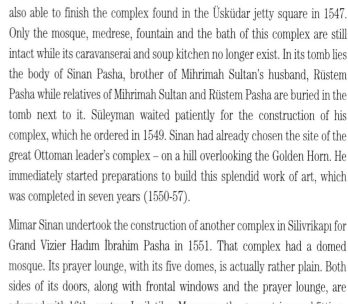

also able to finish the complex found in the Üsküdar jetty square in 1547. Only the mosque, medrese, fountain and the bath of this complex are still intact while its caravanserai and soup kitchen no longer exist. In its tomb lies the body of Sinan Pasha, brother of Mihrimah Sultan's husband, Rüstem Pasha while relatives of Mihrimah Sultan and Rüstem Pasha are buried in the tomb next to it. Süleyman waited patiently for the construction of his complex, which he ordered in 1549. Sinan had already chosen the site of the great Ottoman leader's complex – on a hill overlooking the Golden Horn. He immediately started preparations to build this splendid work of art, which was completed in seven years (1550-57).

Mimar Sinan undertook the construction of another complex in Silivrikapı for Grand Vizier Hadım İbrahim Pasha in 1551. That complex had a domed mosque. Its prayer lounge, with its five domes, is actually rather plain. Both sides of its doors, along with frontal windows and the prayer lounge, are adorned with 16th -century Iznik tiles. Moreover, the geometric wood fittings and ivory inlay work on the gate of its mosque reflect the finest of its kind. The mosque constructed in 1555 for the Admiral-in chief Sinan Pasha, brother of Rüstem Pasha is also exemplary of Mimar Sinan's finer works. Here, he repeated the same plan he had applied with his Üçşerefli Mosque in Edirne, where he carried out his first attempt to construct a mosque with six pillars.

Sultan Süleyman the Magnificent ordered his son Crown Prince Mustafa to be strangled to death, for he had revolted against him in Konya. Ottoman soldiers, who deeply admired Crown Prince Mustafa, suspected that Grand Vizier Rüstem Pasha had played a role in his execution, thus triggering a rebellion. This sticky situation forced Süleyman to dismiss Rüstem Pasha, who he replaced with the husband of his sister, Fatma Sultan, Kara Ahmed Pasha, who was also appreciated by the army as Grand Vizier.

The recently appointed Kara Ahmed Pasha took this opportunity to have a mosque built in his name. However, he was strangled to death in Topkapı Palace in 1558 before Mimar Sinan was able to complete it during the same year. This complex consisted of a mosque, medrese, boy's school, and a tomb. The rectangular-shaped mosque has a dome supported by six main pillars, which are in turn supported by four semi-domes. The window niche and cabinet facades are adorned with 16th-century Iznik tiles while the main dome is decorated with calligraphic inscriptions. Kara Ahmed Pasha and his wife, Fatma Sultan, the daughter of Sultan Selim the Grim are buried in its tomb. Mimar Sinan began work on the Rüstem Pasha Complex in Eminönü in 1560. He constructed its mosque by raising it over a rather narrow area. He

Interior of the Kılıç Ali Pasha Mosque. Commodore of the Navy, Kılıç Ali Pasha ordered Mimar Sinan to construct his mosque in Tophane between 1580-81.

also introduced a new structural system based upon eight elephantine pillars, four of which were unattached and the remainder adjacent to the walls. The interior decoration of the mosque as well as its main prayer hall are adorned with Iznik tiles having a total of 41 unique tulip motifs, effectively turning it into a virtual tile museum. Meanwhile, in 1561, Mimar Sinan had just completed the construction of a mosque in Fındıklı for Kazasker Mehmed Efendi, otherwise known as Molla Çelebi. Mimar Sinan undertook another construction job for Mihrimah Sultan after completing her mosque in Üsküdar. Built in Edirnekapı between the years 1562-65, the Mihrimah Sultan Complex consisted of a mosque, a bath, a tomb and a bazaar. The main area of the mosque was covered with a single dome measuring 19 meters in diameter and 27 meters in height. It was expanded later on with three domed halls on two sides. In doing so, Mimar Sinan created his own unique theme. The marble niche in this mosque, which is situated adjacent to the city walls, is adorned with gold leaf whereas the interior domes and walls are adorned with calligraphic art. Only the mosque,

Interior view of Eyüp Sultan Mosque (1469). It was the first to be constructed since the conquest of Constantinople. It was restored during the reign of Selim III as it had suffered damage over the years.

119

medrese and shops still exist in this complex, which offers a commanding view on a high hill.

The era of Sultan Süleyman the Magnificent came to a close with his passing in 1566. Nevertheless, Mimar Sinan continued to produce many splendid works during the subsequent era of Sultan Selim II. For instance, he undertook the construction of a new complex in Kadırga for Grand Vizier Sokollu Mehmed Pasha between 1571-72. Sokollu Mehmed Pasha was born

Kara Ahmed Pasha Mosque (1555-58). Mimar Sinan constructed a mosque for Kara Ahmed Pasha, the husband of the daughter of Sultan Süleyman the Magnificent, Fatma Sultan.

the son of a Christian priest in Bosnia in 1505. Brought to Istanbul at a young age, he was educated in the Palace School. Sokollu Mehmed was distinguished with his brilliant intelligence and thus was posted important positions in the palace. He was appointed to the rank of Admiral-in chief in 1546 and also became the Regional Governor of Rumeli. Highly appreciated by Sultan Süleyman the Magnificent, as he was extremely successful in all his posts, this gratitude transformed him into a son-in-law of the palace in 1562, when the sultan got him to marry İsmehan Sultan, the 17-year old daughter of his son Crown Prince Selim.

The difference in age between the bride and groom was 40 years, but this was not considered unusual for royal families. Though İsmehan Sultan was short and ugly, she was rather intelligent and ambitious, and it was this ambition that drove her to become the most influential and important woman of the palace. Her husband Sokollu Mehmed Pasha was also a very intelligent, successful and serious vizier and it did not take him long to become Süleyman's Grand Vizier. He continued his position as Grand Vizier long after Sultan Süleyman the Magnificent had passed away, during the periods of Selim II and Murad III as well. He exhibited a character of decisiveness and authority. Situated over an inclined piece of property, the Sokollu Mosque in Kadırga is a shining example of Mimar Sinan's skill as an architect. The niche wall of the mosque is adorned with 16th-century Iznik tiles up to the beginning of the dome. Above the windows are Koranic verses on a dark blue background. The niche and the pulpit in the mosque reflect fine stone masonry. Mimar Sinan created an enormous monumental work of art for Sultan Selim II – the Selimiye Mosque in Edirne, between 1569-78, calling it his masterpiece.

During that period, Mimar Sinan returned to Istanbul in 1573 to begin work on the Piyale Pasha Mosque in Kasımpaşa for Piyale Pasha, the Admiral-in chief. Piyale Pasha, who had been recruited to the palace from the Balkans, was educated and raised within the palace confines. He was first appointed as Regional Governor of Gallipoli in 1547, then appointed to the rank of Fleet Admiral in 1553, a post he held for 14 years. He became a son-in-law to the palace after his successful conquests of Algeria and Sakız and Gerbe Islands as well as scoring major naval victories along the Italian and Spanish coastlines. To appease Piyale Pasha, Sultan Süleyman the Magnificent married him off to Gevherhan Sultan, who was another daughter of the Crown Prince Selim. The mosque Mimar Sinan constructed for Piyale Pasha measures 30 meters x 19.5 meters and is rectangular in shape. Its tile-covered mihrab has double niches measuring 7.5 meters x 3 meters. The 13 different styles of 16th-century tiles inside the mosque are just beautiful.

Frontal windows adorned with tiles bear Koranic verses in white on a dark blue background. Above the second-storey windows are the "İhlas" and "Cuma" Koranic verses, once again in white on a dark blue background. The inscriptions are the work of Circassian Hasan, who was a student of Ahmed Karahisari. There are colorfully painted and gold leafed motifs on both sides of the window shutters in the women's section. A portion of the mosque's main prayer area is covered on top while the other part is open. Numerous columns were used here. The octagonal shaped Tomb of Piyale Pasha lies right behind the mosque, whereas children other than his own are also buried in this tomb.

Upon Selim II's death in 1574, his son Murad III ascended to the Ottoman throne. Mimar Sinan continued his work for 14 more years during the reign of Murad III as well. Thus, his work spanned the reigns of three sultans. He constructed the Pavilion of Murad III in the Topkapı Harem and the Muradiye Complex in Manisa for Murad III as well.

Mimar Sinan began the construction of a new mosque for Sokollu Mehmed Pasha, who was still standing as a strong symbol of authority in 1577. Situated at the foot of today's Atatürk Bridge in Azapkapı, the Sokollu Mehmed Pasha Mosque is a scaled-down version of the Selimiye Mosque in Edirne, with a main dome measuring 12 meters in diameter. Sokollu Mehmed Pasha, who never made compromises and put the interests of the state above everything else, was killed on 11 October 1579 while leaving a Council Assembly at the Topkapı Palace by somebody disguised as a beggar. He was buried in the tomb Mimar Sinan had constructed for him in Eyüp ten years earlier.

After Selimiye, one of Mimar Sinan's other greatest works is that of the huge Atik Valide Complex, which was constructed in Toptaşı, Üsküdar, between 1577-83. Nurbanu Valide Sultan, who was the wife of Selim II and the mother of the reigning Sultan Murad III, had commissioned Mimar Sinan to erect that complex on the slopes of Üsküdar. It is comprised of a mosque, medrese, bath, small hospital, soup kitchen, hospice and a tomb. A caravanserai was also added to accommodate caravans that arrived in the city from Anatolia. The Iznik tiles used in the swath of inscriptions as well as in the niche also date back to the 16th century.

Mimar Sinan built the Zal Mahmud Pasha Complex in Defterdar Caddesi in Eyüp in 1580. Zal Mahmud was infamous as the one who carried out the death order of Sultan Süleyman the Magnificent to strangle Crown Prince Mustafa on the plains of Konya. He had been appointed to the rank of fifth Vizier in 1568 and married Shah Sultan,

another daughter of Selim II to become a member of the royal family. The complex bearing his name consists of a mosque, two medreses, a fountain and a tomb.

Quality 16th-century Iznik tiles were set all around the marble niche in its mosque. Koranic verse in white on a dark blue background is seen above the frontal windows. Zal Mahmud Pasha, who died in 1580, was buried with his wife in the octagonal-shaped tomb of this complex.

Mihrimah Sultan Mosque (1562-65). Mimar Sinan constructed this mosque for Mihrimah Sultan, the daughter of Sultan Süleyman the Magnificent in Edirnekapı.

Mimar Sinan built his smallest complex in Üsküdar by the waterfront for Vizier Şemsi Ahmed from the Isfendiyaroğuls in 1580. Measuring 8 meters x 8 meters, this square-plan complex situated on the seashore has a splendid view. The Tomb of Şemsi Pasha is also found here as well.

Mimar Sinan constructed the Kılıç Ali Pasha Complex in Tophane between 1580-81. It was comprised of a mosque, medrese, fountain, bath and a tomb. Quality 16th-century Iznik tiles were used in the construction of its prayer

hall. Koranic verse is on both sides of the portal. Moreover, the frontal windows of the mosque are adorned with Koranic verse in white on a dark blue background. Windows are also decorated with frames. Above the niche, up to the bottom of the upper windows, is an inscription that bears Koranic verse in white on a dark blue background. Beside these, Mimar Sinan decorated the mosque with an abundance of calligraphy. Behind the niche wall is the Tomb of Kılıç Ali Pasha, while mounted on the wall over looking the avenue is a fountain.

In 1585, Mimar Sinan constructed the Kazasker İvaz Efendi Complex over the Blachernae Palace terrace in Ayvansaray. This complex consisted of a mosque, medrese, fountain and a school with only the mosque and fountain still intact. The mosque's main dome is surrounded by five semi-domes, and its niches feature splendid tiles of the period. Having been trained by Mimar Sinan, Davud Ağa built a mosque in Çarşamba, Fatih in 1585 for Ramazan Efendi, who was the Head Eunuch at the time. He was the follower of his master Mimar Sinan in all his works. Despite his advanced age, Mimar Sinan was still working in 1586 when he constructed the Ramazan Efendi Mosque in Kocamustafapaşa. He had Sai Mustafa Çelebi, who would pen his biography, write the inscription of the mosque, while he decorated the mosque with 16th-century Iznik tiles.

In 1586, the architect Mahmud Ağa constructed the Sadrazam Mesih Pasha Mosque, which is located at the intersection of Ali Pasha Sokak and Mütercim Asım Sokak in Fatih. Mesih Pasha was promoted to palace statesman from the ranks of the eunuchs. He was notoriously ruthless when he was the Governor of Egypt. He had his mosque constructed later on while he served in the capacity of Grand Vizier to Murad III. One encounters bright daylight inside as it built with many windows. Tiles decorate the space around the marble niche and frontal windows. The geometrically designed pulpit enriches the mosque.

The octagonal Tomb of Mesih Pasha lies in the courtyard where a fountain would normally have been placed. Situated on a steep hillside, the mosque has shops and a fountain on its ground floor. By 1588 Mimar Sinan was quite old and no longer able to work anymore. Davud Ağa strived hard to fill in for the master when he undertook the construction of the Vizier Nişancı Mehmed Pasha Complex in Çarşamba, Fatih. When Mimar Sinan passed away in the same year at the age of 90, he left behind a legacy of literally hundreds of complexes, bridges, mosques, hamams, and tombs. He was buried in his tomb in Süleymaniye. With his passing, the Classical-Ottoman era came to an end and a comparatively less fruitful period began.

Neo-Classical Era Mosques

"Istanbul is the only city that truly excites and inspires painters." Lamartine

Mimar Sinan died in 1588, leaving an indelible mark on 16th-century architecture. Though construction projects all over the city slowed down considerably after his death, a scattering amount of attractive works were still being carried out. Among these was a mosque that was commissioned by Takkeci İbrahim Ağa. Based on a square plan with a wooden roof, this mosque has an ablution fountain as well as a public fountain. The intervals below all the windows are decorated with 16th-century Iznik tile panels showing bunches of grapes hanging between branches. Tiles depicting cypress trees and compositions embellished with vases filled with bouquets of carnations add even more beauty to this mosque, which was restored by Mahmud II in 1831.

Situated on the road that runs into Kocamustafapaşa from Aksaray, the Cerrah Mehmed Pasha Complex was constructed by Davud Ağa in 1593. Cerrah Mehmed Pasha was initially the Palace Surgeon, but as he proved his success over time, he was promoted to the rank of Grand Vizier. Situated on a hilly road, the complex on Cerrahpaşa Caddesi consists of a mosque, two hamams and the Gevher Sultan Medrese. Subsequently expanded on both sides, the dome of this complex is supported by six columns. Constructed by Mimar Sinan's student, Davud Ağa, this complex is not as architecturally astute as similar structures built in the past. However, it is still quite noteworthy for its many windows and wide interior area. Known as the conqueror of Tunisia and Yemen, the Albanian expatriate Koca Sinan Pasha served as Grand Vizier for some time. He commissioned the architect Davud Ağa in 1593 to construct the Koca Sinanpaşa Complex along Divanyolu Caddesi while he was Grand Vizier. Comprised of a tomb, medrese and a fountain, this complex has no mosque, as it was built in a confined area. This disadvantage was overcome by converting one of the school classrooms into a prayer room. The Sedaret Kethüdası Hafız Ahmed Pasha Complex was constructed in the district of Fatih in 1595. Other than its tomb and fountain, the buildings of this complex are still intact as they were restored several times. The mother of Murad III, Safiye Sultan, who was originally from Venice, wanted to have a complex as well, so she commissioned the architect Davud Ağa to construct the Yeni Mosque and Complex near the shore in Eminönü in 1597. Utilizing the same system his master Mimar Sinan had

applied in Büyükçekmece, Davud Ağa solidified the foundation by pounding tall stakes into the ground and tying all of them to each other with lead bands. However, just as the structure began to rise above its foundations, the architect Davud Ağa succumbed to the plague that broke out in Istanbul in 1599. Just prior to his death, he was able to complete the Kapıağası Gazanfer Ağa Complex, which is located alongside the Valens protective walls in

Although small in size, the Takkeci Mosque is famous for its 16th-century İznik tiles. Seen here are some details of the tiles and tile panels covering its walls.

A panoramic view of the Sultan Ahmed Mosque, one of the most magnificent structures of the neo-Classical era. (Preceeding overleaf).

Saraçhanebaşı. Thus, after Mimar Sinan, the architect Davud Ağa left behind some immortal works of art. Upon his death, Dalgıç Ahmed Çavuş was appointed in his stead as Palace Architect. He was able to continue the construction of Yeni Mosque as its walls rose up to the lower window level. However, as Mehmed III had passed away in 1603, Safiye Sultan was exiled to the Old Palace in Bayezid, whereby the construction of her Yeni Mosque was put on hold for what was to be many years. Ahmed I succeeded to the throne after Mehmed III. During the first few years of Ahmed I's reign, all contracting work in Istanbul led by Dalgıç Ahmed Çavuş was postponed until 1605. The Celali Revolts, which continued sporadically throughout the 17th century, weakened the empire considerably, forcing the palace to focus more on military operations. Thus, the state was not in the economic position to afford as many construction works as before. Nevertheless, Ahmed I commissioned Sedefkar Mehmed Ağa to build the striking Sultan Ahmed Mosque, which truly reflects the splendor of the early 17th century.

Sedefkar Mehmed Ağa was promoted to the rank of Palace Architect of the Empire upon the death of Dalgıç Ahmed Ağa in 1605. Sedefkar Mehmed Ağa was recruited into the Ottoman palace from the Balkans in 1562 and trained at the Apprentice School. Upon graduation, he was appointed to the Privy Gardens. He was fond of music, architecture and interested in working with mother-of-pearl. As Mimar Sinan's apprentice for 21 years, he accompanied the master on trips to Egypt, Arabia, Mecca, Medina and Jerusalem, steadily accumulating knowledge and experience prior to his appointment as Palace Architect in 1605. The following year, Grand Vizier Kuyucu Murad Pasha commissioned the construction of a complex in Şehzadebaşı. The school of this complex is still used as the research center of Istanbul University's Literature Department. Also, Defterdar Ekmekçioğlu Ahmed Pasha had his own complex constructed in Vefa in 1610. Though these two complexes were built during Sedefkar Mehmed Ağa's service as Palace Architect, we still have no definite proof that they were his works, so we must regard them as anonymous works of art.

As Sultan Ahmed died at a young age, the rest of this complex, along with his tomb were completed during the periods of Mustafa I and Osman II. After Osman II, Murad IV ascended to the throne at a very early age. Consequently, his mother, Kösem Sultan exercised her authority as the Dowager Sultan and began ruling the country herself.

Murad IV died upon returning from his Baghdad campaign. His mother, Kösem Sultan commissioned Mimar Kasım Ağa to build a complex for herself before he passed away in 1640. Located in Toptaşı, Üsküdar, this complex is comprised of a mosque, medrese, primary school, fountain, charitable fountain and two hamams. The mosque is named the "Çinili" Mosque because its interior is decorated with 17th-century Iznik tiles. A unique architectural application was used for its wooden prayer room, which surrounds the structure on three sides. The facade windows have "Ayet-ül Kürsi" Koranic verse inscribed on tiles, whereas there is another thin band of "Fetih Ayeti" Koranic verse inscribed above the window. Kösem Sultan continued her sultanate as Dowager Sultan during the reign of her other son Sultan İbrahim, who succeeded Murad IV. However, as İbrahim proved to be unsuitable as sultan, Kösem's seven-year old grandson Mehmed IV was instated in 1648. But a ruthless dispute soon arose between Mehmed IV's

Interior view (opposite page) and niche (below) of Çinili Mosque in Üsküdar. The wife of Ahmed I and mother of Murad IV, Kösem Sultan commissioned Mimar Sinan to build this structure in 1640.

mother, Valide Hatice Turhan Sultan and Kösem Sultan as the latter insisted on imposing her authority in palace matters.

In the end, Kösem Sultan was strangled to death in 1650, bringing her long sultanate to an end. Regarded as a clever woman, Dowager Sultan Hatice Turhan appointed Köprülü Mehmed Pasha as Grand Vizier, who with full control of the state, ended the infamous iron rule of the women, which had lasted about a century. Henceforth, she devoted herself to religion and only requested that a mosque to be constructed in her name. Instead of erecting a new mosque from scratch, Grand Vizier Köprülü Mehmed Pasha suggested that she continue the construction of the Yeni Mosque Complex that had been abandoned for 65 years since the time of Safiye Sultan. She was conducive to the idea and ordered the completion of this complex. In the meantime, Palace Architect Koca Kasım Ağa passed away in 1660 and

Mustafa Ağa was appointed as his replacement. He worked very hard to complete the complex between 1661-63. As a consequence, the Yeni Mosque Complex was to be the last major work by architects trained under the aegis of Mimar Sinan.

The Köprülü family, which held the political reins of the empire during the 17th century, was also involved in the field of architecture. In 1661, Köprülü Mehmed Pasha commissioned the construction of the Köprülü Complex along Divanyolu Caddesi, having his son Ali Bey complete the job in 1683. In the same year, another complex was built along Divanyolu Caddesi, which was commissioned by Merzifonlu Kara Mustafa Pasha. Another member of the Köprülü family, Grand Vizier Amcazade Hüseyin Pasha, commissioned a complex to be built on his behalf at Saraçhanebaşı at the start of the 18th century. Built over a large area of land, this complex was comprised of a

Interior view of Laleli Mosque. The architect Tahir Ağa was commissioned by Mustafa III to construct this structure between 1759-63.

small mosque, medrese, library, shops, fountain as well as a charitable fountain. The octagonal style mescids of both the Köprülü Mehmet Pasha Complex and Amcazade Hüseyin Pasha Complex are covered with domes. These were built separate from the medreses and took on a certain identity when they were converted into classrooms.

The sultanate of Ahmed III (1703-30) coincided with the start of a new era. Besides the cultural enlightenment that took place, new architectural styles also emerged during the Tulip Era (1718-30). Nevertheless, Dowager Sultan Gülnuş Emetullah had a complex which applied the old school of architecture built in Üsküdar Square in 1708. This complex consisted of a soup kitchen, a primary school, a tomb and a public fountain. Right in the middle of the column-supported courtyard is an octagonal fountain fashioned from richly ornamented marble. The tomb lies in the outer courtyard of the complex in an open-air architectural style, whereas the

public fountain is next to the tomb. One can observe the transition made in Ottoman architecture styles from Classical to Baroque with this complex.

Located behind today's Istanbul City Hall, the Abdülhalim Medrese was constructed in 1707. The following year, Çorlulu Ali Pasha, who was the Grand Vizier of Ahmed II, had a small complex built on Divanyolu Caddesi in an architectural style similar to that seen in the earlier complexes built along this avenue. Some innovations in Ottoman art were initiated by the Grand Vizier of Sultan Ahmed III, Nevşehirli Damat İbrahim Pasha. Cultural relations with France started during his period, which led to the French influence that was easily seen in the cultural life of the Ottoman Empire. Grand Vizier Şehirli Damat İbrahim Pasha had his own complex constructed in 1720 on Dede Efendi Sokak, next to the Şehzade Mosque. The single-domed mosque within this complex was constructed from brick and stone and is based on a square plan, with its dome supported by eight columns.

Interior of the Nuruosmaniye Mosque, regarded as the greatest works of the Turkish Baroque period. Construction commenced during the rule of Mahmud I and was finished by Osman III in 1755.

Measuring 31 meters x 22 meters, the courtyard has a central fountain, rooms of instruction on the sides, medrese, public fountain, library and a marketplace. The engravings found in these structures reflect the characteristics of the Tulip Era. The tombs of Nevşehirli Damat İbrahim Pasha, his wife Fatma Sultan and their relatives are found in the cattle-pen of the mosque. Grand Vizier Nevşehirli Damat İbrahim Pasha was in favor of furthering the art of tilemaking in the Empire and thus he ordered some tile kilns to be built in Tekfur Palace in 1725. Tiles produced in these kilns were utilized in many of the structures constructed later on. The officer in charge

of shipyard affairs, Eminzade Hacı Ahmed Ağa ordered the construction of Ahmediye Complex. Built between 1722-30, this complex was comprised of a soup kitchen, primary school, fountain, public fountain and a tomb. The Tulip Era came to an abrupt end with the start of the Patrona Halil Rebellion, especially when Ahmed III was toppled by the rebels and succeeded by Sultan Mahmud I. The grand vizier of this period, Hekimoğlu Ali Pasha commissioned Çuhadar Ömer and Hacı Mustafa to build him a complex in Cerrahpaşa in 1734. The Hekimoğlu Ali Pasha complex consisted of a mosque, library, tomb and public fountain. Ali Pasha and his family lie at rest in this tomb. Tekfur Palace tiles were used in its mosque, which was the final example of Classical-era architecture constructed in the Ottoman Empire. Grand Vizier Seyyid Hasan Pasha called for a complex to be built that consisted of a shop, an inn, medrese, public fountain and a fountain on the other.

As Head Eunuch during the periods of Ahmed III and Mahmud I, Hacı Beşir Ağa had a complex built in 1745 in Cağaloğlu right across today's Police Headquarters. Above its gate is an inscription written by Yesarı-Zade Mustafa İzzet. There were 17 shops on its ground floor. Another architect, Çelebi Mustafa Ağa designed and constructed the fountain of this complex. Known as a philanthropist, Hacı Beşir Ağa ordered the construction of some charitable establishments in Mecca and a school, public fountain, and a library built in Eyüp.

The Nuruosmaniye Mosque achieved the importance of new architectural elements and is one of the principal structures featuring Baroque influences. Sultan Mahmud I wanted a mosque to be built in his name in 1748. Simeon Kalfa began the construction of a complex over the site of a previous mescid situated outside the main entrance of the Covered Bazaar. However, Mahmud I passed away before it was completed. It was left to his successor, Osman III, to finalize the construction of the Nuruosmaniye Mosque, which was named after him, in 1755. Surrounded by a wide outer courtyard with two gates, the complex is comprised of a medrese, library, soup kitchen, clock house, fountain and a public fountain along with 142 shops. Covered entirely in marble, the square-plan mosque has 14 domes supported by 12 columns. Its central dome measures 26 meters in diameter and is illuminated by 174 windows. There is a band of "Fetih Ayeti" Koranic verse on the wall. Above the main entrance are the Muezzin's Quarters and the Sultan's Loggia to the left of the niche. Şehsuvar Sultan, along with some crown princes, lies in its tomb instead of the sultans who had it constructed. This mosque, which is the greatest example of Turkish Baroque style, is held in the same high regard as the Classical-era complexes. Ascending to the throne in 1757,

Exterior of the Empiric-style Nusretiye Mosque (1822-26). Sultan Mahmud II commissioned the architect Kirkor Balyan to build it as the 16th "Selatin" Complex in Istanbul.

Mustafa III gave great importance to the construction of new buildings and while he had both the Fatih Mosque and the Üç Şerefeli Mosque in Edirne reconstructed, he also commissioned several works during his 17-year sultanate. Among these were the Baroque style Ayazma Mosque in Üsküdar, built for his mother, Mihrişah Sultan, between 1757-60. He also commissioned the architect Tahir Ağa to construct his own complex in Laleli between 1759-63. The Sultan Mustafa III Complex is comprised of a soup kitchen, a bath, a soup kitchen, an inn, a marketplace, a tomb and a public fountain. Reduced to rubble by the earthquake of 1765, Mustafa III's successor Sultan Abdülhamid I commissioned the architect Seyyid Mustafa Ağa to restore the mosque in 1782. The square-plan mosque has a courtyard with 18 domes supported by 18 columns. Its central domed fountain is supported by eight columns. The tomb and the public fountain of the complex overlook the main avenue. Sultan Mustafa III and his son Selim III lie at rest in its 10-cornered tomb. In 1769, the sister of Sultan Mustafa III, Zeynep Sultan commissioned the architect Tahir Ağa to construct a complex in her name in Alemdar Caddesi, of which the primary school and Baroque style mosque are still intact. Abdülhamid I continued to commission public works whereby he ordered Tahir Ağa to construct a complex his own name in Bahçekapı in 1774. Completed in 1780, it was comprised of a medrese, small mosque, soup kitchen, soup kitchen, library, tomb, fountain, kindergarten, and a public fountain. Most of the buildings of this complex are in ruins today. While the Dorduncu Vakfı Inn was being constructed here, its fountain and public fountain were moved to the corner of the Zeynep Sultan Mosque, which is located opposite Gülhane Park. The medrese with its two-storey cells had an important place in the complex. Basements were later added under those cells. Its marketplace was a complex of shops in a row. Today, its medrese is used as the Stock Market building. A marble tomb is at the southern end of the complex. In 1777, Abdülhamid I commissioned Tahir Ağa to build a complex in Beylerbeyi for his mother, Rabia Sultan. This consisted of a medrese, soup kitchen, bath, primary school, soup kitchen, and a tomb for crown princes and two public fountains. The most significant building of this complex is its waterfront mosque, which is appreciated by those passing on ferryboats. It is quite appealing with its dome measuring 15 meters in diameter. Esma Sultan ordered a fountain and a prayer hall built in Kadırga in 1779, at the time of Sultan Abdülhamid I. The flat area above the cistern was used as a prayer hall. Constructed in 1780, the Emirgan Mosque was to be last work of art commissioned by Sultan Abdülhamid I. One of Sultan Abdülhamid I's wives, Fatma Şebisafa Kadın ordered a complex to be built on Unkapanı Caddesi in 1787. While most of this complex was burned

down during the construction of the main road, the single-domed Baroque mosque can still be seen. Ascending to the throne upon the death of Sultan Abdülhamid I, Selim III possessed the emotional character of a poet and composer. He was quite fond of his mother, Mihrişah Sultan, and commissioned the architect Arif Ağa to build a complex in her name in Eyüp in 1792. This work was the first characteristic work of the Sultan Selim III period. Completed in 1795, the complex consisted of the Tomb of the Dowager Sultan, a school, soup kitchen, and a fountain. Its two-storey tomb was constructed in white marble. Its shape, with 12 segments in Turkish

Interior view of Hırka-i Şerif Mosque (1851). It was constructed in Fatih next to an older building during the reign of Sultan Abdülmecid. The Prophet's Cloak is preserved in the octagonal mosque. The eight verses on its dome were inscribed by Mustafa İzzet.

Rococo style, distinguishes this tomb from others. The soup kitchen situated in the center is striking with its monumental kitchen chimneys and ablution fountain along with its public fountain on both sides in Baroque style. The sister of Selim III, Shah Sultan commissioned the architect İbrahim Kamil Ağa to build a complex in Eyüp in 1800. This one consisted of a school, soup kitchen, primary school, tomb and a public fountain. Selim III had his complex, which was comprised of a school, bath, clock room and a tomb, built in Haydarpaşa between 1801-05.

Selim III, deposed by a rebellion in 1808, was succeeded to the throne by Mustafa IV. Ruscuk Senator Alemdar Mustafa Pasha attacked the palace with his army of 20,000 men in an effort to have Selim III regain his throne. But as Selim III was executed during the attack, Alemdar Mustafa Pasha deposed Mustafa IV and instated Crown Prince Mahmud to the throne. While the Baroque style continued during the Sultan Mahmud II period, one sees the emergence of the Empirical style as well. The start of a combination Baroque-Empircal style was marked with a complex built in 1819 for Cevri Kalfa, who had saved Sultan Mahmud II's life. It consisted of a school, fountain and a public fountain. Sultan Mahmud II commissioned Kirkor Balyan to build the Nusretiye Mosque Complex between 1822-26. Its Baroque style dome measures 33 meters in height and 7.5 meters in diameter. A calligraphic inscription on the segmented Baroque style door is the work of Hattat Rakım.

The Sultan's Loggia has four rooms and is accessible by a flight of 24 steps. The "Amme Suresi" Koranic verse is inscribed inside the mosque. A clock house across the avenue has since collapsed and two fountains have been moved over to their present spot. Nusretiye Mosque is a fine example of the Turkish Empirical style. Situated in the Fatih Mosque, the white marble Tomb of Nakşidil Sultan, the mother of Mahmud II, is a fine example of the Turkish Baroque style. Mahmud II was interned a year after his death in 1839 in a marble tomb built in the Empirical style along Divanyolu Caddesi. The mother of Abdülmecid, Bezmialem Valide Sultan, Sultan Abdülaziz and Abdülhamid II were all buried in the same tomb. Upon Mahmud II's death, his son Abdülmecid ascended to the throne at the age of 16. He ordered Dolmabahçe Palace to be built. It took ten years for its construction. Three years after it was completed,

The Ortaköy Mosque. The architect Garabet Balyan was commissioned by Sultan Abdümecid to build this elegant mosque on the Bosphorus shores in 1854.

he moved here from Topkapı Palace. The mosque his mother, had built in 1845 in her name, is also known as the Gureba Hospital Mosque. Abdülmecid commissioned the Küçük Mecidiye Mosque to be built at the entrance of Yıldız Park in Beşiktaş as well as the Hırka-i Şerif Mosque in Fatih in 1848 and 1850, respectively. The Keçecizade Fuad Pasha Mosque and Tomb were built in Yerebatan in 1848. Bezmialem Valide Sultan commissioned the architect Nikoğos Balyan to construct the Dolmabahçe Mosque outside Dolmabahçe Palace. It was completed in 1853 by her son Sultan Abdülmecid after she had passed away. With its wide windows, this mosque is a fine example of the

Exterior and interior views of the Dolmabahçe Mosque, which was commissioned by Dowager Sultan Bezmialem in 1853.

Turkish Baroque-Empiric style. The interior the mosque is adorned with calligraphic art. Situated on a pier surrounded by water on three sides, the Ortaköy Mosque was built by the architect Garabet Balyan and is striking for its rich decoration. Built in 1854, this mosque has a two-storey Sultan's Apartment that stretches along its western facade.

This mosque, with its two minarets complements the view provided by the Bosphorus Bridge. Abdülmecid, who commissioned the construction of more palaces and pavilions than mosques, died at a young age in 1861. He was succeeded by his brother Abdülaziz. During his reign, both Europe and the Ottoman Empire experienced the Eclectic style, which was a hodgepodge of architectural styles ranging from Gothic to Indian and everything in between. Abdülaziz's mother, Pertevniyal Valide Sultan, ordered the architects Montani and Sarkis Balyan to build one such mosque in her name in Aksaray in 1871.

Sultan Abdülaziz ordered the Sadabad Mosque, next to the Kağıthane Stream, to be built in 1862. He was deposed on 30 May 1876 but not before leaving us with such giant works of art as the Çırağan Palace and Beylerbeyi Palace. Sultan Murad V succeeded him to the throne but reigned for just 93 days. He was succeeded by his brother Abdülhamid II. The French architect Vallaury, along with his Italian counterpart Raimondo d'Aronco, the latter of whom was appointed Palace Architect by Sultan Abdülhamid, worked in Istanbul during his reign to come up with such wonderful works of art as the Archaeological Museum and the Museum of Ancient Oriental Works.

The Eclectic style Hamidiye Mosque in front of Yıldız Palace was built on orders of Sultan Abdülhamid in 1885. Also, many mosques, such as the Hidayet Mosque in Eminönü, were built in the last era. Mahmud II ordered its construction in 1813 while Sultan Abdülhamid commissioned Vallaury to restore it in later years. The restoration work of the Cihangir Mosque, built by Mimar Sinan for Sultan Süleyman the Magnificent's son, Crown Prince Cihangir, was carried out in Baroque style in 1889 after a fire destroyed it. Built during the reign of Selim III in 1791, the Teşvikiye Mosque was restored in later years by Abdülmecid and Abdülhamid II, respectively.

The Galip Pasha Mosque (1898) in Erenköy and Suadiye Mosque (1908) in Suadiye are considered significant works of art of the last era. While the architect Vedat Tek constructed the Hobyar Mosque behind the main post office in Eminönü between 1905-09, the architect Kemaleddin, who was a leading voice of the Neo classical school, added to the historical mosques of Istanbul by constructing the Bostancı, Bebek, Bakırköy-Kemer Hatun Mosques, respectively.

The Fatih Complex

Surrounded by schools, the Fatih Complex was the first center of science in Istanbul.

After he conquered Constantinople, Sultan Mehmed II converted the Church of Hagia Sophia into a mosque and also ordered another one to be built in his name. The decision was made to build this mosque in Fatih, one of the seven hills of Istanbul. Situated on this site was the Church of the Apostoleion, which was constructed by Justinian in the 6th century. But that sacred church was in a state of ruin when the decision was made to construct a complex in its stead in the mid-15th century. This complex consisted of a mosque, soup kitchen, medrese, small hospital, hospice, caravanserai, library and hamams. Today's Shoemaker Market is in one of the buildings belonging to the complex, whose mosque is accessible through Çörekçi Kapı and Boyacı Kapı from the west and Çorba Kapı from the east. An inscription above the entrance gate tells us that the architect of the mosque was Atik Sinan and that he started construction in 1467 and finished it three years later. However, this mosque was badly damaged in the 1766 earthquake. Mustafa III later ordered the architect Mehmed Tahir Ağa to restore it.

The center of this monumental mosque is covered with a dome 26 meters wide and 44 meters high, with four semi-domes surrounding the main dome. Arches holding up the great main dome and semi-domes are supported by four large elephantine pillars. These arches separate the center from its sides as well. The tops of its sides are also covered with three smaller domes supported by high columns. Thus, the mosque consists of a vast area measuring 2400 m2 without any divisions. Its niche was constructed in colorful marble. The original architectural style of the inner courtyard in front is still maintained. It is covered with 22 domes supported by 18 columns of granite and Eğriboz marble. It is accessible through three doors, two of which are on the sides and the other is in front.

The gate that opens into the courtyard with a fountain along with its inscriptions belongs to the original building while the decoration seen on its walls and domes are from an earlier period. The mosque and its medrese surrounding the main complex were once the center of science. According to rather old records, the complex hospice provided accommodations for 200 people, with one being able to stay for three days for free. Four of the eight medreses in the outer courtyard faced west while the remaining four faced east. Called the "Mediterranean" and "Black Sea" medrese, each had 19 classrooms. The additional "Tetimme" medreses of the complex as well as the library and school next to the Çörekçi Kapı and Boyacı Kapı on the western side no longer exist. The hospital situated outside the southern Çorbacı Kapı is currently used as a Koranic study center. This hospital is a structure surrounded by domed arches supported by 16 columns. Its caravanserai, which no longer exists, was situated just south of hospital. To the west of this was the soup kitchen, which served hot meals to 2,000 people

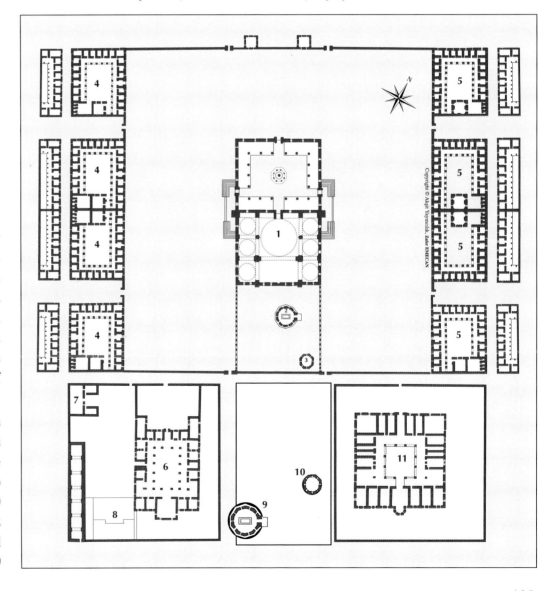

Aerial view of the Fatih Complex.

Plan of the Fatih Complex:

1. Mosque; 2. Tomb of Fatih; 3. Tomb of Gülbahar Sultan; 4. Mediterranean Medrese (School of Theology) ; 5. Black Sea Medrese; 6. Hospice; 7. Soup Kitchen; 8. Caravanserai; 9. Tomb of Nakşidil Sultan; 10. Tomb of Münire Sultan; 11. Hospital (no longer extant).

daily. The mental asylum was directly across from the hospital. But no traces remain of this structure, which served both the mentally and physically handicapped. To the southeast was the bath (hamam), which burned down in a fire in 1916. The Tomb of Nakşidil Sultan, who was the wife of Abdülhamid I and mother of Mahmud II, lies next to the ruined mental hospital. Cevri Kalfa who had saved the life of Mahmud II is also buried in this marble tomb, which was built in 1817. The inscription on the tomb belongs to the famous calligrapher Rakım Efendi. Nakşidil Sultan had a public fountain and a school built in the opposite corner. In addition, the Tomb of the Fourth Favorite of Sultan Abdülmecid, Gülüstü Sultan is found here as well.

The Tomb of Sultan Mehmed II (the Conqueror)

Sultan Mehmed the Conqueror who had initiated a New World Order, so to speak, prepared his army for a military expedition to Italy. He kept it secret and gathered his army in Gebze so that the enemy would not suspect such a campaign. Sultan Mehmed the Conqueror was supposed to be in that military camp to start the expedition but never showed up as his health took a sudden turn for the worse. His ex-patriate Venetian doctor had been slowly poisoning him to death, administering steadily increasing doses until his lungs collapsed due to a high dose of poison. He expired on 03 May 1481. But news of his death was kept from the army until the arrival of Crown Princes Cem and Bayezid in Gebze. Once they arrived there, his death was publicly announced and his body was brought to Istanbul in a covered carriage to be buried in the courtyard of the Fatih Mosque with great ceremony on 21 May. Later on, his coffin was transferred to a tomb constructed for him in the southern end of the mosque. It became customary for subsequent Ottoman sultans to don their swords in Eyüp, and then visit the Tomb of Sultan Mehmed the Conqueror. Situated to the south of the mosque, this dome-covered tomb has 10 segments. His tomb collapsed in the 1766 earthquake and was later rebuilt by the architect Tahir Ağa, who also added eaves during the construction. This tomb was restored during Abdülaziz's reign whereas Sultan Mehmet V Reşad commissioned an Italian decorator to redecorate the interior of the tomb. The tomb was last restored in 1953. The octagonal tomb of the wife of Sultan Mehmed the Conqueror, Gülbahar Sultan, lies a bit further down the path. This tomb was also damaged during the 1766 earthquake but it was later rebuilt over what had remained standing. The stone building in the corner was constructed as a library by Mahmud I in 1742. The tombs of Gazi Osman Pasha and some other famous Ottoman officials are also found around her tomb.

Interior view of the Tomb of Sultan Mehmed the Conqueror. (left)
Interior of the Fatih Mosque. (right)

Şehzade Mosque

"The Şehzade Mosque is a work of art belonging to my apprenticeship days."   *Mimar Sinan*

The son of Sultan Mehmed the Conqueror and Hürrem Sultan, Crown Prince Mehmed died of smallpox at the age of 21 while serving as Regional Governor to Manisa in 1543. His father Sultan Mehmed the Conqueror commissioned Mimar Sinan to build a complex with a mosque in his name. The great architect called the Crown Prince Mehmed Complex and Mosque (1544-48), which was to be his first of many complexes, a work of art from his apprenticeship days. Apart from the mosque, the complex consisted of a soup kitchen, hospice, medrese, caravanserai, a school and various tombs. Based on a square plan, the Crown Şehzade Mosque measures 38 meters x 38 meters in area and has a front courtyard. Measuring 18 meters across and 37 meters high, the main dome of the mosque is supported by semi-domes in four corners. The upper structure system was set into four elephantine pillars. Its body walls are supported by buttresses on four sides. The pulpit of the mosque is adorned with geometrical and plant figures in a low-relief technique. Its marble niche is skillfully decorated. The muezzin quarter is a very elegant piece of art, propped up by eight columns. Mimar Sinan did not use tile in all parts of the mosque, but rather preferred to embellish the dome with calligraphy. Thus, it has quite a plain design. This mosque is accessible through three gates. Its courtyard is surrounded with 16 domed arches supported by 12 columns. The ablution fountain in the middle of its courtyard was constructed during the sultanate of Murad IV. The mosque has two 41.1 meter-high minarets with double balconies, while the exterior of the minarets is adorned with relief decorations. The Crown Şehzade Mosque set the benchmark for architects of other mosques to follow after Mimar Sinan. The structure located opposite the northern entrance known as the "Twisted Minaret Mescid," was ordered built by the Moslem Judge to Egypt Osman Efendi, who died in 1554. The Nevşehirli Damat İbrahim Pasha Complex is situated on the corner of Dede Efendi Sokağı where the caravanserai of the complex is also located. As it was Mimar Sinan's first example of a complex on such a large scale, the other structures found inside the complex carry great importance, too. Let us just briefly discuss them below.

Structures of the Complex

A medrese with a rectangular courtyard surrounded by domed arches is located northwest of the complex. Study rooms lie to the south whereas hospices are located in all the other directions. The previous medrese is currently used as a restaurant. The soup kitchen of the complex is situated to the south of the medrese and merges with the hospital in an "L" shape. The soup kitchen had two symmetrical sections widened with vaults in the middle to allow a vast dining area. There are two kitchens each in the north and south. The hospital is covered with eight domes on top of its walls in two

The Şehzade Mosque. Mimar Sinan labeled this work of art as one from his apprenticeship days..

Mimar Sinan paid particular interest to the minaret decoration during its construction.

Plan of the Şehzade Complex:

1. Mosque; 2. Courtyard; 3. Tomb of Şehzade; 4. Tomb of Rüstem Pasha; 5. Tomb of Fatma Sultan; 6. Tomb of İbrahim Pasha; 7. Tomb of Hatice Sultan; 8. Tomb of Prince Mahmud; 9. Tomb of Destari Mustafa Pasha; 10. Medrese; 11. Hospice; 12. Caravanserai; 13. School

rows. These structures are used by the Vefa High School today. Right across the road is the caravanserai structure, the inner courtyard of which is based on a square-plan without a portico consisting of two separate sections with six domes each.

The sections to the east consist of the kitchens, while those to the west house the provisions storage and employee rooms. A single-domed school building is situated next to the caravanserai.

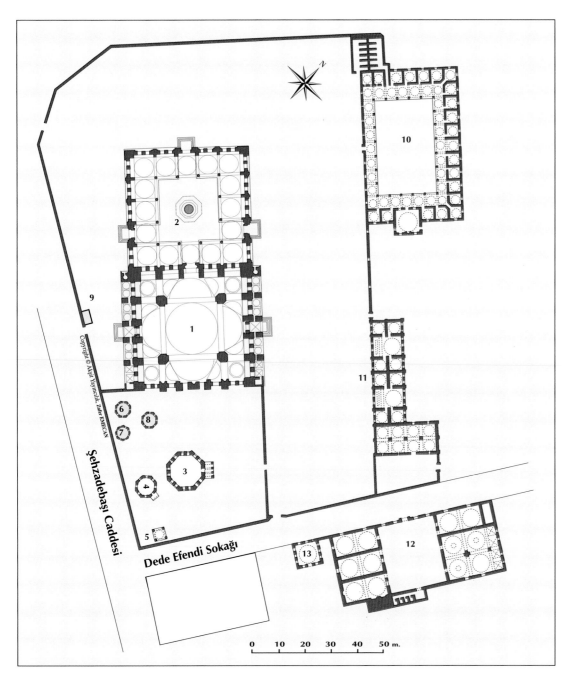

Tombs

The tombs are situated in the tombyard to the southeast of the mosque. When Crown Prince Mehmed died in 1543, his tomb, which was also a work of Mimar Sinan, was rapidly completed in 1544. The octagonal tomb was constructed of two-colored stone and is covered with a dome. A portico supported by four columns lies in front of the tomb with stained-glass windows. There are tiled panels on both sides of its entrance gate. The interior dome of the tomb is adorned up to the top of walls with the finest tiles from the period when light green was predominant. Thus, Sinan eliminated the gloomy atmosphere from the tomb and gave it into a spring-like atmosphere. Measuring 3.5 meters in height, a wooden cage is mounted on the throne-like coffin of Crown Prince Mehmed. There are four wooden coffins in the tomb belonging to Prince Cihangir, the daughter of Crown Prince Mehmed, Hümaşah Sultan, Crown Prince Mehmed and an unknown person.

When he passed away in 1561, the Grand Vizier Rüstem Pasha, who was married to the daughter of Sultan Süleyman the Magnificent, Mihrimah Sultan, was buried in a tomb built by Mimar Sinan in the Şehzade Mosque courtyard. The octagonal tomb has a single dome while its interior is adorned with Iznik tiles up to top of the inner windows. Compositions of vases filled with flower bouquets adorn a white background along the bottoms of the windows. Between the top and bottom windows are tiles depict "sulus" calligraphy styled Koranic verses in white on a dark blue background whereas the dome is adorned with engravings. The two wooden coffins belong to Rüstem Pasha and his son.

The Tomb of Crown Prince Mahmud, who was the son of Sultan Mehmed III, is here as well. The Palace Architect Mehmed Ağa was commissioned to build this hexagonal-planned tomb in 1603. The tomb is covered with a dome while there is a ruined portico at the entrance and hexagon bricks laid on its floor. Two wooden coffins belonging to Crown Prince Mahmud and his mother are in this tomb. Also found here is the Tomb of Bosnian İbrahim Pasha who held the titles of Grand Vizier and Commodore of the Ottoman Navy, and was married to the daughter of Murad III, Ayşe Sultan, as well as a Captain Pasha.

This tomb was constructed by the architect Dalgıç Mustafa Ağa in 1603. The dome covering the tomb sits directly over its walls. This tomb, which appears to be a hexagonal structure from outside, has 16 corners on the interior, and is covered with 17th-century tiles up to the top of the lower windows. There is a band of "Mülk Suresi" Koranic verse inscribed on the tiles. The coffin of Ibrahim Pasha is situated right in the center of the tomb. Next to him are the marble coffins of his son and daughter. The Tomb of Hatice Sultan, whose

Interior of the Şehzade Mosque.

The Tomb of Crown Prince Mehmed (above).

parents are unknown, is also here. This hexagon-planned tomb has a single dome with no decorative elements on the inside. Four coffins belonging to Hatice Sultan, her two daughters and son lie here.

Fatma Sultan was a daughter of Ferhad Pasha and Hümaşah Sultan, who was the granddaughter of Sultan Süleyman the Magnificent. She passed away in 1588, with her open-air canopy-type tomb being completed the following year. The coffins are in the shape of marble sarcophagi, the larger one of which belongs to Fatma Sultan, with the smaller one belonging to her husband, Mustafa Paşazade Mehmed Bey. Destari Mustafa Pasha, whose tomb lies by the side of the entrance into the mosque, was a vizier of Sultan Ahmed I. He was raised in the Ottoman School of Palace Pages and married into the imperial family. Murdered in 1614, he was buried in his tomb in the courtyard of Şehzade Mosque.

He ordered his tomb to be built in 1611, well before he was killed. This rectangular tomb is covered with a dome that is set on top of an octagonal-drum of a cupola. It has a portico at the entrance. The five coffins lying in the tomb covered in tiles belong to Destari Mustafa Pasha, his wife Ayşe Sultan and their three children.

The Süleymaniye Mosque

"The Head Architect is completely mad. Do you honestly think such as large complex can be built in two months? You go ask him yourself once again..."

Sultan Süleyman the Magnificent

eferred to by historians as the "Magnificent" and by Turks as the "Lawgiver," Mimar Sinan was commissioned by Sultan Süleyman to build a complex. Heeding the order he received from the famous sultan, Mimar Sinan chose the third of the city's seven hills overlooking the Golden Horn on which to do so. Since the hill had a rather steep incline, it took quite some time to lay the foundation. In the meantime, stone and marble were brought in from quarries and timber from forests from the most far-flung regions of the empire.

On 13 June 1550, Şeyhülislam Ebussuud Efendi laid the first stone in the foundation-laying ceremony. Having completed the foundations, Mimar Sinan waited until they all settled into place. Meanwhile, he had gotten involved in another construction project – that of the Ferhad Paşa Palace. His enemies took the opportunity to complain about Sinan to the Sultan, saying that he was not very interested in the mosque since he was doing something else at the same time. During the many years that went by after laying the foundations, Mimar Sinan succeeded in completing the preparations to start the construction of the complex. He had even determined which columns he was going to place inside the building. He had one of them brought from Alexandria, another from Baalbek ruins, one from the Arcadius Monument in Istanbul and still another from Topkapı Palace.

Mimar Sinan explained how he constructed Süleymaniye to his close friend, a poet and a calligrapher Sai Çelebi, who later recorded everything about it in a book he wrote called "Tezkeretül Bünyan (Book of Buildings), Sultan Süleyman the Magnificent is said to have arrived at the site while Mimar Sinan was consulting with the marble workers. He severely reprimanded him, asking him why he was not working on his mosque, but rather, dealing with some less important work. He insisted that Sinan give him a completion deadline for its construction. Sinan, who, not used to being scolded like that, informed the sultan that he was going to finish the complex in just two months. The sultan, surprised at being told it would take only two months to complete, turned to those around him and said, " The Palace Architect said that he would finish in two months; I want you to be witnesses of what he has just said." But after he had returned to his palace, he ordered his officials back to the site to query once again, saying, "The Palace Architect has gone completely mad. Do you

really think such a large complex can be completed in two months? You go and ask him..." But Mimar Sinan told the same thing to all who asked. He had already completed the infrastructure of the complex and was ready to proceed. That is why he told them he planned to complete the construction of the

Aerial view of the Süleymaniye Mosque, which Mimar Sinan referred to as a work from his Assistant-Master period (left).

Interior of the Süleymaniye Mosque.

The plan of the Süleymaniye Complex:

1. Mosque; 2. Tomb of Sultan Süleyman the Magnificent; 3. Tomb of Hürrem Sultan; 4. Chamber for the Tomb Guardian; 5. "Evvel" Medrese; 6. "Sani" Medrese; 7. School of Medicine; 8. Hospital; 9. Soup Kitchen; 10. Hospice; 11. Tomb of Mimar Sinan; 12. "Salis" Medrese; 13. "Rabi" Medrese; 14. Baths (Hamams); 15. "Darül Hadis" Medrese

The Süleymaniye Mosque and Complex structures.

complex in two months' time. He kept his promise by recruiting all the skilled workmen in the city, working them day and night to complete the complex by the deadline. The complex was to be inaugurated on 15 October 1557. Mimar Sinan had all its gates and doors locked and sent the key to the sultan to commence the ceremony. However, the sultan, having become so impressed with Sinan, sent him back the key and asked him to open the doors, telling him that it was he who was the most deserving of such an honor. So it was that

Sinan, who, having recently turned 67, proudly unlocked the gates of the mosque. The sultan lavished Sinan with gifts, showing how much he cared for him. Records show a total of 3,523 builders worked on the construction and 59,760,180 akçes, the Ottoman currency at the time, was spent. It was a complex that reflected the glamour of Sultan Süleyman the Magnificent. No matter how much Mimar Sinan might have referred to this complex as a work of his apprentice period, it thoroughly reflects his architectural skills and genius since he was able to position the structures of the complex in an aesthetically pleasing manner over 60-acres of sloping land. Even today, the Süleymaniye Mosque, with its silhouette over Istanbul, continues to reflect the grandeur of the period. Mimar Sinan placed the other buildings of that complex around its mosque so that they would not overshadow its magnificence.

Shops in what is known as the Tiryakiler Bazaar are at the side where the main entrance of the mosque is located. At the beginning of the shops was a primary school. This domed structure with an open anteroom is still used as primary school library. Behind these shops are the "Evvel" and "Sani" Medreses, the gates of which are connected to each other via an archway located on the street. The chambers and classrooms behind the domed porticoes are of the Classical Ottoman style. These medreses are currently utilized as the Süleymaniye Library. In addition to them, there was once a School of Medicine having an array of rooms. While only a few cells of that building are still intact, a maternity ward has since been built in its place. A charitable soup kitchen, guesthouse and a small hospital are found along the street to the west of the mosque, with the hospital located at the end of the street. This hospital once offered services to the sick and mentally ill in its mental asylum wing. This structure is in the shape of two consecutive courtyards with porticoed rooms situated around them.

Today, this building is used as a Koran school for girls. The building in the middle was a charitable soup kitchen where the elderly, students and the poor used to eat for free. It consists of domed rooms in a row around a courtyard. Once housing the Museum of Turkish and Islamic Art, this building is currently being used as a restaurant called "Dar-ül Ziyafe." Besides this building, there was a hospice comprised of domed chambers around a courtyard with a pool in the middle. These were used as bread ovens, a kitchen, lodging for traveling merchants, stables for beasts of burden and warehouses to store their goods. A caravanserai was also located on the lower section. To the north of the mosque at the end of the street is the tomb of the creator of this complex, Mimar Sinan. He was buried in this modest tomb when he died in 1588, at the ripe old age of 90. The inscription on his tomb belongs to Sai Çelebi and reads, "Sinan, the patron saint of architects passed through this world." Reflecting the Classical-

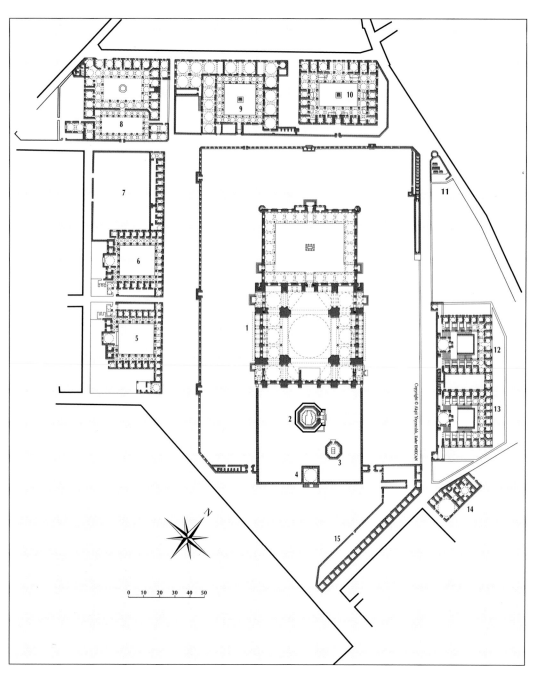

Copyright © Aşçı Yayıncılık, Zafer DİRİCAN

0 10 20 30 40 50

Interior of the Süleymaniye Mosque. Materials used in its construction were brought here from the four corners of the empire. Mimar Sinan shipped the four columns in from Alexandria, one from the Baalbek ruins, one from Arcadius Monument in Istanbul and a fourth one from Topkapı Palace.

Ottoman style, the "Rabi" and "Salis" Medreses are located in this area. The classrooms are situated independently on the western side of the entrance of the courtyard. Also built in the Classical style, the Dökmeciler Hamam of the complex is on the corner, in front of these schools. The "Darülhadis" Medrese is to the south of the hamams. Consisting of a series of domed chambers, the building is accessible via a flight of steps. The Tombs of Sultan Süleyman the Magnificent and his wife Hürrem Sultan are situated behind the mosque. Here, another chamber called "Darülkurra" is also found. With its additional buildings, the complex is every bit as splendid as the mosque. The vast outer courtyard of the mosque is accessible through ten gates. The rectangular-plan inner courtyard is accessible through three gates, one of which is right in the center. Some fine stone masonry is displayed above the central main entrance

gate. Its inscription bears the "Kelime-i Tevhid" Koranic verse. Twenty-four columns of porphyry, white marble and red granite are said to have been brought from the Imperial Loggia in the Hippodrome called "Kathisma," while its floor is paved with marble. A portico with 28 domes surrounds the courtyard. A decorated rectangular-shaped fountain lies right in the middle of it. Two of the four minarets are located in the corners of the northern façade, each with two balconies. Situated behind the mosque, the other two minarets with three balconies are higher than the first two. The minarets have a total of ten balconies, as Süleyman the Magnificent was the 10th sultan of the empire. Measuring 63 meters x 68 meters, the nearly square-plan mosque has a dome measuring 26.5 meters across and 53 meters in height. The mosque is accessible through two gates, one in the

front and the other on its western side. In addition, there are two other gates that open into the Sultan's Loggia and a yard where a stone bier is located. Measuring 6.20 meters x 5.10 meters, the central dome is set upon four arches supported by four elephantine pillars on either side. In addition, semi-domes cover the niche and the main entrance. The area between the elephantine pillars covered with five smaller domes gives the devout ample room to pray. All gates of the Süleymaniye Mosque are made from ebony. Its niche and pulpit are elegant examples of marble etching. The mosque is filled with a total of 138 windows, which give the inside of the mosque an elegant and fresh look. Panels on either side of the niche are made from 16th-century Iznik tile and bear inscriptions on a dark blue background. The inner part of the domes is also covered with calligraphy.

The acoustic setup of this mosque is another clear indication of Mimar Sinan's mastery. He installed 255 small jars all around the mosque to achieve these acoustics and to prevent candle soot. Four porphyry columns were positioned inside the mosque between the pillars facing the northern and southern sides. Like the other material, these columns were shipped in from all over the empire. They measure 9 meters in height and 1.14 meters in diameter. The interior of the Süleymaniye Mosque measures 5,364 m2. All calligraphic inscriptions belong to Ahmed Karahisari and his student Hasan Çelebi, whereas the stained window glasses are the work of İbrahim the Drunkard. Both the Süleymaniye Mosque and the tomb that Mimar Sinan constructed for Sultan Süleyman the Magnificent can be considered two of the wonders of Ottoman architecture.

The Tomb of Sultan Süleyman the Magnificent

Sultan Süleyman the Magnificent suffered a lot of misery throughout his 46-year reign. He had to give orders for the execution of his sons Crown Prince Mustafa and Crown Prince Bayezid as they rebelled against the state. He also lost his other sons, Crown Prince Cihangir and Crown Prince Mehmed. On top of the sorrow of losing his sons, his wife Hürrem Sultan, with whom he was deeply in love, died in 1558. He outlived her by eight years and passed away while on his military expedition to Zigetvar on 06 September 1566. Grand Vizier Sokollu Mehmed Pasha hid his death from the army by secretly bringing his corpse to Istanbul to bury him in the tomb constructed by Mimar Sinan. Eight columns support the dome of his octagonal-planned tomb on the inside. Another 29 columns support the tomb, which is surrounded by porticoes, from the outside. Four green porphyry columns are located on either side of the main gate, where there are also strikingly beautiful Iznik tile panels. The gate wings of this monumental Classical style tomb structure have ivory inlays and engravings. One of the gates bears the verse "La ilahe İllallah," which means,

"There is only one God," and the other "Muhammedin Resulallah," which means "Mohammed is his Ambassador." 16th-century Iznik tiles bearing floral motifs decorate the interior of the tomb. Pendentive medallions made from tiles bear names in white calligraphic inscriptions against a dark blue background. Above the lower windows is a band of Koranic verse in white on a dark blue background. There are some Byzantine-type painted panels resembling marble above this band, and above this section, there are triple windows. Its dome was constructed using the "malachite" technique. The materials of the dome and the red and white stone arches complement each other. The tomb has seven coffins, with that of Sultan Süleyman the Magnificent lying in the middle. To his left, are those belonging to Sultan Süleyman II, who died in 1691, Sultan Ahmed II, who died in 1695 and the Favorite Wife of Sultan Ahmed II, Rabia Sultan, who died in 1712. To the right of his tomb are the coffins belonging to his daughter Mihrimah Sultan, who died in 1578, the Third Favorite Wife of Sultan İbrahim, Saliha Dilaşup Sultan, who died in 1689 and the daughter of Ahmed II, Asiye Sultan, who died in 1695.

16th–century tile panel at the entrance of the tomb (below).

Sultan Süleyman the Magnificent died on 06 September 1566 after a sultanate that lasted 46 years. He was buried in the tomb architect Mimar Sinan built next to the Süleymaniye Mosque. The tomb is decorated with 16th century Iznik tiles (right).

The Tomb of Hürrem Sultan

Beside the tomb of Sultan Süleyman the Magnificent is that of Hürrem Sultan. Hürrem, whose real name was "Roxelana," was the daughter of a Russian monk. She was taken prisoner as a child and sold to the Ottoman Palace. Later, this very intelligent concubine was given the Turkish moniker "Hürrem." She finally attracted the attention of Sultan Süleyman the Magnificent, becoming his wife as well as the First Lady of the Empire. Hürrem was to bear him many children. Simply adored by Süleyman, she would write him poems to express her deep love for him. The ordeal she went through to have her sons sit on the Ottoman throne, and the subsequent fratricidal infighting over the throne exhausted her and she fell ill. She was not able to withstand all the palace tragedies and passed away at the age of 54 in 1558. Sultan Süleyman the Magnificent buried her in a tomb he commissioned Mimar Sinan to build in his complex. The tomb is octagonal on the interior, and has 16 sides on the exterior. Covering the ashlar stone tomb are twin domes that sit on a cylindrical drum. A portico with triple-arched vaults stands in front of its main entrance, on either side of which there are tile panels. This tomb is also adorned with beautiful 16th-century Iznik tiles. Inscriptions containing Koranic verse are etched onto the panels and above the gate. Its doors and windows represent the finest examples of wood craftsmanship.

Iznik tiles cover the interior of the tomb up to the bottom of the top windows, as well as the niches between the windows. Pretty dark-blue, white, turquoise peonies and pointy leaves are used as decoration on the niches. The tops of the walls are crowned with "sulus"-style Koranic verse inscribed in white on a dark blue background. Three coffins lie in the tomb; the largest one belongs to Hürrem Sultan while the others belong to the son of Selim I, Crown Prince Mehmed and the granddaughter of Süleyman the Magnificent, Hanım Sultan.

Interior of the Tomb of Hürrem Sultan. Hürrem Sultan used coercion to have her sons ascend to the Ottoman throne. She died in 1558 at the age of 54. The interior of the tomb is decorated with Koranic verse in white on a dark blue background. Some detail is seen above.

Rüstem Pasha Mosque

The Rüstem Pasha mosque looks more like a tile museum than a mosque.

In 1560, Rüstem Pasha commissioned Mimar Sinan to construct the mosque in Tahtakale that is renown for its tiles. Born in Bosnia in 1500, Rüstem Pasha was a Croatian expatriate who was recruited into the palace at an early age. He was educated and raised here where he impressed Sultan Süleyman the Magnificent with his intelligence. Promoted rapidly through the ranks, he was appointed Regional Governor of Diyarbakır while he was quite young. Sultan Süleyman the Magnificent wanted him to marry his daughter Mihrimah Sultan. But Rüstem Pasha was said to have leprosy. The sultan dispatched a delegation to learn if the rumor was true. The doctor in that delegation submitted his report to Sultan Süleyman the Magnificent, stating that he had found lice in his underwear and lice could not exist on a leper. Seeing that Rüstem Pasha was fit to marry his daughter, the sultan went ahead and gave his approval for their marriage, which took place in 1539. As it came to be, Rüstem Pasha became both a son-in-law to the imperial family and, by replacing Hadım Süleyman Pasha in 1544, the Grand Vizier.

Rüstem Pasha and Hürrem Sultan were accomplices in many plots to execute the eldest son of Sultan Süleyman the Magnificent, Prince Mustafa, and when they finally managed to do so, this paved the way to the throne for Hürrem's sons. However, the army, which had much respect for Prince Mustafa, connected Rüstem Pasha to the murder and demanded that Sultan Süleyman the Magnificent dismiss him from the duties of Grand Vizier, which is what happened. Some time later, Rüstem Pasha had the new Grand Vizier, Kara Mustafa Pasha, killed with Hürrem Sultan's help, which enabled him to regain his post of Grand Vizier in 1555. Remaining at this position until 1561, he commissioned Mimar Sinan to build his mosque on the site of the Halil Efendi Mescid in Tahtakale. As it was situated on a narrow plot of land, shops were built on its ground floor in order to elevate the mosque. Thus, the mosque rises over a terrace and is surrounded by porticoes on three fronts. The courtyard is accessible by a flight of steps in two directions. The mosque is rather distinct in that it does not have the customary fountain. The courtyard ends with a series of arches and a double congregation chamber.

The dome of this rectangular-plan mosque sits on eight columns, four of which are octagonal and independent, with the other four set on eight pillars that rise along the northern and southern walls. Fifteen meters in diameter, the dome is supported by four semi-domes and four arches. The interior of the mosque is divided into three sections. There is an anteroom on each side of the main inner hall. These anterooms are also divided into three sections – by two large arches, the sections of which are covered by small vaults. Three large windows on top of each other illuminate the interior and increase even further the impact the wonderful tiles already have on the ambiance. All the walls of the mosque are decorated with tiles up to the skirts of the dome.

Interior of the Rüstem Pasha Mosque which is adorned with splendid 16th–century Iznik tiles (opposite).

Koranic verse inscriptions on the upper galley above the windows (below).

These tiles represent the most spectacular period of Iznik tiles, made possible with the discovery and use of the color red. An abundance of rich motifs were used on these tiles. For instance, 44 different tulip motifs appear on them. The elephantine pillars are adorned with tiles as well. Thus, the mosque bears the quality of a museum displaying 16th-century Iznik tiles. The façade of its last outer congregation hall is also embellished with these tiles. The two niches on either side of the entrance are adorned with tiles on both the inside and outside. Covered with tiny domes, this section is separated by six columns into five smaller sections. Its single minaret is erected to the left of the mosque. When Rüstem Pasha died on 09 July 1561, he was buried in his tomb in Şehzade Mosque, which is also completely covered with 16th-century Iznik tiles.

Plan of the Rüstem Pasha Mosque
The outer congregation area of the Rüstem Pasha Mosque is also adorned with tiles (right).

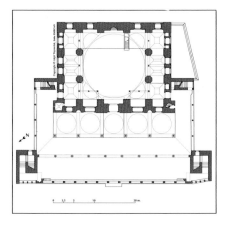

The Iznik tiles give the Rüstem Pasha Mosque a magnificent appearance.

156

Yeni Mosque

Dowager Safiye Sultan gave the order to begin the construction of Yeni Mosque, but it was only completed 66 years later by Dowager Hatice Turhan Sultan.

Safiye Sultan, who became the Dowager Sultan when her son Mehmed III ascended to the throne, wanted to have a mosque built in her name, so she gave an order to Palace architect Davut Ağa to commence with its construction. Davut Ağa, a student of Mimar Sinan, laid the foundation of Yeni Mosque, near the shore, in Eminönü in 1597. To strengthen the foundation, he knocked wooden planks into the ground below sea level and connected them to one another with lead diagonal beams.

In the meantime, Davut Ağa succumbed to the plague during an epidemic that struck Istanbul in 1598. Though he was replaced by Ahmed Ağa as Palace Architect, Sultan Mehmed III passed away in 1603 just as the foundations of the complex were starting to take shape. As a consequence, Safiye Sultan no longer held the title of Dowager Sultan and the construction of Yeni Mosque was subsequently put on hold. Years passed, and sultans came and went but the construction site remained untouched. Finally Sultan İbrahim ascended to the throne and his wife, Hatice Turhan Sultan bore him a son they named Mehmed. Their child ascended to the throne at the age of seven as Mehmed IV, while his mother, Hatice Turhan Sultan, became Dowager Sultan. Known as a very compassionate and religious person, she informed her son and the Grand Vizier that she desired to have a mosque built in her name. The Grand Vizier, Sokollu Mehmed Pasha suggested that she have the unfinished mosque completed in Eminönü instead of constructing a new mosque all over again. She agreed to the idea, whereby Grand Vizier Sokollu Mehmed Pasha gave orders to the architect Mustafa Ağa to resume the construction of Yeni Mosque once more in 1660, after a break of 59 years. Mustafa Ağa commenced building the complex according to the plans of the previous project. He also built the nearby Hünkar Pavilion for Hatice Turhan Sultan to stay and observe the construction work.

This complex was comprised of a mosque, hamam, hospital, school, marketplace, tomb, clock tower and a fountain of which its hamam, school and hospital no longer exist. The Yeni Mosque Complex, which was started by one Dowager Sultan was to be completed by another Dowager Sultan, was inaugurated with pomp and circumstance in 1663. A wall and main entrance gate used to stand in place of today's Osmanlı Bank, while an İşbank branch office occupies the land where the school once stood. The primary school was located to the west of that building. The marketplace of the complex was named "Mısır Çarşısı," as goods imported from Egypt were sold there. It is still called the Egyptian Bazaar although one can find genuine Turkish goods on sale there as well. The marketplace surrounded the Tomb of Turhan Sultan while the public fountain was positioned next to it. Due to the low

Exterior and interior views of Yeni Mosque which is one the most magnificent of all the Dowager Sultan mosques constructed along the seashore.

ground the mosque was situated on, it was raised by a flight of steps from three directions. Its courtyard is surrounded with 24 domed porticoes supported by 20 columns. A fountain with an octagonal dome is situated in the center. Called the Yeni Mosque, it is a replica of the Şehzade Mosque. The dome of the square-plan mosque measures 18 meters in diameter and 36 meters in height, and is supported by four elephantine pillars. It also has four semi-domes, the corners of which are covered with smaller domes. The plan is more rectangular with the upper and lower galleries on the side of the courtyard. The interior of the mosque is adorned with Iznik tiles, which are not considered to be of the same high quality as those that are seen in the Sultan Ahmed Mosque. The pavilion and loggia inside the mosque are connected to one another via a gallery with three pillars. The interior of the pavilion is decorated with marble and fine tiles. Some of these tiles were removed about a century ago by a Frenchman named Sorlin Doringny and taken to France. This splendid mosque has two minarets with three balconies each.

The Tomb of Dowager Sultan Hatice Turhan

Constructed with ashlar blocks in a square plan, the Tomb of Dowager Sultan Hatice Turhan lies behind the Yeni Mosque within the extension of the Egyptian Bazaar. It has the distinction of being the largest tomb in Istanbul. Born in Russia in 1627, Sultan Hatice Turhan was brought to the Ottoman Palace as a concubine and later became the wife of Sultan İbrahim. She fought over the reins of power with Kösem Sultan when her son Mehmed IV ascended to the throne. She was able to eliminate Kösem Sultan by ordering some officials to strangle her whereby Turhan Sultan took control of the empire, as her son Sultan Mehmed IV was only seven years old at the time. She managed to govern the empire with shrewd decisions and good intentions. When Hatice Turhan Sultan died in 1694, she was buried within the Yeni Mosque Complex in a Classical-Ottoman style tomb that the architect Mustafa Ağa built for her in 1682.

The triple-arched portico lies in front of the tomb, which is illuminated by 47 windows. This section is decorated with tile panels. Its gate is strikingly adorned with mother-of-pearl and ivory. The interior of the tomb is decorated with elegant, beautiful tiles, the color of which has faded over time. But they are still more precious and of higher quality than those inside the mosque. The "Mülk Suresi" Koranic verse is inscribed on the inner tile panels of the tomb, with the dome and upper part of the walls being adorned with calligraphic art.

In addition to Hatice Turhan Sultan, her son, Mehmed IV (1648-87), Mustafa II (1695-1703), Ahmed III (1703-30), Mahmud I (1730-54), along with his mother Saliha Sultan, and Osman III (1754-57) all lie at rest in the same tomb. In a room next to the tomb is the coffin of Murad V (1876). This makes a total of six sultans. The crown princes and wives of Sultan Abdülmecid and Sultan Abdülhamid lie in another chamber next to the tomb. Including the wives of Sultan Ahmed III, Hanife Sultan and Zeynep Sultan, there are a total of 44 coffins at rest within the Tomb of Hatice Turhan Sultan.

Sultan Ahmed Mosque

*With six slender minarets that seem to touch the sky, the Sultan Ahmed Mosque is also called
"The Blue Mosque" because of its splendid blue tiles and calligraphy decorating the interior.*

When Mehmed III suffered a fatal heart attack on 21 December 1603 at the age of 37, his son Ahmed I ascended to the Ottoman throne as the 14th Sultan. He was only 14 years old at the time, but in spite of his youth, he was devoutly religious. This led him to have a mosque built in his name.

In the meantime, the architect Davud Ağa had recently succumbed to the plague. One of Mimar Sinan's students, Mehmed Ağa, was appointed Palace Architect as his replacement. Mehmed Ağa had been recruited from the Balkans in 1562 and brought up in the apprenticeship school. He was at first fond of music but then got involved in architecture and mother-of-pearl (sedef) craftsmanship. That's why he was called Sedefkar Mehmed Ağa. He was also a student of Mimar Sinan for 21 years, during which time he learned quite a lot from his master. Sultan Ahmed I commissioned Sedefkar Mehmed Ağa to construct a vast mosque for himself.

After meticulous studies and research, he was able to determine the place of the prospective mosque. However, there were some palaces on the site that belonged to Grand Vizier Sokollu Mehmed Pasha, as well as Mesih Pasha. He purchased the buildings, razed them and prepared the site for the mosque. In 1609, the sixth year of his reign, Sultan Ahmed I struck the first ceremonial shovel into the ground to begin work on the foundation. The mosque was finally finished after eight years. However, the inaugural ceremony of the mosque took place before the addition of the structures that would turn it to a complete complex was completed. Ahmed I died of typhoid at the age of 28 on 07 September 1617. He was buried in the tomb of his complex, which was finally completed in 1620.

We have learned the story of its construction from a book named Risale-i Mimari written by Cafer Çelebi in which he narrated the life of Palace Architect Sedefkar Mehmed Ağa.

Besides its mosque, the Sultan Ahmed Complex was comprised of a sultan's pavilion, tomb, primary school, medrese, hospital, fountain, public fountain and a marketplace. The architecture of the medrese next to the tomb is of the Classical Ottoman style. Situated behind the tomb is a white marble cloakroom consisting of a single chamber, which dates from the 18th century. Public fountains and the primary school lie on both sides of the courtyard. A separate building to the north of the mosque was the Sultan's pavilion and is currently used as a carpet museum. Below this building are shops selling souvenirs. A bath was situated next to this "Arasta" marketplace, once known as the "Sipahiler Çarşısı." There were shops lining the Hippodrome which still doing a brisk business in souvenirs. The charitable soup kitchen and a hospital used to be on the semi-circular terrace on the side of the Hippodrome near the Sea of Marmara. The Classical style

Interior view of the Sultan Ahmed Mosque (preceding overleaf).

Aerial view of the Sultan Ahmed Mosque. This monumental neo-Classical mosque was built by the architect Sedefkar Mehmed Ağa between 1609-17 (left).

Tile panel of the Sultan Ahmed Mosque (below).

horseshoe-shaped hospital lies behind a structure belonging to Marmara University. However, the hospital and the printing house of that complex are not longer extant.

The mosque is surrounded on three sides by an outer courtyard, which is accessible through eight gates, three of which are in the front. Accessible from the outer courtyard through three gates, the floor of the inner courtyard is paved entirely with white marble. The inner courtyard is surrounded by a portico covered by 30 domes supported by 26 columns. Two of these columns are porphyry while the remaining are pink granite and marble. In the middle of the courtyard is an elegant fountain with an octagonal dome supported by six marble columns. This mosque is the only one in Istanbul with six minarets. Four of them have three balconies, with the

remaining two having two each, for a total of 16. The Sultan Ahmed Mosque is comparable to Hagia Sophia in many ways but it is larger and more impressive than Hagia Sophia. Measuring 23.5 meters in diameter, its central dome is based on four enormous arches, the corners of which are pendentive.

The arches are supported by four round, grooved elephantine pillars measuring 5 meters in diameter. The main dome is surrounded by four semi-domes on each side. Its corners are also surrounded by small domes. Galleries are situated above and on both sides of the main entrance. Thus, it has an area measuring 64 meters x 72 meters. Next to the Sultan's Loggia, in the left corner, is the Ordeal Cell of Ahmed I. The plan of the Sultan Ahmed Mosque is similar to that which was incorporated by Mimar Sinan into the

Şehzade Mosque: a single main dome supported by four semi-domes. However, Sedefkar Mehmed Ağa worked on this masterpiece as if he was crafting mother-of-pearl. His calculations on illuminating the interior of the mosque, as well as the harmony of the color of tiles both show the perfection of his masterpiece. Some 260 windows were used to illuminate the interior. Its stained glass windows were restored over time, erasing the mystic atmosphere of the mosque, but giving the tiles a brighter appearance as well. The marble niche is enriched with engravings. The gold leaf used on the pulpit gives it a more precious and imposing appearance. One-third of all walls and pillars are covered with magnificent Iznik tiles up to the upper cornices. 21,043 Iznik tiles were used to decorate the interior of the mosque. The Sultan Ahmed Mosque is known as the "Blue Mosque" as the tiles and engraving work seen inside give it a bluish effect. More than 50 tulip motifs of various colored tulips, daffodils, carnations and other flowers were crafted on its tiles on a white background.

The wooden ceiling below the Sultan's Loggia is adorned with gold leaf embossed embroidery. The wood craftsmanship in the Sultan Ahmed Mosque is as beautiful and striking as its tiles. Sedefkar Mehmed Ağa adorned its doors and windows with beautiful tortoise shell and mother-of-pearl artwork. The calligraphy decorating the interior was inscribed by Kasım-ı Gubari.

The Tomb of Sultan Ahmed

Sultan Ahmed I ascended to the Ottoman throne on 21 December 1603. One of his wives, Mahfiruz Sultan, bore him many children. Presented to the palace by the Bosnian Pasha, the concubine Mahpeyker Sultan became his Favorite in 1609. She would later be called Kösem Sultan and take over the reign of the empire after her husband's death as the Dowager Sultan.

Though his mosque was finished, the tomb was incomplete when Ahmed I died in 1617. It was soon completed and he was buried there afterwards. Ahmed I, who died at a very young age, had changed the Succession Law of Sultan Süleyman the Magnificent that had allowed for the eldest member of the royal family ascend to the throne. In doing so, he ended the fratricidal struggles over the throne by having his younger brother Mustafa ascend to the throne upon his death.

The Tomb of Sultan Ahmed I was constructed by Sedefkar Mehmed Ağa on the side of the mosque overlooking Hagia Sophia. Based on a square plan, this trisectioned marble portico lies in front of the tomb. Tile panels are on both sides of the main entrance gate. The interior of the tomb is brightly illuminated by 52 windows. Its walls are decorated with 17th-century Iznik tiles, with motifs of tulips, daffodils, flower bouquets and leaves in blue, green, red and turquoise on a white background. There is a band of inscription containing the "Mülk Şuresi" Koranic verse. The upper parts of the tomb along with the inside of the dome are adorned with calligraphy. The elegant craftsmanship of the doors and windows belongs to Sedefkar Mehmed Ağa. A total of 36 imperial members, including three Ottoman sultans lie at rest in this tomb. In addition to Ahmed I, the son of Mahfiruz Sultan, Osman II, the son of Kösem Sultan, Murad IV, the wife of Ahmed I Kösem Sultan all lie at rest alongside many crown princes and sultans.

Interior (opposite) and exterior (below) of the Tomb of Sultan Ahmed I, where 36 members of the Imperial family lie at rest.

Tombs of the Sultans

Respect was shown to the Ottoman sultans who were the Islamic Caliphs as well, by having splendid tombs built in their names.

ifferent civilizations had various burial traditions in Anatolia over the centuries. Some buried their dead under mounds of soil, some under rocks and still others in mausoleums. Having defeated the Byzantines, the Seljuks reached into Anatolia and built cupolas to show respect to their dead. Today, we can see their cupolas in Ahlat around Lake Van in the East as well as in central Turkey in places like Sivas, Kayseri and Konya. After founding their own state in Anatolia, the Ottomans developed the architecture style they derived from the Seljuks. In particular, the Ottomans took the tomb architecture of the Seljuks and enhanced it by introducing a variety of different plans. Naturally, the most splendid of the tombs were built for the Ottoman sultans.

The tombs of the first six Ottoman sultans are in Bursa. Istanbul became the final resting place for subsequent sultans, as the city was chosen as the capital of the Ottoman Empire. There are 15 tombs in Istanbul. Ottoman sultans did not have their tombs constructed during their lifetimes. That task generally fell to the successive sultan. Besides the sultans, dowager sultans, grand viziers and pashas would have their own tombs in Istanbul. The majority of these tombs were built in complexes that had been constructed in their name. Sultans whose tombs are located in their own complex include Mehmed the Conqueror, Bayezid II, Selim the Grim, Süleyman the Magnificent, Mustafa III, Ahmed I and Abdülhamid I.

Other Ottoman sultans, such as Selim II, Murad III, Mehmed I, Mustafa I and İbrahim, were buried in the sanctity of Hagia Sophia. There were also those who were entombed in the tombs previously built by their parents. For example, six Ottoman Sultans lie side by side in the Tomb of Dowager Hatice Turhan Sultan.

Some viziers, pashas and dowager sultans wanted to be buried in another sacred place: Eyüp. Ebu Eyyüp Ensari, the Prophet's soldier and flag bearer, was buried there in his own tomb after the conquest of Istanbul in 1453. Other tombs were scattered in districts such as Laleli, Bahçekapı and Divanyolu. The tombs adorning Istanbul, the capital of a giant empire for 500 years, are considered great works of art. The tombs belonging to the

sultans succeeding Sultan Selim the Grim have a distinguished place in architecture, as these sultans held the position of Caliph of Islam at the same time. We are going to describe all of the Sultans Tombs below. We will also mention some important Grand Vizier and Dowager Sultan Tombs. It is impossible for us to mention all the tombs in Istanbul, as the total number is over 600, 119 of which are maintained by the Official Directorate

Interior of the Tomb of Sultan Selim II, which was built in the garden of Hagia Sophia by Mimar Sinan in 1577 (left).

Tile inscription over the entrance gate of the Tomb of Selim II (below).

of Tombs, with 30 open to the public. Tombs located in complexes shall be mentioned in the section that discusses Complexes. The conqueror of Constantinople, Sultan Mehmed II headed fresh military conquests, while beautifying Istanbul at the same time. One of his most outstanding accomplishments was to have his own complex constructed. The Fatih Complex was built over a Byzantine church by the architect Mimar Sinan-i Atik between 1463-70. After he died en route to Europe on one of his military expeditions, Sultan Mehmed the Conqueror was brought back to Istanbul and buried in his own tomb. The tomb of Grand Vizier Mahmud

A close up of the tile panel next to the gate of the Tomb of Selim II.

Pasha is near a mosque by the Covered Bazaar built in 1473 in his name. This octagonal tomb made of ashlar blocks is decorated with dark blue and turquoise tile inlays. The Tomb of Rum Mehmed Pasha in the mosque in Üsküdar dated 1471 is next to the Tomb of the Davut Pasha Mosque dated 1485. Bayezid II commissioned the architect Yakub Shah Bin Sultan Shah to build the Bayezid Complex in Bayezid Square between 1501-1506. His son Sultan Selim the Grim later had his father's tomb built next to the mosque.

By deposing his father Bayezid II, Sultan Selim the Grim ascended to the Ottoman throne in 1512 and reigned for a short period of only eight years. He was always on horseback during his short sultanate, going from one war to another. He is the sultan who brought the Caliphate to the Ottomans. He once said, "Whoever fills up our treasury with money shall deserve to stamp his seal on the treasury gates. Otherwise, my seal stays put." Sultan Selim the Grim gave orders for his own complex to be built on one of the hills overlooking the Golden Horn. But since he died in 1520, his son Sultan Süleyman the Magnificent gave orders to the architect Acem Ali to construct his father's tomb in this place. On a tile of the entrance is an inscription saying the tomb was ordered built by Sultan Süleyman the Magnificent in 1523.

This octagonal tomb is covered with a main dome and has a portico supported by four marble columns in the front. Engravings decorate the dome and the areas above the windows. Selim's coffin is embellished with mother-of-pearl inlays and covered with the caftan his tutor's horse splashed mud on during his Egyptian Campaign. Two identical glazed tile panels decorate both sides of the main gate of the tomb. The inner niches of these panels are filled with motifs of yellow, white and turquoise flowers and arabesque decoration on a dark blue background, while the borders of the panels are done in ivy. Two rows of inscriptions on a dark blue background crown the top of the main gate.

The octagonal Tomb of the Crown Princes is situated across the Tomb of Sultan Selim. The 16th-century tile panels inside the tomb are adorned with engravings. Five coffins belonging to the daughters of Sultan Selim the Grim and the sons of Sultan Süleyman the Magnificent lie at rest inside the tomb. Inside Sultan Selim's complex are the tombs of Sultan Abdülmecid, who had Dolmabahçe Palace constructed, and Sultan Selim the Grim's wife, Hafsa Sultan, whose tomb is in ruins. Also, a little further down the road is the tomb of the daughter of Sultan Selim the Grim, Shah Sultan, who was the wife of Grand Vizier Lütfi Pasha. Sultan Süleyman the

Magnificent, otherwise known as Sultan Süleyman the Lawgiver, commissioned Mimar Sinan to construct the Süleymaniye Complex during his long-lasting reign. In 1566, he was buried in the tomb situated right in front of the niche of the mosque, which is inside this complex. We have already described the tombs of Sultan Süleyman the Magnificent and Hürrem Sultan in the section concerning the Süleymaniye Complex. The plain tomb of Mimar Sinan is located right behind the Süleymaniye Mosque. Mimar Sinan also constructed the Tomb of Barbaros Hayreddin Pasha in Beşiktaş in 1541. Barbaros Hayreddin Pasha was the Commodore of the Ottoman Navy during the reign of Sultan Süleyman the Magnificent. In addition, Sinan constructed the Tomb of Hüsrev Pasha near Bali Pasha Mosque in Fatih in 1546, the Tomb of Yahya Efendi in Beşiktaş in 1570 as well as the Tomb of Ramazan Efendi in Kocamustafapaşa in 1588. The tombs of many several Ottoman sultans lie in the garden of Hagia Sophia.

The Tombs of Hagia Sophia

Selim II ascended to the Ottoman throne upon death of his father Sultan Süleyman the Magnificent. Selim II, who had commissioned the construction of the famous Selimiye Mosque in Edirne, died in 1574 after eight years as sultan. Mimar Sinan constructed a tomb for Selim II in the courtyard of Hagia Sophia and buried him there three years later.

The entrance and walls of this octagonal white marble tomb are adorned with 16th-century Iznik tiles. The tomb, which has four columns and a small dome with eaves, rests on eight marble columns. The inner part of the tombs dome is decorated with engravings. A glazing technique was used on the symmetrical tiled panels on both sides of the main entrance gate to produce motifs of flowers and large twisting leaves in blue, red and green on a white background. Considered one of the finest examples of 16th-century tile work, one of these panels is original, while the other one is a copy, as the original is on display in the Louvre Museum in Paris.

Tiles with motifs of dark blue, blue, red and green flowers and rosettes on a white background are used in the interior of the tomb up to the top part of the lower windows. A strip of Koranic verse winds along the top of the window. 41 coffins lie in the tomb, which is one of the most elegant examples of Turkish art. In the tomb, besides Selim II, his wife Nurbanu Sultan along with their daughters and many other crown princes lie side-by-side.

Murad III ascended to the throne upon his father Selim II's death. After he died in 1595, he was buried in his tomb in the courtyard of Hagia Sophia. The architect Davud Ağa constructed a hexagonal marble covered tomb

for him in 1599. A portico supported by four columns lies in front of the tomb, the gate of which is adorned with mother-of-pearl. The dome of the tomb, which has two rows of windows, is supported by six columns. Its walls are adorned with Iznik tiles. Symmetrical glazed tile panels on both sides of the main entrance gate are from the 16th century. Tiled panels are between the windows inside the tomb. A strip of Koranic verse is on top of the window, whereas the inner part of the dome is decorated with Classical-style engravings. Sultan Murad III, his wife Safiye Sultan, three crown princes and their daughter lie side-by-side in the tomb. Also buried

Interior "malachite" decoration of the dome of the Tomb of Sultan Selim II.

173

The Tomb of Sultan Mahmud II, who died in 1839. His sons Abdülaziz and Abdülhamid II lie alongside him in Cağaloğlu.

in the tomb are the crown princes of Sultan Ahmed I and Sultan İbrahim along with the latter's two daughters, the 19 siblings of Mehmed III who were murdered on orders of Mehmed III so that he could ascend to the throne, and other members of the Imperial Family. This makes a total of 50 coffins in the tomb. We encounter the Tomb of Mehmed III, who ascended to the throne after Murad III, in the courtyard of Hagia Sophia. Ahmed I, the son of Mehmed III, who died in 1603, commissioned the architect Dalgıç Mehmed Ağa to begin the construction of his father's tomb. But, as this architect succumbed to the plague, another architect, Sedefkar Mehmed Ağa completed the task in 1608.

This octagonal tomb has an outer portico that was later rebuilt in Baroque style. Tiles adorn the walls up to the top of lower windows. The "Cuma Suresi" Koranic verse is inscribed along a 120 cm-wide strip on top of the window. As the tiles inside the tomb have faded, their quality is poor. The dome is decorated with engravings. The coffin of Sultan Mehmed III is surrounded by those of his wife Handan Sultan, as well as Ahmed I's six sisters, three princes and 14 daughters. The daughter of Murad III, Ayşe Sultan, also lies in this tomb. There is a total of 26 coffins in the tomb. Constructed by Mimar Sinan in 1570, the Tomb of the Crown Princes is right next to the Tomb of Murad III. While this tomb is octagonal from the outside, its interior is rectangular, with the dome resting on pendentives. The inside of the dome is decorated with engravings that were all done during the late period. In this tomb are the brothers and sisters of Murad III who died while still very young. Moreover, Hagia Sophia's baptism chamber was converted into a tomb where Sultan Mustafa I and Sultan İbrahim were buried.

Tombs belonging to other sultans

Ahmed I ascended to the throne after his father Mehmed III. He died in 1617 after reigning for 14 years. Ahmed I commissioned Sedefkar Mehmed Ağa to build the Sultan Ahmed Mosque during his reign. After his death, he was buried in his tomb overlooking Hagia Sophia, next to his mosque. We mention this tomb in the section covering the Sultan Ahmed Mosque. Mustafa I, who ruled after Ahmed I, was buried in the baptismal chamber that was converted into a tomb, in the courtyard of Hagia Sophia. Osman II and Murad IV, who ascended to the Ottoman throne after Mustafa I, both lie in the Tomb of Sultan Ahmed. Sultan İbrahim I, rising to power upon the death of Murad IV in 1640, was buried next to Mustafa I in 1648. Mehmed IV, who succeeded his father Sultan İbrahim I, was buried in the tomb of his mother Hatice Turhan Sultan in Yeni Mosque. Süleyman II, who followed Mehmed IV, as well as Ahmed II, lies in the Tomb of Sultan Süleyman the Magnificent. Mustafa II, who ascended to the throne after Ahmed II, as well as Ahmed III, Mahmud III, and Osman III, respectively, lie in Tomb of Hatice Turhan Sultan.

Mustafa II, who became Sultan upon the death of Osman III, was buried in his own tomb located in the complex he ordered the architect Tahir Ağa to construct during his lifetime. Built in 1763, the tomb has a single dome and 10 corners. This ashlar block tomb was built in Baroque style; its interior is adorned with 16th-century glazed tiles in coral-red and blue-white. There is a strip of Koranic verse on top of the windows and its dome is decorated with engravings.

This tomb holds the coffins of Sultan Mustafa III and Selim III, as well as eight other coffins belonging to the daughters of Mustafa III. Abdülhamid I, who ascended to the Ottoman throne after Mustafa III as the 27th sultan, was the 92nd Islamic caliph. He died a sad death upon receiving word that his army had been defeated by Russia on 27 March 1789. He was buried the following year in his own tomb – the one that the architect Tahir Ağa had constructed in Bahçekapı, Eminönü. Most of the buildings of the complex have been deteriorated over time but his tomb is still intact.

Twenty-six windows illuminate this marble tomb. His son Mustafa IV had

the footprint of the Prophet Mohammed placed in his polygonal tomb. This marble tomb, the corners of which are rounded, was constructed in Baroque style with a dome on the top and a portico at the entrance. Its windows and doors are embellished with mother-of-pearl inlay; the "Mülk Suresi" Koranic verse is inscribed on the wall against a marble background.

The Tomb of Sokollu Mehmed Pasha in Eyüp. He was famous for his fearless manner of running the affairs of the Empire. His children lie alongside him in this octagonal tomb.

One of the intricate gridworks and tile panels of the Tomb of Eyüp Sultan. The tomb's interior and exterior is decorated with 16th-century Iznik tile (below).

The silver grid work of the Tomb of Eyüp Sultan which was a gift from Selim III (opposite).

There is also another Koranic verse on top of the gate. The coffin of Abdülhamid I as well as those of his son Mustafa IV, and 20 relatives lie side-by-side in the tomb.

Selim III, succeeded Abdülhamid I, was deposed and executed during the Kabakçı Mustafa Rebellion of 29 May 1807 and was buried in the Tomb of Mustafa III, which is located in Laleli. Subsequent sultans who ascended to the throne were Mustafa IV and Mahmud II, respectively. Mahmud II, who ascended to the throne in 1808, ordered the construction of a tomb in the Fatih Complex in 1817 for his mother, Nakşidil Sultan. In addition to his mother's coffin, there are 15 others belonging to Cevri Kalfa and Mahmud II's children in this tomb. Upon Mahmud II's death in 1839, his son and successor, Abdülmecid had the architect Ohannes Balyan construct a tomb for his father along Divanyolu Caddesi. Completed in 1840, this octagonal tomb was constructed in the Empiric style. It is covered by a dome that is supported by its walls. The tomb has seven windows and a gate. Decorations in Empiric style were embellished into bas-relief plaster. Its walls are covered in marble on the outside. The "Besmele" prayer is inscribed in "sülüs" calligraphic style on the outside of the main entrance gate, while the "Rahman Suresi" Koranic verse is inscribed on the inner face. The inscription inside the tomb on a marble background belongs to the calligrapher Haşim. While the coffin in the middle belongs to Sultan Mahmud II, the ones on the right belong to Sultan Abdülaziz and Abdülhamid II. Those to the left belong to the wife of Sultan Mahmud II, Dowager Bezmialem Sultan, her sister Esma Sultan and their daughter Atiye Sultan. Behind the coffin of Mahmud II are those belonging to other members of the Imperial Family. There is a total of 17 coffins in this tomb. The coffins belonging to six wives of Mahmud II and the wives of Sultan Abdülaziz and Sultan Abdülhamid II lie at rest in the annex next to the entrance of this tomb, to the left. In the garden of the tomb, which is surrounded by high walls, are the tombs belonging to some important imperial statesmen as well as some of those from the Republican period, such as Sadullah Pasha, Said Halim Pasha, Fethi Ahmed Pasha, Muallim Naci and Ziya Gökalp. Abdülmecid ascended to the throne after his father Mahmud II. He had Dolmabahçe Palace constructed and moved from Topkapı Palace into his new premises. Abdülmecid died in 1861, leaving behind many works of art such as palaces and pavilions. He was buried in his bare tomb situated in the courtyard of the Yavuz Sultan Selim Mosque. He was succeeded by his brothers Sultan Abdülaziz and Abdülhamid II, who were buried in their father's aforementioned tomb in Cağaloğlu. Murad V, whose sultanate lasted a brief period of 93 days, was buried in an additional chamber in the Tomb of Hatice Turhan Sultan in Eminönü. Mehmed V Reşad, who came to the throne after Abdülhamid II, was buried in a tomb that the architect Kemaleddin had constructed for him in Eyüp. As the last Ottoman sultan, Mehmed Vahideddin was exiled; his tomb is in Damascus, Syria.

The Eyüp Tombs

The District of Eyüp is a part of Istanbul filled with tombs. The first of them to be built is the one belonging to Eyüp Sultan. Ebu Eyyüb Ensari, a friend of the Prophet Mohammed and his flag bearer as well, participated in such battles as the ones in Uhud and Hendek. He also took part in several of the

The Tomb of Dowager Sultan Mihrişah in Eyüp, the mother of Selim III.

Arab sieges against the Byzantines. He finally became a martyr in one such siege in 669. After the Ottoman conquest of Constantinople, Sultan Mehmed the Conqueror ordered a tomb to be constructed in 1458 in Eyüp for Ebu Eyyüb Ensari, whose real name was Halid Bin Zeyd.

The bronze-engraved hacet window of this octagonal tomb, which faces the mosque courtyard, was ordered built by Ahmed I. The tomb was thoroughly restored during the reign of Mahmud II. The panel bearing the footprint of the Prophet Mohammed, which is found in the cell inside the tomb, was a gift of Mahmud I. The silver grid work was donated to the tomb by Selim III. Both its interior and exterior are adorned with 16th-century Iznik tiles. The interior tiles are adorned with verses from the Koran. At the foot of the coffin is a well that supposedly was a spring when it was discovered. The public fountain to the right of the tomb was donated by Haydar Ağa. Its small hospital was ordered built by the mother of Osman II, Mahfiruz Sultan. Sokollu Mehmed Pasha commissioned Mimar Sinan in 1568 to build for his children who died at a young age a complex in Eyüp consisting of a mosque, a medrese, and a tomb. He was also buried there soon after he died in 1579. The tomb, the body of which is prismic in shape, is octagonal on the outside, with 16 corners in its interior. Its walls are made from coarse sandstone. Inside its dome is a wide strip of Koranic verse glazed in white on a dark blue background. The letters are filled in with blue. Sixteen other relatives of Sokollu Mehmed Pasha lie here. Located right across from this tomb is the Tomb of Siyavuş Pasha, who served as grand vizier for some time. Embellished with alluring tiles that are fine representatives of 16th-century Iznik tiles, it was constructed by Mimar Sinan in 1584. This was the first of the polygonal-type tombs that were first seen at the end of the 16th century. Siyavuş Pasha and his sons lie at rest in this tomb. Constructed in 1589, the Tomb of Mirimiran Mehmed Pasha, which is quite near this tomb, has a plan based on 12 corners. Mirimiran Mehmed Pasha was a grand vizier during the reign of Murad III. In the same place is another tomb with 16 sides belonging to Ferhad Pasha, who was a grand vizier during the reign of Mehmed III and died in 1595. The tomb, which is the eternal resting place for 12 coffins, is thought to have been constructed by the architect Davud Ağa. The tomb of Zal Mahmud Pasha and the nearby Tomb of Nakkaş Hasan Pasha, both based on a square plan and date back to 1623, are in Eyüp as well. Near the Golden Horn is the Tomb of Selim III, which is situated within the complex of his mother, Mihrişah Sultan, and dates from 1794. The architect of the tomb was Arif Ağa. The tomb is attractive, with marble covered interior and exterior walls and Baroque-style decoration. Inside is a bas-relief band of Koranic verse inscribed by calligrapher Mahmud

Celaleddin. Besides Mihrişah Sultan, there are the coffins of five other women of the Harem: Beyhan, Hatice, Rafet and Perestü. Selim III commissioned the architect İbrahim Kamil Ağa to construct a tomb on the Defterdar Road in Eyüp for his daughter, Shah Sultan, in 1800. Built in the Baroque-Empiric style, the tomb is situated in a complex consisting of a public fountain and a school. In a group of tombs belonging to Hüsrev Pasha and Mahmud Celaleddin Efendi (Prince Sabahattin) at the Bostan Quay in Eyüp is another tomb dating back to 1860. Constructed in the Empiric style, this tomb belongs to the daughter of Mahmud II, Adile Sultan. The tomb of Prince Sabahattin is also in the Empiric style and has a dome covering the building. It forms a rectangular structure comprising the tombs of Hüsrev Pasha, Halil Rıfat Pasha and Adile Sultan. In addition, there are other tombs in Eyüp belonging to Hasan Hüsnü Pasha, the minister of the navy of the time, the poet Fitnat Hanım and Hubbi Hatun. One of the architects of the late-Ottoman era, Kemaleddin Bey, constructed the Tomb of Mehmed V Reşad, who was the 35th Ottoman sultan. This octagonal tomb lies on the banks of the Golden Horn. Its inscriptions were done by calligrapher Ömer Vasfi and its tile decorations were the work of Kutahyalı Hafız Emin.

Interior of the Tomb of Mihrişah Sultan.

Aqueducts, Fountains and Baths

From an architectural standpoint, the structures supplying the water needs of Istanbul are a very distinct feature of the city.

During the Roman and Byzantine periods, Constantinople was supplied with water from Halkalı, which was brought via aqueducts and stored in a number of cisterns. While the old cisterns were abandoned, the aqueducts were repaired and utilized during the Ottoman period. Today, there are three main networks that provide water for the European side of Istanbul: Halkalı, Kırkçeşme and Bahçeköy-Taksim. The water requirement for the Anatolian side is supplied by the Elmalı Dam. Halkalı was also Istanbul's sole source for water during the periods of Mehmed II, Bayezid and Selim the Grim. However, Sultan Süleyman the Magnificent commissioned Mimar Sinan to repair existing aqueducts and construct a new one from Kırkçeşme. Thus, water collected in the Belgrade Forest Dam was first conveyed to the Eğrikapı distribution station, then throughout the city via this waterway. Water flowed to all of the city's complexes, mosques and hamams as well as to about 400 fountains.

The network which brought water in from Bahçeköy to Beyoğlu's Galata District was bolstered by dams and reservoirs constructed during the reigns of Mahmud I and Abdülhamid I. Mahmud II enhanced these aqueducts in order to distribute this water in a more efficient manner by adding a canal to the network and ordering a distribution station to be constructed in Taksim. Finally, water flowing in from the valley of Hamidiye, between Kemerburgaz and Cendere, was added to the network during the reign of Abdülhamid II and distributed to Galata and the Bosphorus region.

Water that flowed from Belgrad Forest was once collected in a number of historical reservoirs, such as those in Karanlık, Büyük, Topuzlu, Ayvat, Valide, Kirazlı, Şamlar, and Mahmud II, which were constructed in 1620, 1723, 1750, 1765, 1796, 1818, 1828 and 1839, respectively.

After adjusting the pressure in the "rock towers," otherwise known as "water scales," water conveyed from distribution stations was piped to fountains located on street corners. Today one can see examples of these "water scales," which were fashioned from Roman examples, next to the Şehzade Mosque, across from Hagia Sophia as well as in the courtyard of Topkapı Palace. Aqueducts constructed to carry water through the valleys and into town are considered to be distinctive works of art in their own right. Several were erected by Mimar Sinan. One such aqueduct was the twin-level Moğlova Aqueduct (1554-64), which measured 35 meters in height and 257 meters in

length with its four arches. He also constructed the Avasköy Aqueduct, with 120 arches and the 207 meters-long Kovuk Aqueduct, with 47 arches. Sinan built the latter in 1563 over the foundations of an older Byzantine aqueduct. He also constructed the 771–meter-long twin-level Uzunkemer Aqueduct, with 97 tapered arches, once again over the foundations of Roman and Byzantine works. Sinan also erected the Güzelce Aqueduct during the same year. Floods that hit the region in 1563 destroyed many aqueducts,

Uzunkemer Aqueduct in Kemerburgaz supplied Istanbul water for many centuries (left).

The waterways of Halkalı, Kırkçeşme and Bahçeköy supply water to the city. These are seen on the map along with their viaducts and reservoirs.

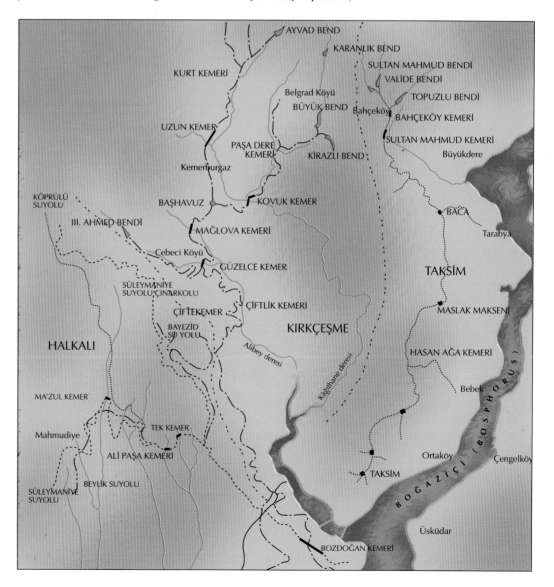

The mother of Selim III, Dowager Sultan Mihrişah ordered the construction of the Göksu Fountain to be built next to the Küçüksu Summer Palace (below).

The Sultan Ahmed III Fountain. Situated at the outer gate of Topkapı Palace, this was built in 1728 by the architect Mehmed Emin Ağa (opposite).

whereupon Sinan undertook the task of repairing several of these between 1563-64. Those that could not be repaired, such as the Paşakemeri Aqueduct, had to be reconstructed. Istanbul's water network was operated by an organization called the "Water Travelers" up until 1926, when the municipality took over and renovated the system. As a consequence, though a great majority of the fountains no longer receive water, they still exist as colorful monuments of the past. Most of those still standing are products of the era of Sultan Süleyman the Magnificent. With their harmonious and well-balanced architecture, they are reflective of Classical-Ottoman style. There are also very interesting fountains which were built in the Baroque style during the Tulip Era. The Ottomans gave great importance to fountains and constructed numerous ones as well as "sebil," or charitable fountains, throughout Istanbul in the 18th-19th centuries. They were named according to their function, as well as their location.

Fountains that were constructed at stopover points for caravans, army and "Sürre" (yearly processions to Mecca) were called "Ayrılık" (Separation) and "Namazgah" (Prayer Hall), whereas those constructed at stopover points for the commanding officer of the sultan's bodyguards were called "Bostancıbaşı." Fountains were also named according to the site at which they were constructed. For example, "Duvar" (Wall), "Köşe" (Corner) and "Meydan" (Square). Wall fountains built into the façades of structures were constructed in various styles until the 20th century. Works found on the corners of streets and buildings were constructed single-faced in the earlier periods and double- or triple-faced in later years. Open-air fountains with engraved surfaces first appeared in the 18th century and were essentially monuments that decorated public squares. Rather than mentioning all the fountains, we shall give you information regarding some of the more magnificent open-air fountains.

Square Fountains

These are considered the finest examples of the various types of fountains. The fountain in front of the Imperial Gate at Topkapı Palace that was constructed in 1728 by the architect Kayserili Mehmed Emin Ağa upon the orders of Sultan Ahmed III is the best example of a monumental square fountain. One of the most cultured examples of Baroque style art, this work has a vaulted fountain on each side and charitable fountains on each of its corners. Each of its faces is decorated with tiles and engravings. Lines of poetry from the famous poet of the period, Seyyid Vehbi, are inscribed at the top.

The Tophane Fountain, which is situated next to the Kılıç Ali Pasha Mosque in Tophane, is another square fountain gracing Istanbul. Sultan Mahmud I commissioned the architect Mehmed Ağa to construct it in 1732. The square-plan fountain is covered with a single dome topped by wide, overhanging eaves. It has marble façades ornamented with motifs of flowers, cypress trees and fruits.

Constructed in 1732 on the order of Grand Vizier Hekimoğlu Ali Pasha, the

square fountain in Kabataş represents a fine example of the Turkish Baroque style. It was moved from its previous location at Setüstü and positioned next to the pier in 1955. Reflecting the transition in styles from Classical to Baroque is a fountain called Bereketzade, which was constructed by Defterdar Emin Efendi in 1732. This fountain was recently moved to its new home beside the Galata Tower. During the completion stage of the Yeni Mosque, Mehmed IV's mother, Hatice Turhan Sultan ordered a fountain to be built as part of the complex. Sultan Ahmed III commissioned the architect Mehmed Ağa to construct both the fountain in Üsküdar's İskele Square in 1728-29, as well as the one in Sultanahmet Square.

The square-plan fountain in Üsküdar is covered with a four-cornered dome with engraved overhanging eaves. Though its architecture resembles the one in Sultanahmet, it does not have any charitable fountain windows. Its marble surfaces are engraved with inscriptions with lines from famous poets of the time. Constructed between 1731-32 for the mother of Mahmud I, Saliha Sultan, the fountain found in Azapkapı is based on a different plan. Here, one encounters a pair of overflowing charitable fountains in the middle with two fountains on either side. The other surfaces of the fountain were left unadorned.

The fountain situated between Beşiktaş and Maçka was constructed by Sultan Abdulmecid between 1839-40 on behalf of his mother, Dowager Sultan Bezm-i Alem. One can see lines of poetry on the fountain belonging to two popular poets of the time, Şükri and Zevir as well as Empiric-style reliefs. It is covered with a spire-like rock cone roof while its walls are unadorned.

The fountain in Eyüp, which was constructed in 1795 upon the order of Mihrişah Sultan, has an architecture that combines the fountain charitable fountain design. Its surface was ornamented with common decorations of that period. The Onçeşmeler Fountain in Beykoz is striking for its distinct architecture. First constructed by Behruz Ağa, who was Sultan Süleyman the Magnificent's Keeper of the Privy Chamber, this fountain was renovated in 1746 by Istanbul's Chief of Customs, İshak Ağa. Thus, it is also referred to as the İshak Ağa Fountain. Water still flows from 10 faucets of the arched and domed fountain. Hamidiye water flows from the square Balmumcu Fountain, which has wide eaves. It was constructed in the neo classical style that emerged in the early 19th century. In addition to this noteworthy fountain, there are others such as the Rukiye Kadın Fountain in Eminönü (1738), the Kaptan-ı Derya Hacı Hüseyin Pasha Fountain in Kasımpaşa (1732), the Süleyman Kaptan Fountain, also in Kasımpaşa (1748), the Dowager Sultan Sineperver Fountain in Üsküdar (1780), the Süleymaniye Fountain (1792), as well as the Pertevniyal Dowager Sultan Fountain in Eyüp. Although it is not a Turkish monument, one of the most attractive

square fountains is the German Fountain in Sultanahmet Square. The fountain was constructed by Kaiser Wilhelm II on behalf of Abdülhamid II to celebrate his 25th year on the throne. It was constructed by the German architect Spitta in 1899 and assembled in its place in 1901. Its copper-plated dome is supported by green porphyry columns on an octagonal marble base. Its interior is embellished with a gold mosaic and with the monograms of both Wilhelm II and Abdulhamid II engraved on the mosaic.

Charitable Fountains

Water or sherbet used to be dispensed on certain days from the windows of charitable fountains in exchange for a prayer for the builder or the donor of the fountain, but this tradition has disappeared over the years. Today, Istanbul is decorated with almost 80 of these charitable fountains. First appearing in the 16th century, these charitable fountains, with their polygonal and circular structures, enhance the appearance of street corners and buildings with their Baroque and Empiric styles, and marble and wrought iron craftsmanship. The oldest charitable fountain dates back to 1587 and is found in Süleymaniye at the corner of the Tomb of Mimar Sinan. Others that have survived to the present are Koca Sinan Pasha in Çarşıkapı

The German Fountain. Situated in Sultanahmet Square, it was a gift by Kaiser Wilhelm II to Sultan Abdülhamid II to commemorate his 25th year on the throne in 1901. The gold leaf mosaic decoration inside the fountain's dome is seen below.

(1593), Kuyucu Murad Pasha in Vezneciler (1606), Sultan Ahmed Mosque (1617) and Hagia Sophia (1640-48). Other significant charitable fountains include the one in the Yeni Mosque Complex constructed on the order of Hatice Sultan (1663), Merzifonlu Kara Mustafa in Çarşıkapı (1691), Kaptan İbrahim Pasha in Beyazıt (1708), Damat İbrahim Pasha in Şehzadebaşı (1719) as well as Gazanfer Ağa at the bottom of the Bozdoğan Aqueduct. The Baroque-style Hacı Emin Ağa in Dolmabahçe (1744); the Turkish Rococo-style Seyyid Hasan Pasha in Vezneciler (1745); the Turkish Rococo-style Nuruosmaniye (1775); Mustafa III in Laleli (1763); Recai Mehmed Efendi in Vefa (1775); Koca Yusuf Pasha in Kabataş (1787), as well as many other charitable fountains bedeck the streets of Istanbul.

One encounters the 19th-century Empiric style in charitable fountains located at the edge of Sultanahmet Square, at the bottom of the Cevri Kalfa School as well as the fountain next to the Tomb of Sultan Mahmud.

Hamams

There are no longer any baths belonging to the Roman or Byzantine periods

The Sultan's Baths of Dolmabahçe Palace (left). They are covered with water marble quarried in Egypt, while the taps are made of silver.

The Haseki Baths Dowager Sultan Hürrem ordered Mimar Sinan to construct in 1558 (right).

in Istanbul, the capital of three empires. Nonetheless, it is known that the Romans did build some rather magnificent baths here. For example, historians mention the baths of Arcadius and Zeuxippus. It is known that there were also public baths such as Carosianae, which was completed by the daughter of Valens in 427. There were also baths inside large mansions. One can clearly see traces of Roman influence in baths which were built during the Byzantine and Turkish periods. Also, Turks were inspired to construct numerous hamams in Istanbul in the Roman tradition. Just as there were hamams built inside the grand complexes, there were independently operated hamams as well. Foundations also constructed hamams as a source of income.

Sadly, only a handful of the more than 150 hamams built throughout the city are still operating today. The Balat Hamams in the district of Balat were constructed by the order of Sultan Mehmed the Conqueror in the mid-15th century. The same sultan was also responsible for the construction in 1460 of the hamams next to the Rüstem Pasha Mosque. This structure was damaged in a fire in 1726 as well as in the earthquake of 1894. Utilized as a cold storage warehouse for many years after undergoing some repairs, it has since been converted into a market. Constructed by Grand Vizier Mahmud Pasha in Mahmutpaşa in 1466, only the men's section of the Çifte Hamams is still in use today. In 1558, Hürrem Sultan commissioned Mimar Sinan to construct the hamams located south of Hagia Sophia, which consisted of both sections for men and women. After undergoing a thorough restoration, this bath is currently operated by the Ministry of Culture as a carpet shop. Situated in Çemberlitaş, the Çemberlitaş Hamams were constructed in 1580 by the order of the mother of Murad III, Sultan Nurbanu. Originally constructed as a bath for men and women, only the men's section is open for business these days; the women's half has been converted into a shop. In 1741, Sultan Mahmud I ordered the construction of the Cağaloğlu Hamams on Yerebatan Caddesi in Cağaloğlu as a source of income for Hagia Sophia. It continues to function in this capacity. Apart from these hamams, we can also count the Nişanci Mehmed Pasha Hamams in Kumkapı, the Bayezid Complex Hamams (1505), the Çardaklı Hamams in Kadırga, which were constructed by the Head Servant of the Sultan's Palace, Hüseyin Ağa Hamams (1503), the Barbaros Hayreddin Pasha Hamams, constructed by Mimar Sinan in Zeyrek, the Dökmeciler Hamams inside the Süleymaniye Complex (1550), the Ağa Hamams in Samatya (16th century), and the Ağa Hamams in Beyoğlu, (16th century), the Hüsrev Kethüda Hamams in Ortaköy (16th century), Yeşildirek Hamams in Azapkapı (1570), the Çukurcuma Hamams in Beyoğlu, and finally the Galatasaray Hamams (1715).

Castles, Towers and Fortresses

"Istanbul is the city God has granted to the most magnificent empire in the world"
Sultan Süleyman the Magnificent

A part from the protective walls in Istanbul, there are also a number of sites in and around the city where fortresses are found. One of them is the fortress situated in Anadolukavağı, which is a tourist attraction. Today, one can see the Byzantine Yaros Fortress in all its grandeur at the top of the hill. It was captured by the Genoese as the Byzantine Empire was on its steady decline, which is why the fortress is referred to as the Genoese Fortress. The imposing fortress, along with its towers, is remarkably intact. Engraved onto its marble walls, are a coat-of-arms, and Classical-Greek inscriptions and epitaphs. The fortress was also used during the Ottoman era after extensive restoration. Sultan Mehmed the Conqueror was the first to have repaired the Anadolukavağı Fortress prior to building Rumeli Hisarı. During the repairs, he had a mosque and some wheat granaries constructed on its premises. Armed with cannons, the fortress was strengthened to prevent aid from reaching Constantinople from the Black Sea. While we are on the subject of Anadolukavağı, let's mention Marco Pasha, who had a mansion in Anadolukavağı. The expression "Go and tell it to Marco Pasha" is still heard today. Marco Pasha was a doctor of Greek origin who was appointed to the rank of General during the Ottoman period. He had a famous reputation for patiently listening to complaints voiced by the public. Opposite Anadolukavağı is another touristic site. Known as Rumelikavağı, it was known in antiquity as the site of the Temples of Kybele and Serapis. One can find fortifications here from various periods. In 1642, the Kazakhs showed their displeasure with the Ottoman administration when they moved in front of Yeniköy and Tarabya.

As a consequence, a line of defense was considered against possible danger from the Black Sea. These shores were fortified by Murad IV and successive sultans. The fortress constructed on the shore at Rumelikavağı is rectangular in shape. Along with its counterpart on the opposite side, in Anadolukavağı, this fortress, with its iron gate facing Mecca, was the first line of defense of the Bosphorus. Sultan Murad ordered a mosque and two granaries constructed within the fortress, where the quarters for the fortress guards were also located. 100 cannons of various sizes were stored in the fortress in the past. It is understood that the fortress, which was constructed prior to the Ottoman period, was utilized after it was restored. In 1393, prior to the conquest of Constantinople, the Ottomans constructed the fortress of Anadoluhisarı, also known as "Güzelce Hisar" or "Yenice Hisar" during the reign of Yıldırım Bayezid. While Rumelihisarı, on the opposite shore, was under construction, Sultan Mehmed the Conqueror ordered this fortress to

Two views of Anadolu Hisar, constructed by Sultan Yıldırım Bayezid in 1393, 49 years before Rumeli Hisarı.

be enlarged and had a mosque erected in front of it as well. This mosque collapsed in later years; the one we see today was constructed in 1883. The main fortress is comprised of inner and outer fortress walls, and three towers. The rectangular-planned fortress was constructed over an outcropping of rock.

Beyazıt Tower. It was utilized as a fire tower during the Ottoman period.

One enters the four-storey tower from the southwestern gate. The fortress was once surrounded by elegant houses, which also lined both sides of Göksu Stream. Flowing past the fortress and into the Bosphorus, the Göksu Stream once provided entertainment with the caiques that traveled up and down its shores. We shall mention in another chapter Rumeli Hisarı, which was constructed by Sultan Mehmed the Conqueror and is currently operated as a museum. We only found it proper to do the same for the Yedikule Fortress, which is also a museum. We have already described the Leander's Tower and Galata Tower in the chapter dealing with the Byzantine Empire. Now it is time to mention something about the other towers in Istanbul.

Utilized as a fire watchtower during the Ottoman period, the 85-meter-high Bayezid Tower is situated in the garden of Istanbul University. First constructed from timber, Mahmud II had it built of stone in 1828 after it had suffered from one fire too many. The Bayezid Tower was renovated in 1889 and 1909 and is still intact. An inscription comprised of lines of poetry by the poet İzzettin was engraved by Calligrapher Yesarizade Mustafa İzzet.

Other lighthouses that can still be seen today are those of Ahırkapı, Yeşilköy and Fenerbahçe. The 36-meter-high Ahırkapı Lighthouse was constructed during the Ottoman Era by the Commodore of the Navy, Süleyman Pasha after a collision at sea.

The 22-meter-high Yeşilköy Lighthouse entered service in 1856. The Fenerbahçe Lighthouse was constructed by Grand Vizier İbrahim Pasha in 1720 during the Tulip Era. The 25-meter-high lighthouse served sailors on the Anatolian shores.

In addition to these lighthouses, there are also many clock towers in Istanbul. These include the Dolmabahçe Clock Tower, the Yıldız Clock Tower and the Tophane Clock Tower. The Dolmabahçe Clock Tower was constructed by the Balyans in 1890, many years after the completion of Dolmabahçe Palace. The 27 meter-high tower was last repaired by this author in 1978 and it still runs like new. With inscriptions on all four sides, the Yıldız Clock Tower (1890) is 22 meters tall. The Tophane Clock Tower (1847), which is 15 meters high, is situated in the garden of the Tophane Summer Palace. We have already mentioned the more significant towers of the 16 found in Istanbul. Apart from those, we can count the 52-meter-high Topkapı Palace Justice Tower (1840), the Kandilli Observatory, and the Çubuklu Khedive Tower. Constructed by the Egyptian Khedive Abbas Hilmi Pasha in 1890, the tower of the summerhouse stands 14 meters and was constructed for its commanding panoramic view of the Bosphorus. There are also several other towers that grace the skyline of Istanbul, including the Atatürk Airport Control Tower, the Şişli Children's Hospital Clock Tower, and the Kasımpaşa Naval Hospital Clock Tower.

Yedikule Hisarı

Situated along the protective walls of Istanbul is a fortress named Yedikule Hisarı, which displays features of both the Byzantine and Ottoman periods. The 5,630-meter-long Land Walls that surround the old part of Istanbul start at the end of Marmara Walls. This was where the splendid ceremonial gate of the Byzantines was situated. Constructed by Roman Emperor Theodosius I in 390 A.D, this gate was called "Porta Aura" because it was once gold-plated. Emperors would enter the city after their victorious military campaigns through this gate, which had the status of a victory arch. But in 413 Theodosius II constructed the protective walls that we see today, merging this gate into the walls.

Thus, the gate became one of the splendid gates of the protective walls. As a matter of fact, Michael Palaeologus entered the city on horseback through this gate after winning back the city from the Latins in 1261. Previously used as a triumphal archway, the gate had three arches and marble towers on both sides, as well as two statues positioned overhead; one was of Theodosius and the other was of Nike being pulled by an elephant cart.

These statues were destroyed by a pair of earthquakes that struck in 740 and 866. John V. Palaeologus had the gate repaired in 1389, adding figures in relief depicting Hercules' actions and some mythological scenes. These figures remained here until the 17th century. Five years after conquering Constantinople, Sultan Mehmed the Conqueror ordered some additional buildings to be constructed here and turned this into an inner fortress separate from the protective walls.

Thus, a fortress called "Yedikule," which was comprised of seven towers including those remaining from the Byzantines, emerged here. Even though Sultan Mehmed the Conqueror first used this place to house his treasury, it was to be transferred to the Topkapı Palace later on.

Yedikule Fortress was eventually converted into a dungeon where prisoners such as rebellious ambassadors and other influential people were locked up. For example, the Russian Ambassador Obrekoff and the French Ambassadors Jean de la Haye and Ruffin were a few of those who got on the wrong side of the sultans and ended up here in custody.

One of the most painful events to occur here was when the reformer Osman II, who was deposed when many people including Kösem Sultan provoked the Janissaries. He was subsequently brought here in 1622 and executed in the Eastern Tower. Apart from this, Grand Vizier Mahmud Pasha, Hasan Pasha and Deli Hüseyin Pasha were also executed here. Once past the narrow entrance gate at Yedikule Fortress, one reaches the old ceremonial gate of the Byzantines. The fortress, including the Golden Gate, Ahmed III Tower, Treasury, trunk walls and the entrance gate, was repaired between 1958-70. A minaret is all that remains of the mosque that was constructed for the fortress guards. It is possible to encounter traces of the dungeon inside one of the towers.

Dolmabahçe Clock Tower. Constructed in the garden of Dolmabahçe Palace in 1890, this tower stands 27 m. high.

191

Rumeli Hisarı

In 1393, Yıldırım Bayezid ordered the construction of a fortress called Anadolu Hisarı, also known as Güzelce Hisar, on the site of the ancient Byzantine Temple of Jupiter. Prior to taking Constantinople, Sultan Mehmed the Conqueror ordered the construction of a fortress directly opposite Anadolu Hisarı to prevent aid reaching the Byzantines from the Black Sea. Preparations made for the construction of the fortress were complete in the spring of 1452 while material and skilled workers were brought here from all over the country. Mehmed II arrived there on 21 March and set up camp on the site where the fortress would soon be constructed. In going over the plans one final time, he gave the command to commence construction of the fortress. He first decided to have a fortress constructed just at that point and started to prepare his plans to go further. The Byzantine Emperor protested the construction of the fortress, saying, "I will grant you a site as wide as the hide of a cow, but you can forget about building on land that is wider than that hide." It is said that Mehmet II cut up a cow's hide into a very thin (and long) thong, whereby he commenced building after marking off the stretched piece of cowhide on the ground. When the emperor sent his ambassadors to protest the action, the Conqueror presented them with this cowhide thong adding, "As per your zoning permission, we have only constructed the site as wide as this piece of cowhide. Let us know if we have exceeded your stated limitations, and we will gladly tear it down." Mehmed II appointed Saruca, Zağnos and Çandarlı Halil Pasha the task of building this fortress, ordering them to expedite the job, which they did.

In this way, the slender ray of hope held by the Byzantines was extinguished as Mehmed II had carried out another one of his plans. It is said that between 13 April-31 August 1452, an architect named Musliheddin completed the construction of the fortress in just 139 days; but this hypothesis has never been proven. The task of constructing of the northwest cylindrical tower was given to Saruca Pasha. He built eight storeys into the 28-meter-high tower and covered the top floor with a brick dome. The northeast tower, which was 22 meters high and had 12 corners, was built by the Grand Vizier Halil Pasha. Measuring 21 meters in height, the southeast tower was constructed by Zağnos Pasha. An inscription indicating the name of the architect was engraved on the gate. Along its walls, the fortress is protected by turrets and narrow roads, the latter not connected to the towers.

The five gates inside the fortress are called Dizdar, Hisartepe, Sel, Dağ and İstihkam. A collapsed minaret is all that remains of a mescid that was built during the period of Mehmed II. Situated on an area measuring 60,000 m2, the fortress also has water facilities such as a fountain, a well and a cistern. While Rumeli Hisarı lost its strategic importance after the conquest of Constantinople, it continued to be used to monitor vessels that plied the Bosphorus, and as prison. Known as the "Black Tower," the Saruca Pasha Tower was converted into a national prison. One of Mehmed II's Grand Viziers, Gedik Ahmed Pasha, the Austrian Ambassador, as well as envoys from Venice and Erdel, were all imprisoned here. Guilty Janissaries were strangled here and their bodies tossed into the sea.

The fortress lost its importance in the 17th century, when the defense of the Bosphorus was moved up to the Black Sea coast. It was abandoned during the period of Mahmud II, with a new town quarter emerging from within it. Rumeli Hisarı underwent a complete restoration between 1955-58. The quarter that had placed itself there was removed and it was landscaped with a beautiful garden and inaugurated as a museum in 1958. Cannons and stone catapults as well as a part of the famous chain used to block the entrance of the Golden Horn are exhibited in this museum.

Aerial view of Yedikule Hisarı (below).

Aerial view of Rumeli Hisarı, which was constructed a shortly before Sultan Mehmed II conquered Constantinople (opposite).

Ottoman Palaces

"There is no city on Earth that compares to Istanbul"
The Poet Nabi

Upon his conquest of Istanbul, Sultan Mehmed the Conqueror found the Byzantine palaces in ruins. This led him to have a palace constructed for himself in Bayezid Square, which happens to be on the site where Istanbul University stands today. Later on, this palace became too confining, so he moved the royal family to Topkapı Palace after it was built in 1475. Known as the "Old Palace," the palace in Bayezid was subsequently turned into a site where the previous sultan's wives, mothers and concubines stayed. Several of the villas that used to line the shore below Topkapı Palace no longer exist for a number of reasons. Sultan Süleyman the Magnificent married off his sister Hatice Sultan to his Grand Vizier, Makbul İbrahim Pasha, and presented them with the İbrahim Pasha Palace, which he had constructed in Sultanahmet on a spot where the Turkish and Islamic Art Museum currently stands. Another palace that did not survive till today is the Summer Palace, which was located between Salacak and Haydarpaşa. The only part remaining from this palace is the word "Harem." There was also a palace in Beykoz that we know was still standing in the 17th century, as a traveler at that time mentioned its existence.

Waterfront palaces on the Bosphorus were the fashion during the first half of the 19th century, especially during the reign of Mahmud II. Ahmed II and subsequent sultans were enthusiastic about building such palaces. In addition, renovations of and additions to existing ones, such as those Selim III had the French architect Melling make to one such palace, were not uncommon. After this palace was destroyed by fire, Mahmud II had it replaced by another one, which was to become preferred to Topkapı Palace. Mahmud II had two more wooden palaces constructed, one in Beylerbeyi and another in Çırağan, the latter being the old Çırağan Palace. We know what these palaces looked like only from gravures that remain of them. Mahmud II's residence in Beşiktaş marked the beginning of the end for the Topkapı Palace as a place of residence. His son, Abdülmecid tore down the wooden structure built in Dolmabahçe and paid the architect Garabet Balyan and his son Nikoğos Balyan five million gold pieces to construct today's Dolmabahçe Palace (1843-56). Abdülmecid's brother, Abdülaziz ascended to the Ottoman throne in 1861 and demolished the wooden palace that his father Mahmud II had constructed on the opposite shore of the Bosphorus, replacing it with the Beylerbeyi Palace (1861-65). The two-storey palace that Nikoğos and Sarkis Balyan had made from coarse sandstone was considered for use as a summer residence. In addition to this very ornate palace, which had six halls and 24 rooms, Sultan Abdülaziz commissioned the Balyans to tear down the old wooden palace on the

Bosphorus and construct the Çırağan Palace, which is particularly striking because of its marble craftsmanship. We are familiar with the former palace only through the gravures of d'Ohsson and Melling. Divided into two sections, the "harem" and "selamlık," this three-storey palace is connected to the main road by two monumental gates. The Sultan's Gate opens into the showy palatial

Sultan Abdülaziz commissioned Nikoğos and Sarkis Balyan to build the Çırağan Palace between 1863-71 (opposite).

One of the magnificent gates of Çırağan Palace (below).

garden with the Shore Gate facing opposite. The other gate, the Gate of the Dowager Sultan, opens into the Harem section.

After Sultan Abdülaziz was deposed in 1876, Murad V ascended to the Ottoman throne for a brief 93 days. He was subsequently forced to reside in the Çırağan Palace. This palace was used as the Parliament Building during the Second Constitutional Monarchy (1909) and was rendered unusable by a disastrous fire that struck the following year. Having remained as a burnt-out skeleton for many years, it was later restored and transformed into the Çırağan Hotel. Succeeding Murad V was Abdülhamid II, who had new pavilions constructed to complement existing ones, preferred to conduct his affairs in Yıldız Palace. As we shall examine these palaces in more detail, one by one, we cover them in brief here. However, there are also palaces that no longer exist. One of these is the "Yazlık" (Summer) Palace, which was situated between Salacak and Haydarpaşa. The neighborhood's current name "Harem," is all that remains of this palace. There was also the famous Sadabad Palace, which was constructed for Damat İbrahim Pasha Ahmed III, on the shores of the Golden Horn. Praised in the poems of the poet Nedim, this palace was destroyed in the Patrona Halil

riots, which broke out in 1730. Sultan Mahmud II commissioned Mimar Kirkor Balyan to construct a new palace but that was subsequently left to rot as it was not highly regarded by his son Abdülmecid, who ascended to the throne soon after. Abdülaziz had it torn down, constructing in its place the Çağlayan Summer Palace. Memories of this summer mansion remain only on artists' canvasses. When it was torn down in the 1940s, the last vestiges of the Sadabad Quarter, where fabulous night entertainment could be had once upon a time, were gone forever. When the Tersane Saray, an opulent palace in the vicinity of Hasköy along the Golden Horn, was torn down at the beginning of the 19th century, Selim III ordered a shipyard and a factory constructed here. Only the Aynalı Kavak Pavilion was built on the wide land here. A few remnants are all that is left of the Davud Pasha Palace, which was built in the 16th century for the sultan to salute his army before it started out on a campaign.

Not many structures remain of palaces belonging to those connected with the dynasty. Those that have survived are being used for other purposes today. For instance, the Feriye Palaces, which were palaces of the second degree and were built for the servants of Çırağan Palace, are used as the Kabataş Lyceé and Galatasaray University. These Feriye Palaces consisted of buildings that stretched as far as Beşiktaş. One of the two adjacent palaces in Ortaköy constructed for Abdülhamid's two daughters is currently being utilized as a school. The building next to the mosque in Ortaköy was the Waterfront Palace of Esma Sultan, the sister of Mahmud II. Then again, nothing remains of Esma Sultan's Waterfront Palace on the Eyüp shoreline. It is only through the gravures of the artist Melling that we are reminded that a palace was once located at the foot of the bridge on the edge of the Golden Horn in Ayvansaray – the Waterfront Palace belonging to Hatice Sultan, the sister of Selim III. A school was since been constructed on the site of the Fikirtepe Summer Palace, where Murad V lived before he became sultan. There are also the Çifte Saraylar, two palaces built by the daughters of Sultan Adbülmecid, Cemile and Münire, which are located in Fındıklı.

The one on the Beşiktaş side belonged to Cemile Sultan. Later on, the palace allotted to Adile Sultan was appropriated for use by the Ottoman Parliament and Senate in 1910 and was utilized as the Academy of Fine Arts between 1928-48. This palace was renovated after fire damaged it in 1948. The two structures remaining are now being used as the two main campuses of Mimar Sinan University. The Adile Sultan Palace on the slopes of Kandilli was converted into a school, which unfortunately suffered heavy damage in a fire that struck in some years ago. The Adile Sultan Pavilion in Koşuyolu, on the other hand, is used today as a hospital. Located on the foothills of Beylerbeyi is the Palace of the Last Caliph, Abdülmecid, the conservation of which is being underwritten by Yapı Kredi Bank. Another former waterfront palace, being used as a hospital today, is that of the Baltalimanı Orthopedic Hospital.

Topkapı Palace

This palace was the center of the Ottoman Sultanate for four centuries.

In bringing to an end one era with his conquest of Constantinople and ringing in another, Sultan Mehmed the Conqueror made it the third capital of the Ottomans. At the same time, he began to have a palace made for himself once the construction of public works had gotten underway. Over time, this palace,, which was built in Bayezid Square, proved to be too restrictive for his family, whereby he had a new palace constructed in Sarayburnu. Built between 1460-78, this palace was to be the place where the sultans resided and the state carried out its administrative affairs until Dolmabahçe Palace was constructed about four centuries later. New additions were added by every sultan to the structures that were concentrated around four courtyards. Moreover, in adding the Harem, which reflected a world unto itself, these structures were transformed into a mini city-state, where thousands of people lived. The palace buildings were surrounded by a wide protective wall called the "Sur-u Sultani" (Sultan's Walls), which had several gates. The palace derived its name "Topkapı" much later on from one of the gates where artillery pieces were stored. The most magnificent entrance of Topkapı is that of the Bab-ı Hümayun (Imperial Gate) on the Hagia Sophia side. The Sultan's Summer Palace used to be located on the top floor of this gate and it was from here that the sultans would view ceremonies that were organized in front of the gate. Today, this gate, the upper part of which is no longer extant, opens out into the first courtyard of the palace. Hagia Eirene, which was used as the palace armory, and the adjacent Darphane-i Amire, where the palace firewood and reed matting was stored, are in the western part of this courtyard, which was called the Procession Square. In addition, there was once a summer palace where the people would go to convey their problems to the palace. There were also once structures on the palace side of the square, such as the Women's Hospital and Sultan's Oven.

Other than these, there were also some pavilions within the Sur-u Sultani. Those which have remained intact are the Çinili Pavilion, located in the garden of the Archaeological Museum, the Alay Pavilion, situated over the light rail line, which is known to date back to the period of Murad III, as well as the Sepetçiler Summer Palace, which is in use after having been restored in recent years. While some of the waterfront pavilions and palaces disappeared, particularly in the 1860s, to make way for the railroad, others were removed even before then.

The 2nd Courtyard: Utilized today as the entrance to Topkapı Palace, one passes through the Bab-üs Selam into the second courtyard of the palace. Named the Divan Meydanı (Council Square), the second courtyard is comprised of the main section of the palace and features an area for ceremonies where the administration of the state was carried out. It was the

(preceding overleaf) Aerial view of Topkapı Palace.

The main entrance of the second gate (Bab-üs Selam) of Topkapı Palace.

Another aerial view of Topkapı Palace (below).

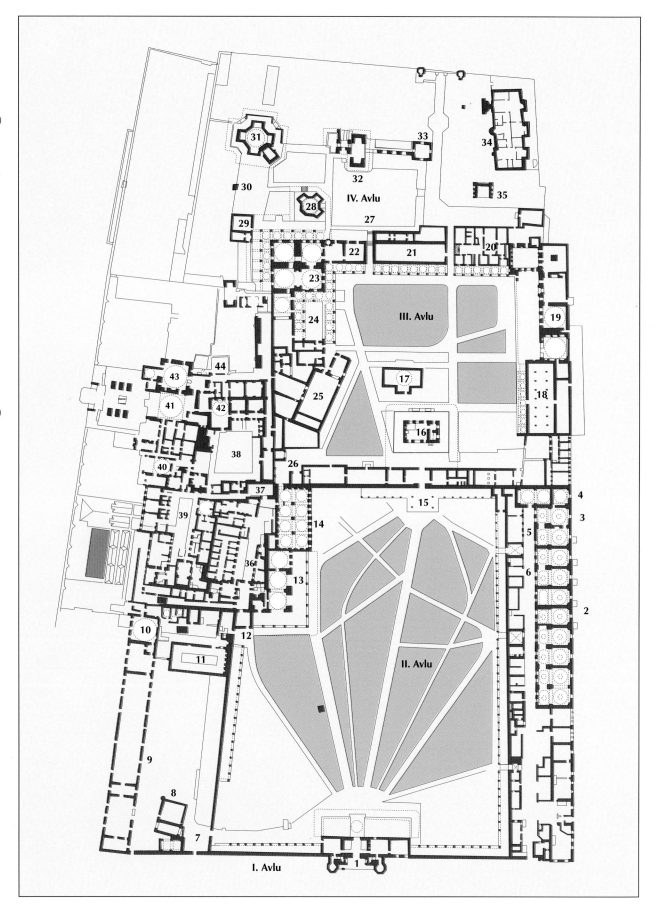

place where the Council would convene and the sultan's coronation ceremonies and ambassadorial acceptance receptions would be held.

On the left side of the courtyard is the Adalet Kule (Tower of Justice), whose shaft was built during the period of Sultan Mehmed the Conqueror. A tower was raised during the reign of Mahmud II in 1820. A pavilion was later added to the tower by Sultan Abdülaziz.

Known as "Kubbealtı," the Divan-ı Hümayun (Imperial Chancery of State) building is located beneath the Tower of Justice. Sultan Süleyman the Magnificent commissioned the Palace Architect Alaeddin to build this edifice between 1527-29. The Imperial Chancery of State consists of three domed spaces adjacent to each other. The first space is the apartment where the councils of state and public receptions were held. The other section belongs to the Imperial Chancery of State Apartment, whereas the last section was used as a Chamber of Archives. After having suffered major damage during the fire of 1665, these apartments were repaired during the reign of Mehmed IV. According to the inscriptions found here, they were also repaired in 1792 and 1819, during the sultanates of Selim III and Mahmud II.

Dating back to the 16th century, the colonnade section in front of the Tower of Justice was restructured with decorative wooden Rococo-style fringe in the 18th century. Sultans would follow the council meeting from the window above the apartment called "Kubbealtı." It was here that Grand Vizier and Council Viziers as well as the Anatolian and Rumeli chief military judges would meet to discuss the matters of the day and make related decisions. Grand Viziers would receive ambassadors in this place where the state was administrated. Receptions were held according to protocol in this place where several other ceremonies were also organized. The structure to the east of Imperial Chancery of State is that of the Foreign Treasury. Used by Grand Viziers, this treasury was set aside for state expenditures. Currently utilized as the Weapons Museum, where Turkish and Iranian weapons, as well as those of the Mamluks, are on display, this eight-domed structure remains from the period of Sultan Süleyman the Magnificent. The descending path next to Kubbealtı leads to the Sultan's Stables, where the palace horses were sheltered. Preserving rich riding costumes, the Raht Treasury is found at the northern edge of these barns. Moreover, the Corps of the Palace Guards and the Beşir Ağa Mosque are also found in this section.

The Tower of Justice. Topkapı Palace

The Palace Kitchens are located on the right side of the Second Courtyard, which is entered through three gates. It is known that these kitchens were constructed together with the palace. However, they were expanded later on by Sultan Süleyman the Magnificent. Destroyed by fire in 1574, the kitchens were completely renovated by the renowned architect of the era, Mimar Sinan. Today, the creamery and pantry structures of the kitchen are utilized as the palace archives and fabric warehouse. Comprised of four sections added during the era of the Süleyman the Magnificent, the

Confectionery and Beverage wings currently house the glassware, Yıldız porcelain and Turkish kitchen utensil collection. The precious Turkish-made glassware, as well as the coffee cups and dishes with pictures of sultans, are very attractive items. European porcelain and Ottoman flatware can be seen in what used to be the Cooks' Quarters, while Chinese and Japanese porcelain ware is on display in the main kitchen section. Now, let's talk a little about this world-famous Chinese porcelain collection.

Chinese and Japanese Porcelain ware: The Chinese began exporting their porcelain to the Middle East and Near East in the 9th-10th centuries, and later it came as far as Anatolia via the Silk Road, entering the Ottoman Palace. Today, the Chinese porcelain collection is comprised of 10,358 pieces, several of which are on display in the old palace kitchens. The Chinese porcelain collection at Topkapı Palace represents one of the three most important collections in the world. Moreover, the collection provides an uninterrupted chronology running between the 13th-19th centuries, allowing one to view the historical developments of Chinese porcelain.

Belonging to the Yuan, Ming and Qing dynasties, these porcelain specimens are categorized as "Celadon," "Blue-White," "Mono color" and "Poly colored." The 1,354 pieces of green-glazed celadons, which are believed to give off telltale signs whenever poison is put inside them, comprise of an important component of the collection. On display is a variety of items that include dishes, bowls, vases and ewers with decorative motifs, such as dragons, phoenix birds, fish and rosettes, on them.

The most important stage in Chinese porcelain was the use of cobalt blue in the 14th century. As a consequence, the first blue-white porcelain was produced during the Yuan period. There are currently 5,373 pieces of blue-white Chinese porcelain dating between the 14th –19th centuries in the collection. The fact that this collection possesses 40 of the 200 blue-white Yuan pieces that exist in the world today is a clear indication of its importance. The blue of this period was dark with black dots. The vessels in the shape of jars, dishes, bowls, vases and water flasks are decorated with mythological creatures such as Chi-ling, Phoenix and dragons, and floral designs. One of the 54 pieces of Ming-period blue-whites, called the "Annam Vase," dates to 1450. Crafted in Vietnam, the vase bears the name given to Vietnam during the T'ang period when it was a Chinese protectorate. There are mono-colored pieces in white, yellow and navy blue. Poly colored porcelain was produced starting from the first half of the 16th century. There are red, green, and pink colored porcelain works in this collection, which the 16th-century sultans who used them had the imperial jewelers decorate with gold leaf rims. These make up 273 pieces of the collection. The designs found

Ewer with lotus design painted in red enamel and gilt. Qing Dynasty, 18th century.

Blue-white Chinese dishes, vase and cup from the 14th-15th centuries.

in Chinese porcelains also had an impact on Ottoman craftsmen. This can be seen in the blue-white Iznik tiles. In addition to the Chinese porcelain in the Topkapı Palace, there are also upwards of 600 pieces of Japanese porcelain, comprised of dishes, vases, bowls and jars of large dimensions.

The Third Courtyard: One passes from the 2nd Courtyard into the 3rd Courtyard through the Bab'üs-Saade (Gate of Felicity). Ottoman sultans would ascend to the throne in front of this gate and receive the tributes of state notables here. This is where religious holiday greetings would be exchanged, and funeral processions for sultans who had passed away held.

Called the Akağalar Kapısı (Gate of the White Eunuchs), as it was the official residence and office of the white eunuchs of the palace, one passes into the Privy Court where the Inner organization of the palace is found. Although this gate was one of the first to be erected, it acquired its late 18th-century Rococo-style

appearance during the periods of Abdülhamid I and Mahmud II. Found here is the Library of Ahmed III, the Sultan's Audience Chamber, the Privy Chamber in the eastern corner, a mosque, as well as the dormitories of the Inner Court School, which opened into the courtroom in the south, with its pavilions.

One of the earliest structures in the Topkapı Palace, the Sultan's Audience Chamber, is situated just past the Gate of the White Eunuchs. It was Sultan Mehmed the Conqueror who said, "Above all, there should be an Audience Chamber. Let my viziers, military judges and head of the financial department meet here four days a week." The Sultan's Audience Chamber served as a functional and ceremonial hall of the palace. Here sultans would ascend to the throne and receive ambassadors. The structure's interior decoration was renovated for the last time in 1856 in the Empiric style.

The Library of Ahmed III is situated behind the Sultan's Audience Chamber, in the middle of the courtyard. It was constructed during the Tulip period in 1719 and functioned as the Palace Library. It has a fountain in front of it and staircases on both sides leading up to its entrance. The interior walls are covered in tiles whereas its cabinets are inlaid with mother-of-pearl and tortoise shell. The Kapı Ağası Dairesi (Apartment of the Gate Eunuch) is located just to the right of the gate. Further down the way, at the corner, are the Hamams of Selim II, which were used later on as the Palace School. Next to this was the Campaign Pages Quarters, where servants who ceremoniously washed the sultan's garments and turban were housed. Today, the costumes of many of the sultans are on display here.

The halls referred to as the Fatih Pavilions are currently utilized as the Treasury section. Moreover, a room in the adjacent bath has been cordoned off as a part of the Treasury. Situated next to this is the administrative part of the palace, which used to be the Pantry Staff Quarters. This is where those who prepared the sultan's meals and set his tables would stay. Next to this was the Treasury Pages Quarters.

The building known as the Treasury of the Guards, which has a connection to the Privy Chamber, houses the palace's clock collection.

Here, it is possible to see the most fascinating examples of Turkish clocks as well as those from Germany, Austria, Great Britain, France and Switzerland. In the northeastern corner of the courtyard is a structure called "Office of Sacred Relics." This was a private apartment of the sultans and is where the Throne Chamber was located. Pursuant to the transferring of the Caliphate to the Ottoman sultans in the 16th century, this section was sequestered to store the sacred relics. The structure next to the Office of Sacred Relics was the Mescid of the Privy Servants, which carried out the

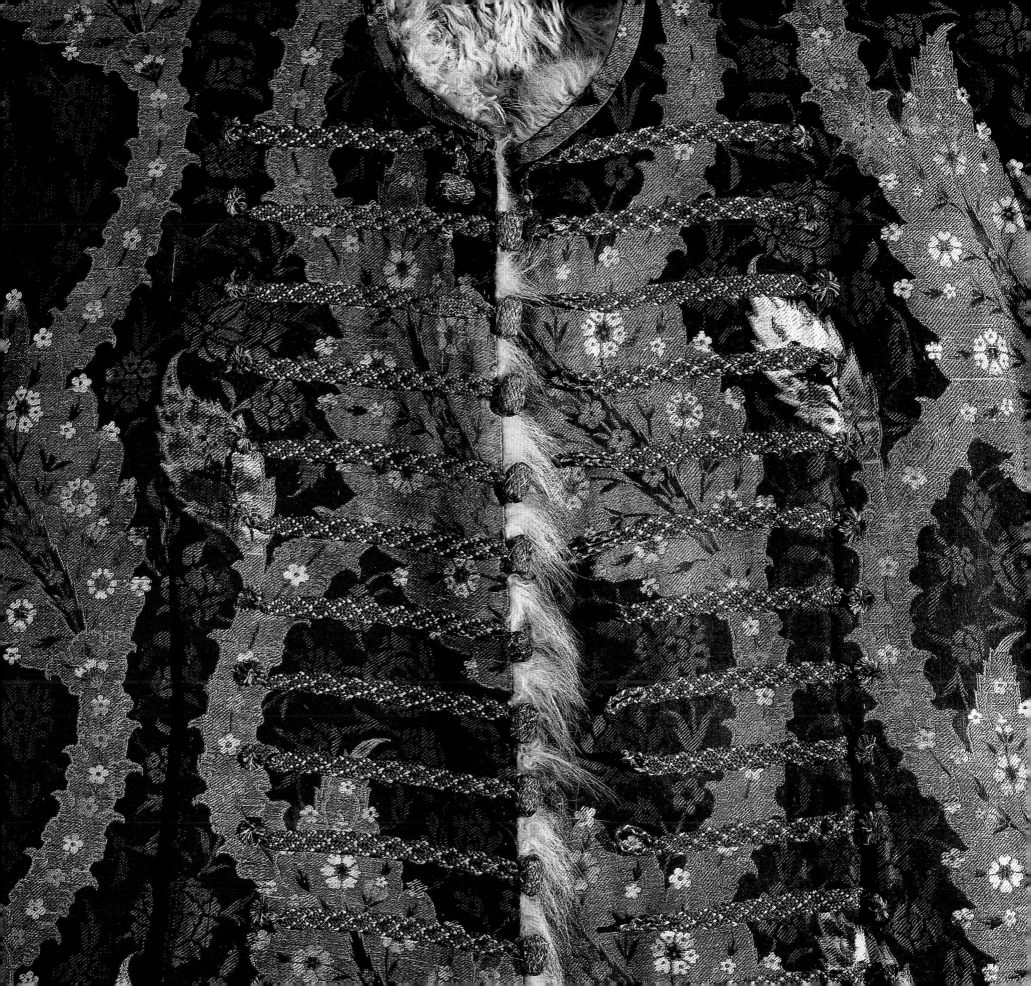

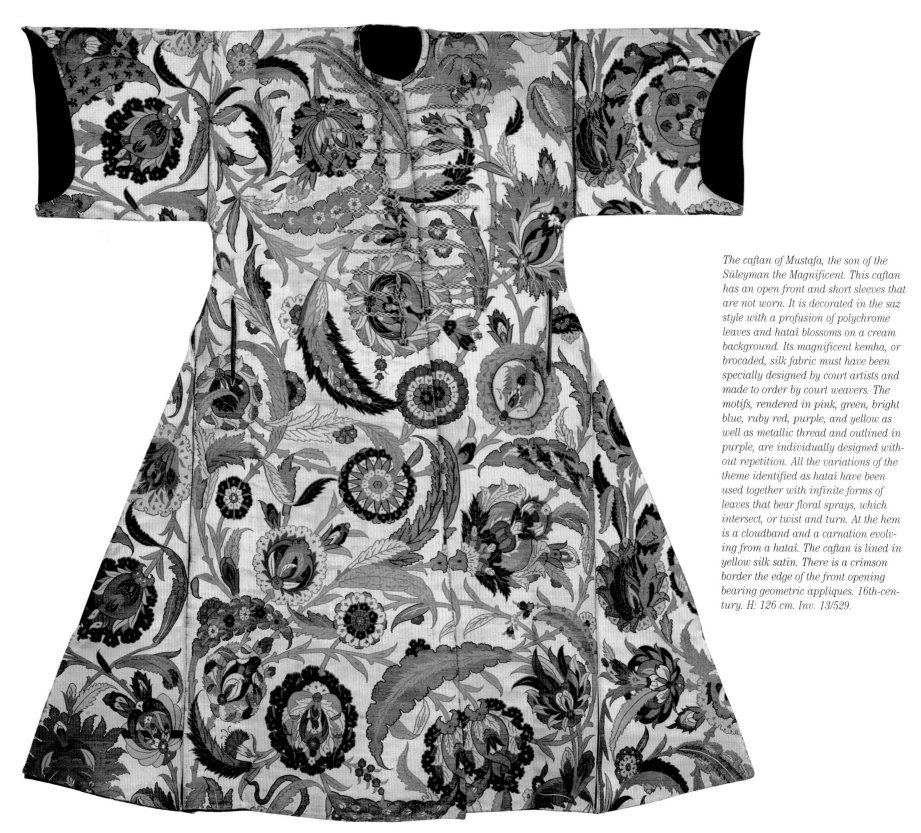

The caftan of Mustafa, the son of the Süleyman the Magnificent. This caftan has an open front and short sleeves that are not worn. It is decorated in the saz style with a profusion of polychrome leaves and hataî blossoms on a cream background. Its magnificent kemha, or brocaded, silk fabric must have been specially designed by court artists and made to order by court weavers. The motifs, rendered in pink, green, bright blue, ruby red, purple, and yellow as well as metallic thread and outlined in purple, are individually designed without repetition. All the variations of the theme identified as hataî have been used together with infinite forms of leaves that bear floral sprays, which intersect, or twist and turn. At the hem is a cloudband and a carnation evolving from a hataî. The caftan is lined in yellow silk satin. There is a crimson border the edge of the front opening bearing geometric appliques. 16th-century. H: 126 cm. Inv. 13/529.

Ceremonial caftan of Şehzade (crown prince) Bayezid (died 1562). Long-sleeved ceremonial caftan, sometimes associated with Bayezid II (1481-1512) but more plausibly belonged to another of Süleyman the Magnificent's sons. It is thought to have been made with cloth specially woven in the palace workshops in finest "Gülistani" kemha. Both caftans share patterns of the "saz yolu" type, with lanceolate leaves and large palmettes on curved stems, on dark green background. This pattern consists of countless variations of hataî, amidst lanceolate leaves in blue, pink, green, yellow and black. H: 150 cm. Inv. 13/37

private service of sultans. It currently houses a portrait collection of all the Ottoman sultans. The Gate of the Aviary is located on the northwest side of the Second Courtyard. Next to the Gate of the White Eunuchs are the Quarters of the White Eunuchs, a section of which displays Ottoman palace embroidery and leather specimens.

There are three interesting sections within Topkapı Palace's Privy Courtyard: The Sultan's Costume Section, the Treasury Section, and the Office of Sacred Relics.

The Section of the Sultans' Caftans: The Sultans' Caftans and Ottoman fabrics are displayed in the Quarters of the Campaign Pages. Because of the fact that Ottoman sultans were also the Caliphs of Islam, the garments they wore were preserved, thus forming the collection of sultans' caftans. The garments of deceased sultans would be saved in cloth bundles with their names labeled on top as a clear indication of which caftans belonged to which sultan. Besides these exquisite caftans, one can also view shirts with talisman motifs as well as children's garments, which were also preserved.

While most of the caftans were made with Turkish material, there are also those that were made from Iranian, Italian and Spanish fabric. The caftans were woven according to designs drawn by Imperial decorators in workshops established on palace grounds. Additionally, the reputation of fine silk garments woven in workshops in Bursa and Istanbul spread throughout the world. Sultan's caftans were fashioned from valuable material such as "kemha" (a compound-weave fabric that uses polychrome silks together with gold, gilded silver and silver metallic threads), "diba," "atlas" and "seraser," which is a very expensive silk woven from silver-gold alloys, and "çatma" (silk velvet, woven with gold, gilded silver, and sheer metallic threads). The sultans' garments have been preserved in chronological order, from Sultan Mehmed the Conqueror to Mehmed V Reşad.

The garments of the latter sultans had European influences in the manner of jackets and trousers, but then again, traditional caftans were still worn. Caftan styles remained the same for hundreds of years though there were some differences in the detail work. It is seen that caftans with Inner linings

Gold binding of the Divan of Murad III (1574-95).
This encrusted and gold worked cover was made by the court jeweller Mehmet Usta by order of Zeyrek Ağa, for the manuscript containing the poems of Murad III. Both the front and rear of the cover are decorated with a central gold oval şemse medallion with finials and four spandrels within a series of gold frames. The gold madallion and frames are decorated with curved stems and floral motifs in repoussé, encrusted with emeralds, diamonds and rubies. 1588 D.37x22 cm. Inv. 2/2107

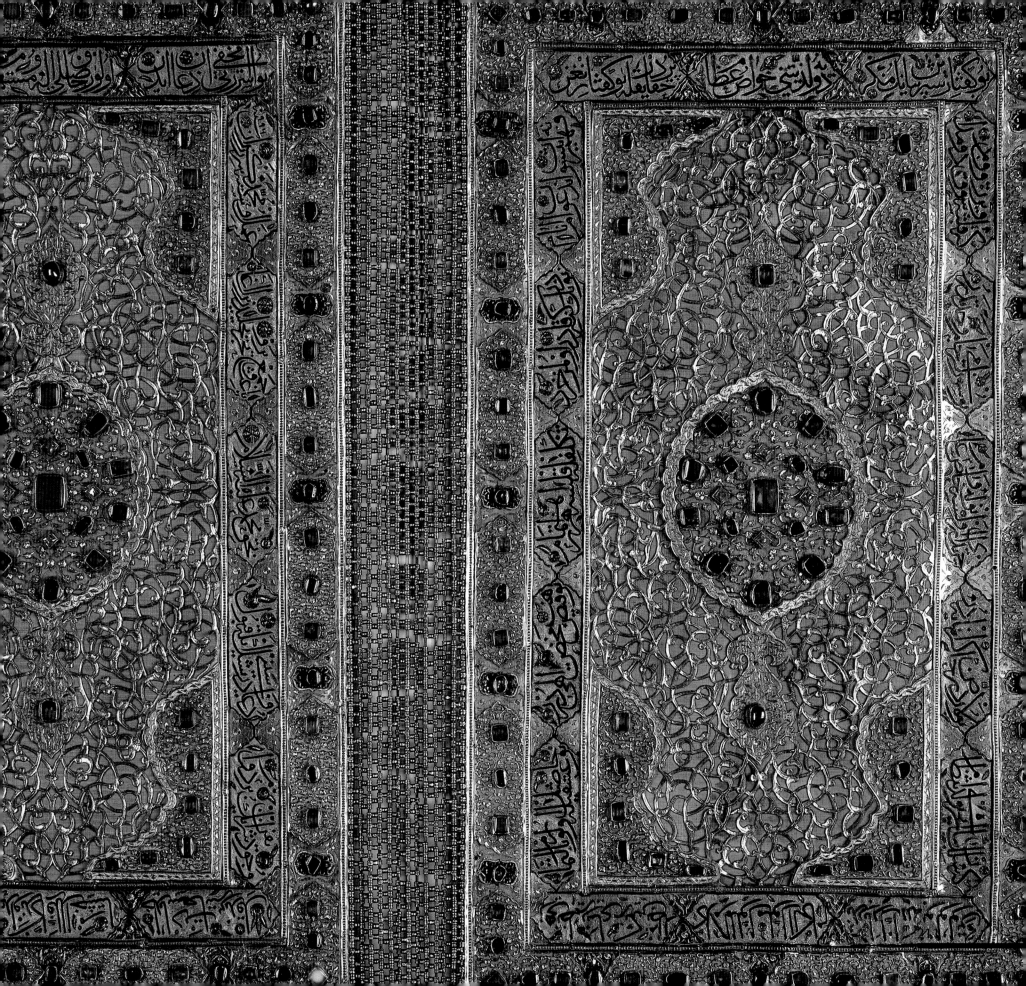

of plain colored silk, with judge's collars and long, loose sleeves open in front were preferred in all periods. The more opulent caftans that sultans would wear on special days and receptions have been displayed with additional pomp and care. Moreover, just as the summer caftans were made of thin material, one sees that winter caftans were made of heavier fabric and lined with fur. Among those on display in remarkably preserved condition are the "serenk" (a compound-weave fabric using two or three colors of silk) caftan of Mehmed II, the "kemha" caftan of Bayezid II, the silk velvet and "seraser" (a compound-weave fabric woven with silver and gold threads) caftans of Selim II, as well as Mehmed III and Murad III's silk brocade caftans with inner fur.

The serenk caftans of Bayezid II and Selim I constitute the finest examples of this material. There are also caftans made from silk. Examples of this can be seen in the caftans of Murad III and Ahmed I. In addition to these examples, there are a number of caftans in the sultan section that were made from other materials. The sultans' caftans constitute the finest examples of amongst a total of 1,550 garments found in this section. In addition to the sultans' garments, there are also around 40 carpets and prayer rugs of Persian designs, as well as samples of Ottoman fabrics.

The Treasury Section: The Topkapı Palace Treasury collection is exhibited in the Third Courtyard in three rooms called the Fatih Pavilions, and a forth connected to them. Though the state treasury was kept in the Yedikule Fortress for some time after the conquest of Istanbul, it was brought here later on. Palace Treasury is where priceless works are displayed. There were several other treasuries in the Ottoman Empire, such as the Foreign Treasury, which currently houses the Weapons Section. There was also the Ambassadors' Treasury as well as the Household Effects Treasury, the latter of which was located in the Sultan's Stables, where precious riding costumes were kept. Let's discuss how the most popular section of Topkapı Palace, and the world's most appealing treasury collection came about. The treasury of Sultan Mehmed the Conqueror was subsequently enriched with war spoils captured by Selim I during his

The Topkapı Dagger (1741)
This dagger, the symbol of Topkapı Palace, was made for Mahmud I in 1741 as a present for Nadir Shah of Persia. It was returned to the palace upon the outbreak of unrest in Persia. There are three 30-40 mm. oval emeralds on one face of the handle, the other side being decorated with enameled and mother-of-pearl fruit motifs. A hinged lid to the hilt, which acts as a setting for an octagonal -cut emerald 30 mm. in diameter surrounded by diamonds, opens to reveal a London - marked watch. The sheath is decorated with floral enamelled motifs on gold, and encrusted with diamonds towards the tip and hilt. Baskets of fruit in enamel are worked on both sides of the sheath. L.35 cm. Inv. 2/160

successful campaigns in Iran and Egypt. This is why Sultan Selim the Grim was known to have said, "If any of my descendents fills the treasury with money, then let his seal be stamped on the gate of the treasury. Otherwise, my seal shall remain." Well, fate should have it that the seal of the treasury gate was never changed throughout the duration of the empire. The treasury was opened by a commission of treasury servants and closed by the same commission. As a part of tradition, Ottoman sultans would have the treasury opened when they were coronated, view it ceremoniously, and make the effort to ensure its further growth. There were several ways money and priceless works would find their way into the treasury. The most valuable pieces of booty acquired from victorious wars would be registered into the treasury. Gifts brought here by ambassadors during ambassadorial receptions as well as gifts presented during coronation ceremonies made up the largest sources of the treasury. Moreover, priceless gifts would also be registered during wedding or circumcision receptions of crown princes as well as the birth of those connected to the dynasty. Craftsmen would also create very fine works and present them to the sultan and receive assistance from him. The wealth of statesmen who were executed or dismissed from their positions was also added to the treasury. Another source for the treasury would be works that were acquired for a price. Other than these, Ottoman sultans would have valuable items crafted for the Tomb of the Prophet Mohammed, which were sent to Kaabe in Mecca as gifts. These had come to make up quite a considerable pile at the tomb, as

every sultan would send these valuable items. They, however, were brought back from the Arabian Peninsula by Fahreddin Pasha and added to the Treasury during World War I in order to counter the concern that these lands were to be captured by other countries. They make up some of the precious items on display in the Treasury. Others there are the gifts exchanged between Sultan Mahmud I and the Iranian Shah Nadir Shah. When peace was finally made between the warring countries, Nadir Shah sent a world-famous throne to commemorate this peace. In return, Mahmud I had his palace jeweler prepare some precious works of art, which were ...quently sent ... with his ...assador to Nadir ... Upon reaching the ...anian border, he learned that Nadir Shah had been assassinated, whereupon he duly returned to Istanbul with the said gifts. Henceforth, they were placed into the Treasury. Among these works of art are the Topkapı Dagger and an arrow pouch adorned with precious gems. Gifts that arrived via in any of these ways were not the private property of the sultan, but rather were registered with the property of the Treasury. So, this is how the Treasury of the Ottoman Empire

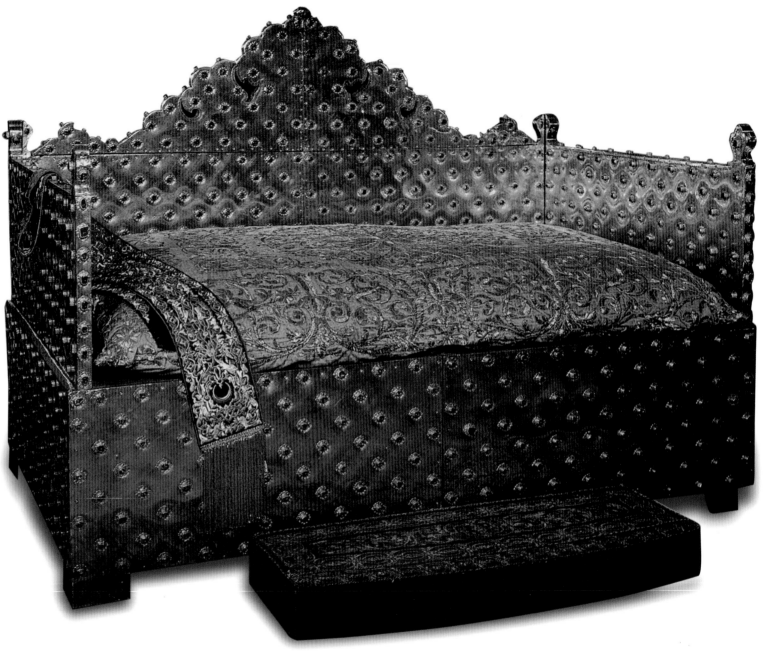

Ceremonial Throne. This throne was made by the master goldsmith at the Court, Ibrahim Bey, in 1585 by order of the vizier of the time, Ibrahim Pasha and presented to Murat III. (1574-1595) It is decorated with ten gold plaques over a walnut frame and is encrusted with 954 chrysolites. The throne weights nearly 250 kg. The throne was used by the Ottoman sultans during ceremonies and for coronations until the late Ottoman period, and is portrayed in a number of miniatures. 1585, D.108x178 cm Inv. 2/2825.

accumulated. It is unequalled in the world and people from all over the world view it with great awe. These works of art were once kept locked up in cabinets. It was Sultan Abdülmecid who began to display a portion of these works. Successive sultans continued to do the same, whereby it became a tradition. The majority of the items found in the Treasury today belong to the 16th - 19th centuries. In addition, there are also a few samples of works belonging to the Byzantine, Seljuk and Memluk periods. These precious treasury items can be categorized in the following way:

Thrones: The most remarkable group in the treasury section consists of its thrones. One of these is an ebony throne belonging to the 16th century. Its side and back surfaces are made of ebony and it has calligraphy designs fashioned from ivory and mother-or-pearl inlays. It is thought that this portable throne was used by Murad IV during his Baghdad Campaign. The second throne made of wood is the Throne of Sultan Ahmed I, or the "Arife" Throne, which had the name of Ahmed I etched into the dome. This throne was crafted by Mehmed Ağa, who was the architect of the Sultan Ahmed

Mosque as well as a manufacturer of inlaid furniture. Displaying the finest of 17th-century craftsmanship, this throne is covered with tortoise shell and mother-of-pearl over walnut. The inlays are decorated with precious stones. There is a clock cabinet adorned with precious stones located above the dome, with an alabaster top piece positioned over this. There is also a throne pendant inside the dome. One of the most important thrones in the treasury is that of the Bayram Throne. Ottoman sultans would sit on this throne during Coronation and Bayam ceremonies and receive those presenting tributes. Imbedded with a total of 954 chrysolite stones, is believed that this gold-plated wooden throne was presented to Sultan Murad III by the Egyptian Khedive, İbrahim Pasha. The most striking and valuable work in the Treasury Section is the Throne of Nadir Shah. Previously known as the Throne of Shah İsmail, recent research has shown that it belonged to Nadir Shah. The Iranian Shah Nadir Shah sent this throne to Ottoman Sultan Mahmud I as a token of peace. The wooden throne is covered in enameled gold plates. Its outer surface is thoroughly adorned

with emeralds, rubies and pearls. Determined to have been crafted on the subcontinent, it is assumed that Nadir Shah acquired it as loot acquired during his campaign there. This Indian crafted throne was subsequently sent to the Ottoman Palace as a symbol of the peace made between the two powers. Another interesting group in the treasury is that of the "aigrettes," which were costume jewelry affixed to the turbans worn by Ottoman sultans or crown princes. In essence, these were the symbol of the dynasty. Decorated with emeralds, rubies, diamonds and pearls, these priceless pieces of jewelry were worn atop turbans or fezzes together with the feathers of peacocks, egrets or birds of paradise. When the sultan passed away, these aigrettes would be placed into their tombs. Later on they were collected in the Treasury, where they came to constitute a separate group.

Pendants that determined the place of the sultan comprised yet another group. These were decorative elements that symbolized the rulers and complimented the thrones and the décor of important places. Several pendants found in the treasury today were made for the tomb of the Prophet. Emerald pendants made for Ahmed I, Mustafa I, Abdülhamid I and Abdülmecid are the most impressive. Decorative pendants with diamonds and enamel over silver of Sultans Selim III and Mahmud II are recognized from their inscriptions and monograms. Another interesting group in the treasury consists of the implements of war imbedded with precious stones. An example of these is the bejeweled suit of armor belonging to Sultan Mustafa III. Comprised of steel braids, the armor was coated with gold in various places. Additionally, his sword and stirrups were also gold covered and studded with precious stones. Another priceless work that goes into this group is a bejeweled helmet. All the swords, daggers, scimitars, "yataghans" and maces are decorated with priceless gems. One can see bow and arrow pouches adorned with diamonds, rubies and emeralds. Several valuable daggers are on display in the Treasury. These include the inscribed yataghan of Sultan Süleyman the Magnificent, the dagger of Sultan Selim the Grim, which has an alabaster handle, as well as the dagger with an

The Spoon-maker's Diamond.
One of the most valuable objects in the treasury is the Spoon-maker's Diamond. The gem is 86 carats and 42x35x16 mm. in size. The entire diamond, with setting, is 70x60 mm. Inv. 2/7610.

Detail of velvet quiver.
This green velvet quiver is decorated with four large gold plaques and four small plaques, also gold encrusted with emeralds, rubies and diamonds. The case is also trimmed with gold. The backside is covered with green ustufa decorated with red flowers. The quiver was among the gifts sent to Shah Nadir of Persia from Mahmut I in 1746, which were subsequently returned on the Shah's death. 1747. D.22x42 cm Inv. 2/454

emerald-studded handle that was given to Mehmed IV by his mother, Hatice Sultan. The one known as the "Topkapı Dagger" is considered to be the tour de force of the treasury. As we mentioned earlier, this dagger was to be presented as a gift to Nadir Shah from Mahmud I, who had it crafted in the palace jewelry workshop. It is one of the finest works reflecting Ottoman jewelry making. There are three large emeralds on the handle of the dagger, which also has an emerald covered clock on the top and a gold sheath studded with diamonds. The most important group in the treasury consists of the works made from alabaster. These are crystals covered with gold and imbedded with precious stones. Among these various small, but priceless, artworks are water flasks, ewers, pen boxes and cups. Making up another group are gifts of art that arrived from abroad, including two statuettes decorated with diamonds, rubies and enameled pearls which were presented to Abdülaziz from the Moslems in India, a gold basin with an ewer and end table presented to Sultan Abdülhamid II from France, an ebony cane which came from India, as well as a oil lamp fashioned from green marble, which was a present from Czar Nicholas II.

Pendant oil lamps, incense holders, rose-water sprinklers, bejeweled pendants and candelabras, which were all made for the Kaabe, are also part of the treasury. The gold candelabras that Abdülmecid had made are amongst the works in the treasury that attract much interest.

Another group in the treasury, of which there are several examples, is the bejeweled book covers. The great majority of them belongs to the 16th century and is covered in gold and embedded with precious stones, such as emeralds, rubies, diamonds and turquoise. Moreover, among these works that show the artistry of Ottoman jewelry making there is the golden Koran holder of the council of Murad III. In addition to these, there is a distinct place for embroidered Koran bags that were used by crown princes and

Aigrette. The body of this 18th-century aigrette is pear shaped and is crowned by five jewel-studded leaf-shaped flanges, from the top of which projects a tall plume. The entire surface of the aigrette is covered in diamonds. In the middle of the pear-shaped body are two emeralds and a ruby. There are four enormous pearls at the base of the jewel-studded crown, which itself is covered with diamonds, with rubies interspersed. On either side of the body of the aigrette, there is a pair of long chains covered with diamonds. Gold sticks to which emeralds are attached hang from the chains. 18th-century. 32 cm in length. Inv. 2/284.

The crest is enameled in green. In the center there is a large diamond framed with rubies. These in turn are surrounded by eight diamonds. Four diamonds are set over the central gem from which spring sprays of pearls and emeralds. Sprays of emeralds and rubies set on gold stems are attached to the crest of the central spray of pearls. The six lateral sprays are encrusted with diamonds, emeralds and pearls. 18th-century. H: 17 cm. Inv. 2/159

sultans during their school days. There are few pieces of women's decorative costume jewelry in the treasury due to the fact that they were the personal belongings of the women. However, it is possible to see examples making up this group in the treasury. Among these are the "Kevkeb-i durri" and "Şebçırağ" diamonds and the branch pin brooches with diamonds. Undoubtedly, the most valuable piece in this group is that of the "Spoonmaker's Diamond." Unearthed in Eğrikapı during the period of Mehmed IV, this diamond was sold to the Palace. It was expertly crafted down to 86 carats in the 18th century and dressed with smaller diamonds. It is simply not possible to display all of the contents of the extremely rich Ottoman treasury at the same time. For this reason, exhibition of items is on rotation.

The Apartment of the Holy Cloak and Sacred Relics: Constructed during the reign of Mehmed the Conqueror as the Sultan's Private Chamber, this apartment is situated in the north corner of the Privy Courtyard. The hall of first entrance is called the Anteroom with Fountain, as it has a water-tank with a fountain in the middle. The first chamber to the right of this anteroom is the "Arzhane," where the sultans received guests. As for the second chamber in the corner adjacent to this, it is the Sultan's Chamber

A miniature depicting the accession ceremony of Sultan Selim II carried out in the ceremonial tent in Belgrad in 1566. Upon the death of Süleyman the Magnificent during the Zigetvar Compaign, Grand Vizier Sokullu Mehmed Pasha requested that Selim II take over his father's position as sultan. Selim II was declared the new sultan at an accession ceremony held inside the Otağ-ı Hümayun (Imperial Tent) in Belgrad. In the miniature, the sultan is accepting those who have come to congratulate him. 1568. Nakkaş Osman, Nüzhet el Esrar el Ehbar der Sefer-ı Zigetvar. Inv. 1339, s111a.

Return of Sultan Mehmed III from the Eğri Campaign. When Mehmed III (1595-1603) returned victorious from the campaign, victory parades were held. Silk cloth was used along the road in order to keep back the crowds. Eğri Fetihnamesi, 1598. Inv. H1609-69a.

Next page:

Revan Pavilion. This pavilion was built during the reign of Murad IV in commemoration of the Revan campaign. Octagonal in plan, it contains one large chamber with three alcoves*. Covered on the interior with 17th century tiles, the chamber is illuminated by shutters that are decorated in mother-of-pearl and tortoise shell inlay. The upper level of the chamber has mosaic polychrome glass lights. Niches in the walls contain panels of 16th century tiles that have tinted glaze. The interior of the dome bears evidence of recent restoration, being entirely covered with decorative motifs of a later period. Four oculi open into the covered dome itself. The façade of the pavilion is partly covered with white and polychrome marble. From the point at which the tile ends, the pavilion is paneled with blue and white tiles up to the drum of the dome. * The pavilion is surrounded by porticos and covered with a dome.

To the left of the Anteroom with the Fountain are the Quarters of the Guards of the Private Chamber, otherwise known as the Destimal Chamber. The walls of all these chambers are decorated with Iznik tiles from between the 16th –18th centuries. The windows and door wings also display some of the finest examples of wood craftsmanship. After the Caliphate passed to the Ottoman sultans with the conquest of Egypt by Sultan Selim the Grim in 1517, the sacred relics which were hitherto under the protection of the Islam Caliphs in Egypt were subsequently brought to the Topkapı Palace. While these relics were stored in various places around the palace, they were gathered up during the reign

of Mahmud II and preserved in a room that had been used as the throne chamber since the reign of Mehmet II. It is called the Chamber of the "Hırka-ı Saadet," as the cloak of the Prophet Mohammed is found here amongst the holy relics. Precious artworks sent to the tomb of the Prophet Mohammed by means of the Ottoman sultans' "Sürre Alayı" (procession accompanied by gifts) were removed from the Arabian Peninsula during World War I and sent back to Topkapı Palace. Thus, the collection of works in this section was further enriched. Decorated with 16th-century tiles and Koranic verses on the walls, this chamber was once utilized as the sultan's throne chamber. It is now the place where the most valuable of sacred relics are housed. The chest of the Cloak of the Prophet is found on a throne that was made during the time of Murad IV by the palace head jeweler, Zilli Mehmed. Next to this, the "Sancak-ı Şerif" is preserved in another chest. The two swords and the bow of the Prophet Mohammed are exhibited in the front part. Personal items such as a letter, a tooth, hair from his beard, a footprint and a seal all belonging the Prophet Mohammed are displayed in the room next door, which is called the Arzhane.

The gold scabbard of Hacer-ül Esved can also be seen in this chamber. Among the priceless Korans found in the section of the Sacred Relics is the one that was being read by Prophet Osman when he was martyred. These works and others are exhibited on a revolving basis.

A number of works such as the scepter of the Prophet Moses, the sword of the Prophet David, the swords of Prophet Ebu Bekir, Ömer, Osman and Ali, the wooden relief of the Mescid-i Aksa, Seven Hairs of the Prophet, and the cover, keys and golden water gutters to the Kaabe Stone, are all part of the collection of the Sacred Relics.

The Fourth Courtyard: One enters the Fourth Courtyard through a gap in the Third Courtyard. The terrace of this courtyard, which is in the direction of the Golden Horn, was expanded in the first half of the 17th century during the periods of Sultan Murad IV and İbrahim, with new pavilions being added on top. There is a pool with a fountain on the marble terrace in front of the pavilions. Surrounding this pool is the Revan Pavilion to the south, the Circumcision Chamber to the west, with the Baghdad Pavilion situated a bit further on. The İftariye Pavilion is also situated between these pavilions. It is thought that the Circumcision Chamber found on the marble terrace was constructed during the period of Sultan Süleyman the Magnificent. It assumed its current appearance after the changes made during the period of Sultan İbrahim.

This pavilion derives its name from the fact that it was where the circumcision ceremony of the crown princes of Ahmed III was conducted.

Baghdad Pavilion (1639)
This octagonal-planned pavilion was built by Murad IV to celebrate the Ottoman conquest of Baghdad. The central dome is flanked by vaulted extensions. They open out into a broad portico on the front covered by wooden eaves and supported by 22 marble columns. Between them run geometric-interlace carved balustrades.

The Circumcision Chamber is famous for its Iznik tiles, which were produced between the 16th-18th centuries. It is understood that these tiles were removed from other places in the palace and assembled here. The most important of these are the blue-white Iznik tiles dating to the 16th century.

Murad IV commissioned the architect Koca Kasım Ağa to construct the Revan Pavilion opposite the Circumcision Chamber, to commemorate the Revan Campaign of 1636. The exterior of the octagonal-shaped plan pavilion is covered with marble up to a certain height, and then covered with 17th-century tiles above that section. There are wide wooden fringes found on the two façades of this pavilion that has three vaulted recesses. A copper brazier graces the inside of the pavilion while its walls are covered with tiles up to the skirt of the dome.

The inside of the dome is decorated with engravings of flora motifs. The top row of the two sets of windows is of the stained glass variety whereas the window shutters are inlaid with mother-of-pearl and tortoise shell. The turbans worn by sultans during ceremonies were preserved here, which is why the Revan Pavilion is also known as the "Turban Chamber." The Baghdad Pavilion is situated in the corner of the "Courtyard with a Pool" overlooking the Golden Horn. This octagonal-plan pavilion having four recesses on the inside and four on the outside was also constructed by Murad IV in 1639. Looking at it from the garden side, it seems to have two storeys. The pavilion is surrounded by a wide wooden fringe resting on 22 marble columns.

The outer lower windows are covered with marble up to the top line while the upper windows are adorned with tiles. The pavilion is covered with a dome that is decorated with engravings whereas its three doors as well as its cabinets and window shutters are inlaid with mother-of-pearl and tortoise shell. Its walls are covered with 17th-century tiles. Koranic verse, which was written between the gaps of the upper and lower windows by Enderuni Mehmed Çelebi in white on a dark blue background, surrounds all of the walls.

The İftariye Arbor is situated between the Baghdad Pavilion and the Circumcision Chamber. This arbor, which is also called the "Mehtaplık," (Moonlight) was erected in 1640 during the Sultan İbrahim era. Made entirely of metal, the inside of the İftariye Arbor was furnished and Bayram greetings and salutations would be made here. Moreover, the sultans would break their fast here during the month of Ramadan, particularly if it occurred during the summer, hence its name "İftariye."

In the section of the Fourth Courtyard to the west of the Courtyard with a Pool is the Anteroom Pavilion. Although there is no exact date as to when it was built, it is understood from its name that it was constructed by Grand Vizier Koca Mustafa Pasha between 1670-83. It has survived to this day thanks to several major renovations. There is a structure to the right of the Pavilion called the Chamber of the Head Doctor or "Tower of the Head Male Servant." This structure consists of a tower on top of the protective walls that encircled the palace of Sultan Mehmed the Conqueror. It derives its name from the fact that the head doctor would care for patients and administer medicine from here. Descending down a marble staircase, one comes through the Tulip Garden to the part where the Anteroom Mosque,

Circumcision Chamber. The square-planned structure, consisting of a pavilion chamber and annex which was built during the reign of Sultan İbrahim on the site of earlier buildings torn down for that purpose. The chamber is covered with a coffered vault embellished with brushwork tracery and the walls revetted with tiles dating from the 16th and 17th centuries.

the Garment Chamber and the Mecidiye Pavilion are all found. The Mecidiye Pavilion was constructed by Sultan Abdülmecid and is the final pavilion to have been built in the palace. The pavilion and the Garment Chamber were built at the same time. With these structures, which were erected opposite an extraordinary view of the Bosphorus and Marmara Sea, we bring to an end the architecture of Topkapı Palace. Let's provide the world the Topkapı Palace in its entirety by also including the Harem, which is a mysterious structural complex in and of its own.

The Harem

Sultan Mehmed the Conqueror had a palace built in Bayezid Square after he took Istanbul in 1453, but it proved to be too cramped for the growing population of the palace. He decided to have what is known today as Topkapı Palace built in its stead. While the palace was under construction, between 1472-78, Sultan Mehmed II also had the first compounds of the Harem put into place. The Harem was continually expanded upon until Murad III, who had it restored and transferred altogether to the new palace. His successors carried on the expansion work in the Harem. With the addition of new sections over time, the Harem steadily grew.

Now, let us begin our tour of the Harem, something that has kept its mystery for 300 years, never to hear the echo of any other men's footsteps but those of the Sultan.

The Main Entrance Gate of the Harem: To the east of the 60 meters x 8-10 meters Eunuchs' Courtyard lies the main entrance gate to the Harem. Today's exit gate, the Gate of the Aviary, lies to the left of this main gate.

Above the gate, there is an inscription bearing Koranic verse describing manners concerning the respect to be shown in entering homes. As one enters through the main iron gate, there is a courtyard with large mirrors on walls where the eunuchs used to post round-the-clock watch. The sections inside were all in control of assistant masters. There are three Inner doors: the one on the very left leads to the Corridor of the Concubines' Quarters, the one in the middle to the Courtyard of the Dowager Sultan, while the third goes to the Golden Way, which measures 46 meters x 4 meters. This gate was used by the sultans and crown princes. After girding his sword, the sultan would return to the Harem with a glorious parade. After saddling up his horse at the Courtyard of the Dowager Sultan, he would follow the route along the Golden Way to his throne. It was traditional for him to toss gold coins at the concubines waiting for their sultan along both sides of the Golden Way. The door in the middle opens into the Courtyard of Dowager Sultan. The chambers of the Dowager Sultan and the Sergeants-at-Arms are situated around this

courtyard. The Dowager Sultans, Sergeants-at-Arms, Favorites and Felicities would reach their chambers through this door.

Courtyard of the Concubines: The door on the left was the one used by the women not related to the sultan's family, concubines, masters and assistant masters. The concubines would keep this door locked from the inside with sliding iron bars. Even the eunuchs would be refused access to the courtyard. In order to be able to reach the concubines or, in another words, the Courtyard of the Sultans' Wives, this door has to be used. The inscription above that door bearing the words, "Our God, who is able to open all gates, please open some lucky gates to us, too!" is clearly reflective of their desires.

Just past the door, there are some stone benches on the left hand side of

An aerial view of the Harem, one of the most interesting sections of the palace.

the corridor. The eunuchs would put trays loaded with meals on them and close the door. Then, the door at the rear end of the corridor would open and a small group of concubines would come to pick up the trays. The "Courtyard of the Concubines," accessible from the end of the passage, was constructed in the 16th century. This courtyard has porches on three sides, a fountain, a large domed bath and the entrance gate to the stairs going to the "Chamber of the Assistant Masters." Right across from the courtyard are the kitchen, cellar, launderette and the toilets. Next to it is the "Chamber of the Sultans' Wives" and the "Concubine Quarters."

The Concubines' Quarters: The door next to the "Chamber of the Sultans' Wives" opens to the stairs called "40 Stairs." The fifth door beside it is the Concubines' Quarters where about 25 concubines were quartered. Inside are two divided sections. Its windows overlook the courtyard and it has a mezzanine supported by marble pillars. The pillar gaps were closed by

The gilded bronze latticework divides and the warming up section of the Sultan's hamam. This hamam was originally designed in the 1580s by Mimar Sinan and was used by sultans and their wives. It was remodeled during the mid-18th century, when it acquired an ornamental fountain, marble tub and sauna done in the western style of the age.

The Chamber of Selim III by the Abdülhamid I Chamber reflects the beautiful samples of Ottoman Rococo.

wooden partitions, with new sections being added to accommodate the increasing concubine population in the Harem.

The novice concubines would be quartered on the bottom floor whereas the more experienced ones would have their stations upstairs. There would be one old concubine stationed to a quarter of ten younger ones. They would straighten their rooms during the day and make their beds to sleep at night. The hearth on the ground floor would heat the entire chamber. The more experienced concubines would inspect the novice concubines, while they would be inspected by the Assistant Masters. The Masters, of course, would inspect their Assistants.

The "40-Step Stairs" next to the Chamber of the Sultans' Wives led down to the Harem Hospital. The cellar of the Dowager Sultan lies at the foot of the stairs, whose total number of steps is actually 52. Since the Concubine Quarters were situated to the east of this courtyard, it was called the Courtyard of the Concubines. Adjacent to them are those of the Patients' Master. There are two sections here, one of which is the Hospital Bath and the other, the Hospital Kitchen. Across the courtyard, there lies a launderette and a place where they used to cleanse dead bodies. Those who died in the Harem would be cleansed there and taken out through the "Meyyit Kapısı" (Door of Death).

The Chamber of the Sultans' Wives: The chambers belonging to the Second, Third and Fourth Wives are located to the right of the courtyard. The Chamber of the First Sultan Wife was located in the Courtyard of the Dowager Sultan next to the Anteroom with a Hearth. As it is known, the wives of the sultans were ranked First, Second, Third and Fourth. The Chamber of the Second Sultan Wife has a wooden door and very low sofa. It has two rooms with walls covered by Kütahya tiles, which were repaired on a number of occasions. From here, one enters a narrow corridor. The toilets were located on the right side and a set of stairs on the left side. This corridor goes into the main hall. On the wall to the right there are some shelves, a hearth and a sink with cold and hot water faucets. The windows on the opposite wall have the look of flower bouquets. The room contains a hearth that has been refurbished. It has a copper brazier in the middle and couches upholstered with silk fabric. The room on the left contains small cabinets in which beds and belonging were kept. The upstairs bedrooms belonged to the Sultans' Wives. While the ceiling of the small room is unadorned, that in the main room has a dome adorned with calligraphy. It is thought that the rooms originally built for the wives of the sultan were later used by the Assistant Masters of the Harem.

The Chamber of the Dowager Sultan: Chamber of the Dowager Sultan

is entered through the Sultans' Wives' Chamber. Once sons ascended to the throne, their mothers would leave the old palace and come to the Harem with pomp and circumstance and settle in the Chamber of the Dowager Sultan. Since they were the head of the Harem, it was natural for them to command many concubines and maids. The Chamber of the Dowager Sultan is reached by walking past two tiny galleries. There lies a spacious courtyard just outside the chamber. The entrance to the chamber is located in that courtyard. After becoming familiar with this courtyard, we will then continue our tour of the chamber. This open-air courtyard became the center of the Harem as its many compounds expanded around it. The Golden Way, which is thought to have been built during the time of Sultan Mehmed, lies to the south of the courtyard, while the quarters belonging to the Masters and Assistant Masters of the Harem are to its west. The Pharmacy of the Harem is located next to these. The buildings situated east of the Chamber of the Dowager Sultan, near the Golden Way, belonged to Haseki Sultans. After giving birth to sons, the wives of sultans were referred to as "Haseki Sultan." The maternity wards are situated next to those compounds. There is a hall with a hearth on the other side of these compounds.

The Haseki Compound is accessible through a door in that hall. Thought to have been built during the reign of Sultan Mehmed, this chamber has a big hall with a hearth. Hürrem Sultan is said to have been the first to use this chamber. Later on, those pavilions were covered and new quarters were added to the building. Access into the Anteroom with a Fountain is gained through a door from the same yard. Since the sultans used to saddle down their horses there after girding on a sword, it is therefore called "The Gate of the Throne," too. The sultans would also bid their mothers farewell there while leaving for a war and, donning chain mail, they would mount their steeds. The Dowager Sultans' Chamber can be reached by walking past two tiny galleries by the Kadınefendi Chamber. The first room just at the entrance belonged to the head maid of the Dowager Sultan. It is adorned with a brazier, tile on its walls, and recessed cupboards covered with mother-of-pearls. The Chamber of the Dowager Sultan can be reached from there. The main entrance of the Chamber of the Dowager Sultan is in the Courtyard of the Dowager Sultan. There are two rooms, the first of which was used as the waiting room for the incoming guests, while the other was the entrance. The stairs opposite where the guards used to stand on duty lead to the rooms upstairs. The Felicities and the Favorites who had passed the night with the Sultan used to stay in those three rooms. Above its door is an inscription dating to 1667, just two years after a devastating fire. Just beyond that door is the vast dining hall of the Chamber of the Dowager Sultan. The hall has two floors. The first floor is covered with 17th-century tiles. The ornaments on the upper floor and on the dome were arranged by Mahmud II in 1817. The dome is adorned with hanging leaves and bunches of grapes. There is also a hearth in the hall. The side of hall where the window is situated was most likely utilized as a dining room. To the left of the dining hall, there is a bedroom, which can be reached through a pair of wooden gates adorned with mother-of-pearl inlays. Its vaulted walls with mirrors are covered with 17th-century tiles. On the left side is a bed, the canopy of which is embroidered with gold leaf. A curtain is draped over the bed. Situated across from the bedroom is the Dowager Sultan's prayer room and connecting the two rooms is a door and two windows with bronze

Valide Sultan's Chambers. Attached to her bed chamber, this tiled room contains a tile painting of Mecca in underglaze, painted in shades of green, also a dominant color throughout the tile revetments covering the walls, some of the finest of the period. The windows are covered with bronze grills.

Selim III had a chamber built for his mother Mihrişah Sultana above the Valide Sultan's Chamber. It has two rooms whose walls are adorned with landscape images.

latticework. On its walls there is a picture of Mecca, dating from 1667, painted in a pleasant light green color.

As the Chamber of the Dowager Sultan was restored numerous times between the 16th-20th centuries, it has naturally lost most of its originality. Its dome was repaired towards the end of the 18th century and decorated with figures reflecting that era. The hearth in this chamber was the last section to have been repaired; it was restored with tiles taken from the Apartment of Cevri Kalfa. Those concubines under the control of the Dowager Sultan were housed on the ground floor. One can see all three floors of the Chamber of the Dowager Sultan from the courtyard. Now something should be said about the Chambers of Mihrişah Sultan and Selim III.

The Chamber of Mihrişah Sultan: The top floor of the Chamber of the

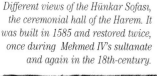

Different views of the Hünkar Sofası, the ceremonial hall of the Harem. It was built in 1585 and restored twice, once during Mehmed IV's sultanate and again in the 18th-century.

Dowager Sultan belonged to the mother of Selim III, Mihrişah Sultan. It is accessible via a set of stairs on the side. Along those stairs, there are landscape figures that reflect the influence of western art. Once her son ascended to the throne, Mihrişah Sultan moved into that chamber with great ceremony. Selim III commissioned the palace architect Melling to construct this chamber for his mother. After he was deposed, Selim III had the chamber converted into a hidden section in which he lived with his mother for about a year. The double-roomed chamber is square-shaped with a flat ceiling. The ceilings of the both rooms are adorned with Baroque and Rococo- style gold leaf. In the interior room is a marble, Baroque-style hearth adorned with European tiles. On both sides of the hearth, there are western-influenced landscape paintings. The sides and the top of the window in the large niche in the second room are decorated with the same sort of paintings.

The Chamber of Abdülhamid I: The bedroom of Abdülhamid I is situated adjacent to the Chamber of the Dowager Sultan opposite the Sultan's Hamam (Bath). It was the practice until the era of Osman III, for Ottoman sultans to spend their nights at the Murad II Pavilion. Designed by Head Architect Davud Ağa in Rococo-style decoration, this chamber was used by Osman II and Abdülhamid I. Because it was Abdülhamid I who had it restored, the chamber has since been remembered by his name. This place is rectangular-shaped and has three covered sections. The walls and the ceilings are all decorated with Baroque and Rococo-style gold leaf. The chamber has a Baroque-style fountain covered with pink and blue European gold leaf tiles. One reaches the Chambers of Selim III and Mihrişah Sultan by passing through this chamber.

The Love Chamber of Selim III: The Love Chamber of Selim III is accessible from the Bedroom of Abdülhamid I. While Osman III had it built, it was Selim III who decorated and used it. The Chamber consists of two rooms called the Chamber of Selim III and the Love Chamber of Selim III. The latter was built in 1790. It has a wooden ceiling and is square-shaped. The walls and the ceilings are all decorated with Baroque and Rococo-style gold leaf. There is a marble hearth in it reflecting one of the finest examples of Turkish Rococo style. Its hearth has white tiles on its interior and blue flower patterned tiles on its exterior.

The Osman III Pavilion: A long narrow corridor connects the Love Chamber of Selim III to the Osman III Pavilion. Construction on this pavilion began during the reign of Mahmud I and was completed by Osman III in 1754. The hanging garden in front of the Sultans' Anteroom is situated over the Inner palace walls and façade overlooking the Golden Horn. The

pavilion, which has a flat courtyard in the front, consists of three interconnecting rooms. The walls are adorned with Rococo and Baroque-style gold leaf. Among those ornaments seen are brown and blue patterned European tiles. In addition, in the niche of the middle room, there are some western-influenced paintings pertaining to the life of the Inner palace. This enormous room is the most opulent room of the chamber.

The Sultan and the Dowager Sultan Hamams: The Sultan and the Dowager Sultan Hamams are found on the right hand side as one walks towards the Sultan's Anteroom from the Chamber of the Dowager Sultan. The most beautiful hamam in the Harem is the Sultan's Hamam, which was fashioned from white marble by Mimar Sinan in the 16th century. Adjacent to this is the Dowager Sultan Hamam, which was restored by Turhan Sultan, the mother of Mehmed IV. It has the same plan as the Sultan Hamam. It was convenient to heat both of them by one stoke hole as they were next to one

another. The Sultan Hamam has three separate sections. The first section was used as the Rubdown and Relaxation Room. From traces remaining on the walls, one assumes that it was decorated with calligraphy inscriptions. There are some wooden couches with white upholstery covers in this tranquil section. The Disrobing Room has a gold leaf wooden cabinet and a crystal mirror with a gold leaf frame. The main bath is in the third section. The caldarium (hot) part of the bath is accessible through the tepidarium (cold) part. It is illuminated by means of both small and large round windows affixed in the dome. The iron cage part to the left was the place where the sultans washed. It was completely enclosed with iron bars to protect the sultans from being assassinated. As we leave this place with elegant taps and small cabins, we can reach the most glorious hall of the palace, that of the Sultan's Anteroom.

The Sultan's Anteroom: Sultan's Anteroom was the hall where sultans would receive their guests and spend their day. The Sultan's Anteroom was built under the supervision of the architect Davud Ağa in 1585, a little after the Murad III Pavilion. This domed hall was completely restored during the 18th century by Mehmed IV after the fire of 1665. Osman III had the balcony and the couches installed underneath, after which it began to be used as a ceremonial hall. It has a total of 26 windows, including those on top. The dome rises on four tapered arches decorated in the Rococo style. Wooden parts of the dome, such as the windows and cabinets, are ornamented with various embroidery designs. The original 16th-century decoration of the arches provides a clue as to the architectural style of the period. The Sultan's Anteroom was covered with blue-patterned Delf tiles on a white background. On either side of his throne, which was positioned opposite the entrance, are large Chinese vases. To the left of the throne are oriental couches with velvet upholstery. The balcony above was where the orchestra played. The symmetrically placed clocks were the presents of Queen Victoria. The wooden armchair in another corner was presented to Abdülhamid II by Kaiser Wilhelm II. The mirror-covered cabinet in the left corner of the hall is, in fact, a hidden door. Sultans would traverse to other parts of the Harem through that door. The "Ayet-ül Kürsi" Koranic verse covers the tile on the walls of the hall. The part above the throne bears the year of restoration (1666) and the name of Sultan Murad IV, who commissioned the work. The inner parts of the tapered arches and pendentives are embellished with 16th-century calligraphy. The original style was maintained during the restoration process.

The Anteroom with a Fountain: One walks through the Anteroom with a Fountain in order to reach the Pavilion of Murad III from the Sultan's

Chamber of Murad III (1578). Built by Mimar Sinan, the walls of the pavilion are decorated with 16th–century Iznikl tiles of the era. A close-up of the fabulous tile work around the hearth (below).

Anteroom. This was the gallery where Crown Princes and Sultans' Wives used to wait outside before they entered the Sultan's Anteroom. The arched, rectangular-shaped anteroom derives its name from the fountain in one of its walls. The name of Sultan Mehmed IV is inscribed over the fountain. The walls of this vast hall are covered with 17th-century tiles; one of its doors opens into the Anteroom with a Hearth. There is a door in the Anteroom with a Hearth that leads into the Courtyard of the Dowager Sultan. This gate was also used by the sultans, hence its other name, the "Throne Gate." The sultans would reach the Anteroom with a Hearth and enter their chamber by walking past the Anteroom with a Fountain. The walls of this chamber containing a vast hearth are decorated with 17th-century tiles. According to the inscription on them, it was restored by Sultan Mehmed IV after the 1665 fire. The Anteroom with a Hearth opens into the Chamber of the Head Haseki. The Chamber of the Crown Princes lies above the Head Haseki chamber. The Pavilion of Murad III is reached through the Anteroom with a Fountain.

View of the Library of Sultan Ahmed I. The Ahmed I library by the Murad III mansion.

The Sweetmeats Room was constructed by Ahmet III in 1705 (opposite).

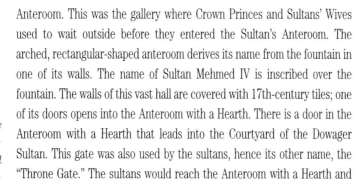

The Pavilion of Murad III: One of the most charming chambers of the Harem is the Pavilion of Murad III. It was built by Mimar Sinan in 1578 and reflects the splendor of the 16th century. The whole chamber is covered with red coral tile scattered on a blue tile background. Highly placed windows illuminate this splendid pavilion. Covering the chamber is an impressive dome that is classically decorated. The symmetrically placed couches are embellished with calligraphy.

The hearth in the chamber reflects all of the beauty of the era. Opposite the copper-coated hearth lies a recessed marble fountain from which water still flows. They used to leave the tap on most of the time to prevent others from overhearing their conversation. Other significant works of art in that chamber include cabinets inlaid with mother-of-pearl, doors reflecting the splendor of the era, oriental couches and braziers. There is the "Ayet-ül Kürsi" Koranic verse winding itself all over the tile that covers the walls. Beneath the pavilion is a large pool. Moving forward, let's enter the Library of Ahmed I through the opposite door.

The Library of Sultan Ahmed I: This is a small square-shaped chamber that is decorated with Iznik tile from a later period than those used in the Chamber of Murad III. This place was built by Sedefkar Mehmed Ağa during the reign of Ahmed I. The library is particularly striking because of its unique cabinets upon which there is a figure of a bull covered with mother-of-pearl. To the left of the entrance lies a fountain in a niche dating to 1608. The upper parts of the walls are covered with blue and white, green and white tiles from the 17th century.

Sweetmeats Room: Found next the Chamber of Ahmed I, the "Sweetmeats Room," also known as the "Privy Chamber of Sultan Ahmed III," it is one of the smallest and most remarkable rooms located in this section. Built in 1705, this room is adorned with engraved panels of sweetmeats on plates and bouquets of flowers. Attracting the attention of visitors in this square-shaped room is the mirror to the left, small niches, the copper-burnished hearth, small crystal candelabras and a round copper tray on the floor. The Crown Prince Chambers are entered from here.

Twin Pavilions (Crown Prince Chambers): After walking past the Pavilion of Murad III, one reaches the Crown Prince Chambers, otherwise known as the "Çifte Pavilions." It consists of two interconnecting rooms accessible by a staircase. These rooms were built in the 17th century by Murad IV and Mehmed IV. The first room, which is almost square-shaped, belonged to Murad IV and is accessed via a narrow door. The room is nearly square in plan and has a dome covered with a variety of gold-gilded motifs. Hidden by a ceiling for many years, it existence was only realized after the

Two views of the Çifte Pavilions. Comprised of two rooms, they are also referred to as the Chambers of the Crown Princes. The walls of both rooms are embellished with the finest tiles of the period.

final restoration work in the Harem was completed and the ceiling was removed. The walls of the rooms are adorned with dazzling 17th-century tiles. The top of the hearth to the right of the entrance was adorned with engravings similar to tile motifs. There is a strip of inscriptions and tiles between the two windows. There is also some writing on the Inner parts of the windows. From this extremely attractive place with its wonderful stain glass windows and faucets found in the Inner windows, one passes through a tiny door and into the second room, which is said to have been used by Mehmed IV. A hearth lies to the left side of the room and a brazier stands on the right side. The vault-shaped mirrored ceiling decorated with geometric and plant motifs, and the mother-of-pearl inlaid cabinets positioned on both sides of the hearth are all of indescribable beauty. The difference in elevation between the two rooms was only realized after the final restoration work was completed. These Privy Chambers, the interior and exterior of which are completely covered in tile, were allocated to the Crown Princes after the 18th century.

The Apartment of the Favorites: After leaving the Crown Prince Chambers, where the princes were once either full of hope or fearful of death, one encounters the "Courtyard of the Favorites" and the "Pool of the Favorites." Down the way is a place called "Şimşirlik." The chambers behind the courtyard are the Apartments of the Favorites, which are comprised of five separate rooms on the upper floors, which were built by Abdülhamid I. The ground floor of these apartments belonged to the sultan and was called the "Mirrored Anteroom of the Sultan." From the anteroom, the first rather large room is accessible via steps that are hidden in a cabinet. The other comparatively smaller rooms are lined up in a row next to this room. They can be reached via the staircase found next to the Golden Way. And, finally the corridor of the Golden Way is come upon.

The Golden Way: Somewhat narrow in width, the Golden Way measures 46 meters in length. It was a street on which the concubines could walk back and forth whenever they felt the need. The Golden Way was witness to many important events in Ottoman history. For example, this is where Cevri Kalfa literally stopped the traitors bent on murdering Mahmud II in their tracks by throwing hot embers into their eyes. While it has a rather uninspiring appearance, it derives its name from the fact that this is the place where sultans would toss gold coins to the feet of the concubines lined up on either side of the path during special occasions. The Golden Way is the last stop of the spellbinding world of the Harem. We exit the Golden Way through the Aviary Gate to emerge back into the Third Courtyard.

Dolmabahçe Palace

This palace was the favorite of the sultans during the final years of the Ottoman Empire

At the beginning of the 17th century, the site where the Dolmabahçe Palace now stands was a busy inlet where the Imperial Navy maintained its warships and organized festivals marking the departure of war campaigns. The Commodore of the Navy, Halil Pasha had an immense amount of soil excavated from a nearby hill and dumped here during the reign of Sultan Ahmed I. After years of filling in this bay with earth, the spot was eventually transformed into picnic grounds reserved for the sultans. From then on, palaces and summerhouses were constructed along the entire shore at various times. Mahmud II found Topkapı Palace too gloomy and at Dolmabahçe Palace after having the wooden palace renovated. When Sultan Abdülmecid ascended to the throne, he chose it as his residence, but not without first having it torn down and then completely rebuilt. In 1843 he commissioned the architect Garabet Balyan to construct what was to become the present palace. Although the building was officially completed until 1854, the sultan did not take up residence here until 1856. Built in the lavishly decorative style of the 19th century, the building was initially called the "Sahil" (Coastal) Palace, but later referred to as the "Dolmabahçe" ("Filled in Garden") Palace because of the fact that it was built using landfill.

Dominating the exterior contours of the palace is the high central Reception Apartment, along with the selamlık and harem apartments, which are connected via corridors. The Apartment of the Crown Prince is at the end of the Harem Apartment while the Apartments of the Dowager Sultan projects 95 meters off from the Harem, adjacent to the Apartment of the Crown Prince. The interior layout of the palace is very simple and regular. Groups of rooms in a straight line open into a larger chamber. For instance, each private bedroom of the Harem opens into a central living chamber. The length of the marble pier, which is adorned with magnificent steel banisters, stretches for about 600 meters. The mother of Sultan Abdülmecid, Bezmialem Sultan eliminated one of the missing elements of the palace when she had the Dolmabahçe Mosque constructed. It was Abdülhamid II who had the fine Clock Tower erected. Thus the composition of the palace was essentially complete. Nevertheless, there were other buildings added to make the palace more serviceable. These were the

Private Treasury of the Sultans, an Upholstery Section, the Glass Pavilion as well as Pasha Apartments in the part extending towards Beşiktaş. There was also a Pharmacy and Sweetmeat Kitchens, which spilled over to the opposite side of the road to Beşiktaş. In addition to these, there were

A façade view of Dolmabahçe Palace, which was constructed on orders of Sultan Abdülmecid between 1843-56 (opposite).

The Palace Treasury Gate (below).

The plan of Dolmabahçe Palace: 1. Sultanate Gate,
2. Ceremonial Gate; 3. Yalı Gates;
4. Dignitaries' Waiting Room; 5. Sultan's
Reception Chamber; 6. Hall of Circular Crystal
Stairs; 7. Zülveçheyn Hall; 8. Library; 9. Baths; 10.
Muayede Hall; 11. Bedroom of the Dowager Sultan;
12. Blue Hall; 13. Room of Atatürk's Death; 14.
Pink Hall; 15. Bedrooms of the Sultan's Wives; 16.
Bedroom of Sultan Reşad
17. Harem Baths; 18. Harem Section
The Hall of Crystal Circular Stairs (below).

service units such as the Carriage House, Palace Stables, a Harem for the Crown Princes as well as a Woodcutters' Apartment, and a Palace Soup Kitchen. All these were located along a strip that stretched for almost another kilometer along the shore, on either side of the main palace, from Kabataş to Beşiktaş. However, over time, some of these have been torn down; others are used as public offices today. There is yet another structure mentioned in the historical sources – the Palace Theater, which was built by Sultan Abdülmecid I and later destroyed in a fire.

The Gates

The palace features two highly elaborate gateways, which are representative of the empire's magnificence. The Treasury Gate faces the Clock Tower, as well as the Sultanate Gate, which faces the main roadway, Beşiktaş Caddesi. There are some decorative elements on the sides of the gateways, such as a pair of columns with composite capitals, oyster shells, leaves and branches, rosettes, strings of pearls and eggs.

The gate pediments are adorned with hanging wreaths, small flower vases and rose windows. Above the Treasury Gate, in green and gold, is the monogram of Abdülmecid (1853). Beneath this is a double-line inscription by the poet Ziver (1857). The Sultanate Gate bears the same monogram (1854).

The other important gates of the palace are the Dowager Sultan's Gate, the Upholstery Gate and the Kitchen Gate. There are also five waterside Pavilion gates along the shore. The palace garden was surrounded with high walls in accordance with the social lifestyle of the Ottoman Palace. However, the way the garden landscaping is situated on a flat area is unlike traditional Turkish gardens. The Chief Gardener Sester and his assistants who worked in the garden during the period of Abdülmecid were all from Germany. Thus, it is quite natural to notice western influences here.

The outer façades of the palace are a combination of Baroque and Eclectic Renaissance styles. Floor levels are separated by different styles of column capitals. Triangular pediments crowning the façades and the marble parapets of the balustrades along the faces blend in a wide range of symmetrical motifs drawn from western designs such as cartridge rose windows, medallions, oyster shells, hanging wreaths, decorative vases, and curled leaves. Mostly the work of Italian and French artists, the interior was made up of primarily alabaster, marble and porphyry.

The furnishings and interior décor are the work of the famed French designer, Sechan, who also created the Paris Opera. One can perceive the influence of the French palaces in the fresco technique in the ceilings, as well as the fine gold leaf embossed designs seen in the doors, doorjambs, windows and window frames made from mahogany and balsam wood. Moreover, scenes of nature and people are also represented on the canvas paintings stretched over the ceiling, which is the most highly decorative section. The three-storey palace is comprised of 285 rooms, 43 halls, six balconies and six Turkish hamams. There are some rather large halls in the Sultan's Private Apartment and Harem apartments with names like "Methal," "Süfera," "Merdiven," "Zülveçheyn," "Küçük Binek," "Muayede"

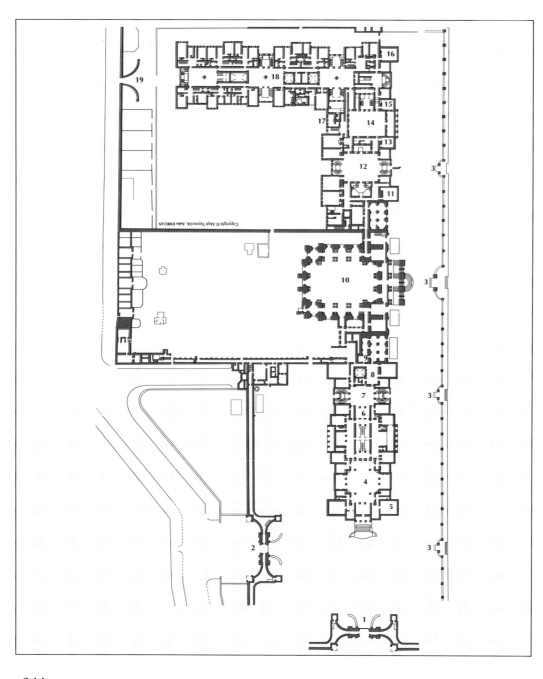

and "Mavi." All of these were the scenes of historical events. These rooms and halls are covered with 131 carpets and 99 prayer rugs measuring a total area of 4,452 m2. Another striking feature of the interior décor is the abundance of Baccarat and Bohemian crystal utilized in the chandeliers and hearths. These sparkle and tinkle, adding warmth and character to the otherwise vast, empty spaces in the palace. The most splendid of the 36 crystal chandeliers hangs from the 36-meter high ceiling in the Muayede Hall. With a total of 750 light bulbs, this behemoth fixture weighs 4.5 tons and was a present from Queen Victoria. The palace includes an Art Gallery with an impressive collection of works by noted artists such as Zonaro, Fromentine, and Ayvazovski. 280 Chinese, Japanese, Yıldız and European porcelain vases, 156 historic and elegant timepieces, 581 candelabras made of silver, crystal and other precious materials, 11 silver braziers, crystal and silver stem and flatware, and room decorations.

It is worth seeing the alabaster balustrades of the staircases on two sides that wind up from the grand entry hall of the Mabeyn. In addition to this set of stairs, there are another five grand staircases as well as six or seven service stairways. An elevator was added during the illness of the Turkish President Mustafa Kemal Atatürk, the founder the modern-day Republic of Turkey. The building was originally heated with braziers and hearths. Sultan Abdülhamid II had tile porcelain stoves built into the palace, whereas finally, Sultan Mehmed V Reşad had the central heating and electricity grid installed during his reign.

The inlaid parquet floors, particularly those in the sultan's private apartments, are another elegant feature, and are extremely unique. As the palaces and the priceless items inside them and even the Ottoman sultans were considered public property, they were transferred to the nation upon the demise of the Ottoman dynasty through Law No. 431, dated 03 March, 1924. Today, these palaces are administered by the Department of National Palaces under the aegis of the Department of the Turkish Grand National Assembly.

The Entrance Hall

The magnificent Entrance Hall is reached by passing through the greens and whites of the gardens, and up a staircase of 11 gray marble steps. Both the balcony and triangular pediment, which are supported by four columns, give this foyer a very distinguished appearance. From here, one passes into the entry hall, whose interior design was changed by the Caliph Abdülmecid Efendi. It is decorated with two matching four-meter high mirrors on the walls on either side of the corridor, as well as with French flower vases that were presented to Sultan Abdülhamid.

The main parquet-floored hall is supported by four columns. Beyond the columns, to the left and right, are smaller lounges. The ceiling is ribbed and colorfully engraved. There are rooms in every corner. The one to the right of the entrance is the Chamber of the Grand Vizier, while the one to the left is the Room of the Sheihkulislam. There are also two sections separated by rows of opposing columns. On the side of the chamber facing land, there are hearths. Ceramic tile covers the base of each of them while the upper portion is made of crystal. The large vases standing in front of the lounges

Dolmabahçe Palace's Hall of Circular Crystal Stairs is lined with artificial marble columns topped with composite capitals. The parquet and wood paneling is very attractive.

on the side were made in the Yıldız Tile Factory. Each is in four parts and feature illustrations by Turkish and French artists. The palace, which was illuminated with candles and coal gas prior to electricity, acquired a central heating system during the renovation work of 1910. At the same time, radiators were placed in various places in the hall.

The Hall of Winding Crystal Stairs

A magnificent crystal-inlaid staircase takes us upwards. There is an enormous vaulted glass dome overhead and a magnificent chandelier hanging down into the hall, which is surrounded by artificial marble columns. There are two projections – one each on the landward and seaward sides. The ceiling and column beams are decorated in panels having gold-gilded reliefs. The ceilings of the sections along the side are also embellished in gold-gilded designs. All of the entry and exit doors to this grand stairwell are made of gold-gilded mahogany. These all give rise, along with the carpet runners on the stairway, to a warm atmosphere. There are four candelabras with crystal stands in each corner of the hall with four more with silver stands in the stairwells. This harmonizes with the smaller crystal chandeliers in the side vaults.

Two silver flower vases of Indian origin are located in the salon's garden-side lounge. The base of one is decorated with images of a lion and a horse while the other contains reliefs depicting stags. The upper portions of both are decorated with colorful raised stones. On the central table is a musical clock. Crafted by artisans in the Shipyard of the Golden Horn, the clock bears the monogram of Sultan Mahmud II and is decorated with gold, rubies and diamonds. The gold embroidered upholstery material on the set of furniture is the same as that used for the curtains. There is also the same arrangement on the seaward side.

The Dignitaries' Waiting Room

The small room in front of the waiting room was reserved for translators. In the waiting room proper, two gold leaf vases from Berlin, each adorned with deep blue enamel, grace the corners of the room. Baroque-style silver candelabras rest on the central table. A gold leaf crystal mirror is located to the right of the entrance. Among the elegant furnishings of the room is a pair of gold leaf bronze clocks and candelabras on the buffet. Constructed in a Gothic style, the ceiling was designed to give the illusion of infinity.

The ceiling is ribbed and decorated with gold leaf. The décor of the main waiting room is made up of many of the fine elements common to most rooms of the palace, i.e., gold leaf, mahogany, and crystal, among others. A carpet covers the entire floor and there are crystal hearths and mirrors on either side of the door. Like other rooms, this one is decorated with a fabulous crystal chandelier. Of particular note here is the unity created by the graceful curtain-like blending of the walls, ceiling and windows. The total effect, although extremely ostentatious, is nonetheless very pleasing to the eye.

The Hall of the Diplomatic Corps

The four corners of this grand hall sparkle with hearths of cut crystal, painted tile, and gold leaf. The cloaks are adorned with Chinese porcelain vases and Sevres candelabras. The ribbed and sectioned ceiling is

Also known as the "Crimson Room," the Dignitaries' Waiting Room derives its name from the matching color of the drapes and furnishings. Dolmabahçe Palace.

decorated with raised, gold leaf roses. There are three recesses, one each on the landward, seaward and garden side, each separated from the hall by two columns. A Baccarat crystal chandelier hangs in the center of this room where the momentous decision was made to change the Turkish alphabet script from Arabic to Latin. In addition to the Hereke-covered furnishings, crystal and silver candelabras complete the room's ambience. The monogrammed piano on the landward side of the room is French and is inlaid with precious metal. Two sets of furniture, one on the landward side and the other on the seaward side, are covered with silk material that matches the curtains.

The Sultan's Reception Chamber

This was the room where the sultan received foreign ambassadors. The entry, where the accompanying delegations would wait, is decorated with a fine cornice encompassing three windows heavily embossed in gold leaf.

Decorated in crimson and gold, the Audience Chamber, also known the Crimson and Gold Room, is filled with paintings depicting victorious battle scenes. A set of candelabras and a Sterling silver vase stand on a marble table in the center of the room.

The room is completed by two red crystal hearths at either side of the entrance. In front of the hearths are small tables, which were gifts to the sultan from Napoleon. One of these depicts the French Emperor with the ladies of his life, while the other depicts him with angels. The lower panels of the walls are solid mahogany, whereas the upper panels are decorated with engravings and gold leaf. One exits this hall through a door that is symmetric to the entryway. After passing through the hall with the alabaster balustrades in the same direction, visitors then enter two interconnecting rooms that open into a small corridor. The one on the inside is the Porphyry Room.

A silver vase crafted in India.

Situated on the first storey of the palace beyond the Hall of the Circular Crystal Stairs and over the entrance, the Hall of the Diplomatic Corps was used as the Dignitaries' Waiting Room. Dolmabahçe Palace.

Sultan's Reception Chamber. Situated in a corner of the Hall of the Diplomatic Corps, this was where foreign envoys were received.

An ivory and silver candelabra.

The Porphyry Room

Located on the upper floor of the Sultan's Private Apartment on the side facing the sea, its name is derived from the artificial porphyry plaster used to make the walls and ceiling. It has two doors decorated with walnut sidings and gold leaf; one opens into a small corridor and the other into the Hall of Winding Crystal Stairs. Between these two doors along the edges are furnishings comprised of a console-shaped marble hearth embellished with reliefs of flowers and acanthus leaves with two vases and a gold leaf/porcelain composite bronze clock, which is a fine example of French Baroque. The ceiling is ribbed and is decorated with artificial porphyry stone. Though there is no chandelier in this room, a row of light bulbs was installed along the bottom of the ceiling. One can see the most artistic parquet flooring of the palace in this room. Among the room furnishings are gold leaf consoles along two of the walls, a vase made of green-veined jasper stone, flower vases and stands, gold leaf bronze candelabras, and an engraved center table with black mosaic stones. This room was one of the important rooms in which the last Ottoman sultans received visitors. Sultan Murad V received visitors presenting tributes upon his coronation, and a concert was held in honor of certain Balkan rulers during the reign of Mehmed V Reşad. A piano recital was also given in this room in honor of the Serbian King Black Yorgovich on 03 April 1910.

King Alexander of Yugoslavia met with Atatürk in this room during his visit to Istanbul on 04 October 1933. Atatürk held a meeting with the King of England, Edward VIII in the Porphyry Room on 04 September 1936. The parquet and ceiling decorations in the room in front of the Porphyry Room are distinctly beautiful.

The Zülvecheyn Hall

"Zülvecheyn" translates into English as "two-sided," and, true to its name, this hall overlooks both the sea and the garden sides of the palace. The hall's ceiling, which is separated into three sections, is supported by gold leaf- covered artificial columns having composite capitals. The entire ceiling is also done in gold leaf. The parquet on the floor is in a pattern of interlocking star shapes. On the seaward side of the hall are mirrors and consoles, which face one another, that are covered with metal having gold-gilded reliefs and the monogram of Abdülmecid. The matching furniture and curtain fabric is of Turkish Hereke manufacture. A carved table sits upon a Hereke carpet. On the table is an 18th-century Chinese bowl with pink designs together with blue-white Chinese and Japanese vases. In the right corner of this hall is an apartment with three rooms that were turned into a library during the time of Caliph Abdülmecid. On the far side of the room is a mirror-topped Bohemian red crystal hearth. On either side of the hearth are mirrored consoles over which a 60-candle chandelier hangs from the middle of the ceiling with crystal column candelabras adding more ambiance.

The marble table under the chandelier with dragon feet is carved and covered in gold leaf while the dark blue Sevres porcelain vase on top of the table is decorated with gold leaf and bronze. This room originally served a religious function for the palace as the site of prayers at religious holidays, funerals, and weddings. When the sultan received "Tranquility" lessons here, he sat at the seaward side on top of a cushioned sofa surrounded by his attendants. Each year during Ramadan, this room was filled with prayer rugs, and a special section was screened off from the women of the Harem. In addition to these religious functions, the Zülvecheyn Hall was one of the most suitable of the large rooms in the palace to hold large dinner receptions. Two major receptions took place here shortly after Sultan Mehmed V Reşad ascended to the throne in 1909, one for the Viceroy of Egypt, and one for the King and Queen of Bulgaria. During the time of the last Caliph, Abdülmecid, two banquets were held in this room, one for his wives and one for his Crown Princes.

This room served as the Presidential Dining Room during Atatürk's presidency. During these times, a Turkish traditional orchestra would perform at on the seaward side, and a western orchestra would play on the side of the room near the stairs. When Jordanian King Abdullah stayed in Dolmabahçe Palace, he received some of his guests in this hall. One goes out the door on the left of this hall into a narrow corridor; the room on the left of the corridor is the Music Room. Beyond the Music Room are the hamams of the Sultan.

The Marble Hamam

The enclaved ceiling of the restroom of the Marble Hamam is adorned in an intriguing architectural composition. The diamond-shaped middle part is decorated with gold leaf reliefs, whereas the crystal chandelier hangs in the center of the room. Entering the room, one encounters a striking huge bath door of gold leaf and plastered mahogany, embossed with the monogram of Abdülmecid. The small entry inside features the bath in two partitions on the right and the toilet to the left. The alabaster of the bath was shipped from Egypt. Stylistically, this bath does away with the Turkish tradition of unadorned hamams as it is decorated and possesses some western elements. This shows us that the two styles were carefully synthesized and used in the palace. The two rooms of this bath open out to a terrace facing the sea. This is why it gets plenty of light, both from the ceiling and the windows. The bath has one large and two small washbasins, all of which have silver faucets. The floor is covered in gray Marmara marble and the doorknockers are made of crystal.

The Harem

Another steel door at the end of the corridor connecting the selamlık with the Harem ensures passage into the entrance corridor of the Harem. The room on the right of this corridor, which faces the sea, is where the Dowager Sultan would receive her guests. The sofas and curtains are made from red Hereke fabric, utilizing the same material as the wall coverings. To the right of the entrance is a marble hearth decorated with gold leaf and reliefs. The oval mirror with its marble reliefed frame above it reaches up to the bottom of the ceiling.

The doors on either side of the hearth are opulently adorned. The floor is covered with a French Aubusson carpet. The middle part of the ceiling is dome-shaped and decorated with battle-axes, helmets, swords amongst garlands with a motif resembling the bow of a ship done up in high relief, using an illusory engraving technique. The other sides are colorfully engraved. Weapons of war are seen in relief form at the bottom of the ceiling. There are small vases sitting on a console in sections separating the windows in the cornice gaps. The red-white crystal chandelier hanging from the ceiling completes the opulence of the room.

Just after leaving the room, an organ can be seen on the right hand side of the corridor. From there, one goes through another door into the Blue Hall, and then into the Bedroom of the Dowager Sultan on the right.

The Bedroom of the Dowager Sultan

Decorated with gold leaf and reliefs and standing on the right hand side of the room is the wooden, canopied bed of the Dowager Sultan. Next to it is a bronze, mother-of-pearl jewelry box, which was crafted in the workshops of the Yıldız Palace in 1902. Its design is commensurate with the abundant gold that appears in the rest of the room's furnishings. The ceiling is made

Zülvecheyn Hall. Stretching from the seashore inland this wide room was where chants were sung and prayers were performed during Ramadan.

The Blue Hall. This hall derives its name from its dominant color. The room in which Atatürk passed away is in a corner of this hall (opposite).

of handmade cloth. Exiting the Bedroom of the Dowager Sultan, one enters the Blue Hall. Stretching from the sea façade to the garden side, many grand receptions and holiday tributes were presented here.

The Blue Hall

This hall received its name from the dominant color of its the curtains, ceiling and walls. The extensions at either end are illuminated by three windows overlooking the sea. The ceiling panels were mounted after being carved and are defined by massive, heavily decorated frames. Nature scenes and floral arrangements are featured on the ceiling panels. A red and white crystal chandelier with 54 candleholders hangs in the center. At the entrance there is a pair of mirrored consoles on either side. The same system has been applied to the other three doors of the hall. In addition, there are elaborate lamps in front of each of the mirrors that help to brighten up the room. The lounge nearest the sea is furnished with a set of light colored, gold leaf quilted furniture. The marble table standing in the center is decorated with reliefs and gold leaf. A French Baccarat vase made on 05 February 1869 that sits on top of the table complements the décor of the room. The walls of the lounge nearest the land are colorfully engraved with the same deceptive composition that appears on the side closest to the sea. Crystal column candelabras have been placed in the four corners of the hall. The carpet in the center is European. The Japanese vases decorated with reliefs are colossal. The groups of dragon fighters on them are depicted in bas-relief and gold leaf. On the side facing the sea, there are two European vases, while on the side facing land there is a blue-white Chinese vase. In addition, there are Baccarat and Yıldız vases on top of the consoles. An elevator was added in the middle of the illuminated space during the Republic period when Atatürk took ill. This is where two large Japanese vases stand today.

Many receptions took place in the Blue Room during Abdülmecid's reign. The sultan also observed his family religious holidays there, in the company of his wives, concubines, and children. Furthermore, Abdülaziz accepted many foreign dignitaries there. The coronations of both Abdülhamid II and Mehmed V Reşad were held there, and in the final years of the Sultanate, the Harem band performed marches in this room.

The Room where Atatürk Died

To the right of the Blue Hall are two smaller rooms. The first was used by Gazi Mustafa Kemal Atatürk as a study. In contrast with the rest of the palace, this room is very simply decorated. The second room served as Atatürk's bedroom, and it was here that he passed away on 10 November 1938. To the right of the entrance, there is a painting depicting the four seasons, which was much beloved by Atatürk. All of the furnishings are made of walnut. The room is highlighted with gold leaf stars and leaves.

The Pink Hall

Named for its dominant color, this room was the gathering place of the women of the Harem. The ceiling is made from engraved plaster. The room is decorated predominantly with mirrors and consoles. A balsamwood table with bronze-inlay stands atop a huge Hereke carpet in the center of the room. The room is lit by the central chandelier having 60 candles and its matching floor-standing candelabra in the four corners. During Atatürk's illness, one of the two glass cabinets in the hall was converted into a bathroom door that opened into the hall. As Atatürk found this hall quite refreshing during his illness, he had his deck chair moved there, where he would rest. Sterling silver braziers in the corners provided heating of this large hall, the façade of which faces seaward.

The Bedroom of the Sultans' Wives

The rooms over the corridor beyond the Pink Hall are those of the Sultans' Wives. The bedroom belonging to the First Wife of the Sultan was located along this corridor at the right. There is a bedstead decorated with gold leaf engraving with walnut planks on three sides, a dressing table, tile stove, cabinets as well as a red room set of furniture with the same fabric as the curtains in the room. The ceiling is made from plaster and decorated with engravings. The second room over from this one belonged to the Second Wife. The walnut-covered bronze bedstead is very beautifully decorated. The ceiling is made from plaster and decorated with engravings. There is the Bedroom of the Third Wife at the end of the corridor. The walls are done up in wallpaper up to the ceiling bottom. The ceiling is decorated with engravings. A white-lacquered bedstead, cabinet and table make up the main furniture of the room, while there is also a matching mirror, console and bedside table there.

The Bedroom of Sultan Mehmed V Reşad

The large room next to this one was the bedroom of the elderly Sultan Mehmed V Reşad. A canopied bedstead with a combination of mahogany and walnut on three sides sits to the left of the entrance. The monogram "M.R." is wrought into the bed railings. The same monogram is seen on the clock on top of the bedside table. Among the other items decorating the room are a crystal chandelier hanging from the ceiling, a center table decorated with gold leaf, a gold leaf console and crystal mirror and a set of furniture of covered with the same velvet as the drapes. Moreover, the

Fireplace in the Bedroom of the The Dowager Sultan.

Pink Hall. Located in the Harem section of Dolmabahçe Palace, the Pink Hall served as the main hall where the women of the harem held their meetings.

cigarette stand, decorated with recessed metal over wood with the monogram of Mehmed V Reşad as well the woodshed in the shape of furniture next to the stove are rare works worth seeing.

Harem Hamam

The Harem hamam is an apartment comprised of a relaxation room, a disrobing room, a washroom and a toilet. The ceiling and the lower half of the walls are covered in gray Marmara marble. The upper half of the wall is covered in Iznik tiles embellished with European designs. The three basins in the washroom have silver faucets. Reflecting the brightest period of Kütahya tilemaking, the stove and its circular tray were made by an Armenian specialist. The tray is currently used as a table.

Bedroom of Sultan Abdülaziz

A room in a corner of the Blue Hall was the Bedroom of Sultan Abdülaziz. Adjacent to the right wall at the entrance is a king-size bed enclosed on three sides with gold leaf and engravings. On the wall is an Aubusson tapestry, which was a gift to Sultan Abdülaziz from the French ambassador. One of the armchairs, which has his monogram on it, was made to accommodate Sultan Abdülaziz's bulky body. Decorative items include crystal mirrors, gold leaf cabinets and Yıldız vases atop consoles.

The Bedroom of Sultan Abdülmecid

As it gets sunlight from three sides, this room receives an abundance of light. A canopied bedstead decorated with mother-of-pearl and covered in silver with mosquito netting is positioned adjacent to the wall facing the entrance. Amongst the precious items in the room are two bronze Sevres vases in the corner, a washbasin with two mirrors, gold leaf console mirror and a garment closet. The colorfully engraved chandelier hanging from the ceiling is made of red, white and green crystals. The sultan, who was quite fond of alcohol and women, died at the age of 38.

The Holiday Reception Hall

This is the central focus of the palace, both from the inside and outside. The women of the court, foreign dignitaries, musicians, and other invited guests would sit in the galleries when observing holiday festivities.

The room takes its name from the traditional receptions given by the sultan before annual religious holidays. A few days before these holidays, Sultan Murad III's throne, which weighs 250 kg, would be brought here from the Topkapı Palace Treasury and set up in the garden side of the hall. Opposite this, a row of chairs for foreign dignitaries would be set up.

After the holiday prayers, the sultan would rest in a small room in the corner of the hall. He would then receive tributes from his Council of Ministers and all the accompanying male members, who would approach him on the throne to kiss his outstretched tassel. The two corner rooms on the landward side have flat ceilings, while those on the seaward side are domed. These rooms are where the sultan would rest before the beginning of a reception. During the time of Abdülhamid II, a hidden staircase was added in the left room on the side facing land so that the sultan could leave the ceremonies surreptitiously.

The hall measures 40 meters x 45 meters. Paired columns support semi-domes, which in turn support the 36 meter-high central dome. The inside of the dome is lined with lead, and engraved with colorful designs. An inscription on the stairs leading to one of the galleries gives the names of three Armenians and indicates that it was they who made the dome. The columns, which were case in a foundry, are made of artificial marble.

The lighting of the hall is provided by four porphyry-based crystal candelabras in the corners of the room, matching pairs of silver column candelabras, and a massive central chandelier. The lower section of this incredible chandelier fell to the floor during an earthquake that struck while a reception was being held by Abdülhamid II. It was determined that the part that fell weighed about 700 kg.

A system which was installed on the ground floor heated up the hall. Thus, according to this, six furnaces were opened in certain places on the ground floor and then covered with metal domes and covers. Warm air would be fed into the hall through gaps in metal plates that opened up from under the pair of columns. Two days before the reception, the lit furnaces would provide the hall with a warm temperature of 18°-20°.

In addition to the exchanging of holiday greetings, the Sultan's Official Hall played host to some historical events in Turkish history. Sultan Abdülmecid gave a huge banquet to honor Field Marshall Pelisser in 1856, and also organized an official reception in honor of the Hungarian Emperor Franz Joseph. In addition, there was a reception held for the Austrian-Hungarian Emperor Carl and his Empress during the final months of World War I.

One of the most important events that took place in these halls was the opening of the first Parliament on 18 March 1877 by Abdülhamid II. Atatürk, who came to Istanbul for the first time as President in 1927, addressed deputies, generals and city notables, and had some nice words to say about Istanbul. When Atatürk died, the people of Istanbul filed past his corpse in this hall.

We have thus become acquainted with yet another Ottoman palace of incredible structure and interior decoration belonging to the late period.

Ceiling decorations of the Muayede Hall.

Muayede Hall. This wide hall was where receptions and holiday ceremonies were held. The women of the harem would watch the ceremonies from the upper galleries. A gift from Queen Victoria, the chandelier gives the room an atmosphere of imposing grandeur.

Beylerbeyi Palace

The palace where French Empress Eugenie stayed is one of the finest examples of late-Ottoman architecture.

There once were gardens called the İstavroz Gardens on the site where Beylerbeyi Palace is today. Later this parcel of land was divided up and became the property of the sultan, who had a summer palace called Şevkabad built on the site. Sultan Ahmed I was fond of Beylerbeyi and so had a mescid and apartments for his attendants built in the woods near the summer palace. Sultan Ahmed I's son Murad IV, who was born in this summer palace in 1612, paid much attention to these venues after he ascended to the Ottoman throne. The district experienced its heyday during the reign of Mehmed IV. This huge plot of land was split up and sold to the public towards the end of the 18th century. Later on, Mahmud II considered the idea of building a palace on this land which had passed through a number of hands. It was legally expropriated in 1832, after which a wooden, two-storey, yellow-painted palace was constructed on the site.

Many important dignitaries visited this palace, banquets were held for western princes and crown princes, and Abdülmecid, the eldest son of Sultan Mahmud II, was circumcised here. Abdülaziz had the old palace torn down after he became the sultan and had today's Beylerbeyi Palace built on the site between 1861-65. The palace architect was the master builder Sarkis Balyan, who had received his inspiration from the French Baroque architectural style.

Balyan constructed the palace entirely of marble and coarse sandstone, which was shipped from Bakırköy. It is heavily decorated on both the exterior and interior. The lowest floor is subterranean, while the two floors above are comprised of six halls and 24 rooms on the sides. The Pool Room on the bottom floor separates the Harem and selamlık. The entrances of the Harem and Reception Apartment sections are in two directions. One encounters a magnificent view while entering the palace via the wide staircase in the Reception section. All the furnishings in the palace were imported from France. Reed matting was laid throughout the palace to counter the effects of excess seaside humidity. Carpets are spread over these reeds. The large Sevres vase and Bohemian chandelier in the entrance hall are both quite striking. The Adjutant Room is on the seaward side of the hall, while those on the landward side were set aside for the servants. The room which opens into the Pool Room is called the Captain Pasha Room, which is decorated with ropes.

Sultan Abdülaziz commissioned Sarkis Balyan to construct Beylerbeyi Palace between 1851-65.

The entrance hall of Beylerbeyi.

There are two ways to go upstairs from the Sultan's Official Hall – from the Entrance Hall as well as from the Pool Room. The Hall of the Men's Quarters and the Sultan's Official Hall on the second floor are strikingly ostentatious. In passing from the Sultan's Official Hall to the Harem, the final room is the Official Reception Room.

The rooms located in the Sultan's Official Hall section on the upper seaward side are also of interest to visitors. The walls of these rooms are covered in wood siding. The prayer room is on the second floor of the Mabeyn.

Like that of the Sultan's Official Hall, there is a richly decorated hall in the

Beylerbeyi Palace Pool Hall. This hall features many marble columns around the pool.

entrance of the Harem section. There are a number of rooms which were placed on the landward and seaward sides. One goes upstairs from this hall via a two-sided staircase. It is assumed that the room upstairs to the right of the corridor on the seaward side was that of the Dowager Sultan. French Empress Eugenie stayed in room number 24 in this section. A bath was also constructed at the end of this room.

The interior decoration is very much different from the exterior. There are a lot of 19th-century European Baroque influences in the furniture, mirror, chandelier, consoles and cornices. Abdülaziz brought an artist from Poland during the decorative phase of the palace.

The sultan is believed to have prepared sketches for the decoration of the palace, which he commissioned this painter to carry out. It is known that the sketches were preserved in an album by the wife of the painter. Amongst the oil paintings decorating the ceilings in the several of the palace rooms and halls are those of warships showing the Ottoman flag. In addition, the calligraphic Koranic verse inscribed on the ceiling and walls is also quite striking.

One disembarks at the pier with its double wrought iron gates to enter the palace garden. There are two tiny seaside pavilions situated at either end of the seawall. The tent-shaped roof becomes sharply pointed at the top. The sea-façade is diagonal, whereas there are portico-domed parts positioned in front of the entry on the landward side. The garden extends in sets towards the rear, and is decorated with rare trees, pools, and marble and bronze statues, all of which were made in Paris in 1864.

The artists and the date the works were completed are etched on the bases of the statues. Measuring 80 meters x 30 meters and three-meters deep, the marble pool on the garden's uppermost terrace is surrounded by three pavilions, named "Serdab," "Sarı" and "Ahır." Found to the right of the large pool is the three-storey Sarı Pavilion, which derives its name from the color of its stucco. Its basement consists of a hall and two rooms, whereas the upper floors each have an entrance, one hall and two rooms on the sides. This is one of the surviving parts of the old Beylerbeyi Palace.

The Serdab Pavilion is located behind the pool, and it is also known as the Marble Pavilion. It has an anteroom and two rooms and its façade is covered with white marble. There is a marble fountain pool in the center of the anteroom. Moreover, the ornamental marble fountains which are recessed into the right and left walls complement the pool. There are elegant earthenware pots that widen towards the bottom in order for the water to

Blue Hall, upper floor of Beylerbeyi Palace. The palace was named for the blue color of its columns. (left)

Ceiling ornamentation of Beylerbeyi Palace (above)

flow evenly in the ornamental marble fountains. Water flowing from here flows into the pool from the trough. This pavilion is also a part of the old Beylerbeyi Palace.

Located to the right of the pool is the Ahır Pavilion, which was built to care for the sultan's horses. There are wide glass doors and windows in the part of the pavilion that extends outward. There are engravings in the ceiling that depict colorful coats-of-arms consisting of stirrups and girths, as well as beasts of prey attacking other animals. There are 20 partitions with iron bars for the horses.

The floor is decorated with bricks placed upright. The palace was renovated in 1909, during the final years of the empire. Reconstruction of the pier was carried out according to blueprints drawn up by French naval construction engineer Eugene and Harbor Captain Miralay Mustafa Bey. The first prominent guest of this summer palace was Empress Eugenie.

The empress resided in Beylerbeyi Palace on behalf of Napoleon III in reciprocation of the visit Adbülaziz had made to France. Other esteemed guests to stay at Beylerbeyi Palace during their stay in Istanbul include Iranian Shah Nasruddin and Karabağ King Nicola.

The ex-sultan Abdülhamid II, who was living in Thessaloniki, returned to Istanbul at the outbreak of the Balkan War to settle here. He chose one of the rooms overlooking the sea on the lower floor to live out the last years of his life. He passed away here in 1919.

Atatürk was the last notable guest to have stayed here, having resided in the Harem Apartments twice.

Yıldız Palace

This palace is comprised of pavilions situated in the middle of a woodland.

Like Topkapı Palace, this beautiful green area known as Yıldız Woods, is home to several pavilions, which are collectively referred to as Yıldız Palace. The first pavilion was constructed by Sultan Ahmed I in the early 17th century. Sultan Selim III also had a pavilion built here for his mother Mihrişah Sultan at the end of the 18th century. Mahmud II had the Yıldız Pavilion constructed in these woods, along with a beautiful garden. It has been called "Yıldız" ("star") ever since. Sultan Abdülmecid had these pavilions torn down in 1842 to make way for a pavilion called Kasr-ı Dilkuşa for his mother Dilkuş Sultan.

Sultan Abdülaziz first had a structure built on the inner part called the Büyük Mabeyn. He then had the Malta, Çadır and Çit Pavilions constructed in the garden. He also had a bridge connecting Çırağan and Yıldız erected.

As he did not feel secure enough at Dolmabahçe, Sultan Abdülhamid II moved to Yıldız, where his sultanate continued for another 33 years. Later on, the 500,000-m² Yıldız Palace was surrounded by high walls. It was transformed into a small city, possessing such elements as a theater, museum, workshops, a library, a pharmacy and parks. Abdülhamid II had an army base constructed just beyond the all-encompassing walls, and in this manner was able to protect himself and his throne.

The presence of various architectural styles in the buildings at Yıldız Palace indicates that several architects were involved in their construction. For instance, we know that architects such as Sarkis and Agop Balyan, Raimondo d'Aronco, Garabet Balyan, Vasilaki Joannidis and Vallaury were employed here at various times. We also know that the Büyük Mabeyn, a section of the Chalet Pavilion, as well as the Malta and Çadır Pavilions, were the work of Agop and Sarkis Balyan. All the buildings in Yıldız are gathered around three gardens and are entered through four large gates. Constructed in 1866 by Sultan Abdülaziz, the Büyük Mabeyn is in the first courtyard. Measuring 30 meters x 40 meters and comprising one of the monumental structures of the palace, the Büyük Mabeyn is the work of Agop and Sarkis Balyan. The palace is entered via a double set of stairs. Inside, the ceiling, gate and walls are all decorated with gold leaf. The porcelain stove and chandeliers are some of valuable furnishings that are worth seeing. Constructed by Sultan Abdülaziz, the Çit Pavilion is north of the palace,

above this same garden. It is where he received foreign ambassadors. The Adjutants' Apartments and Armory buildings are located to the east. The palace's Building of Fine Arts presently serves as the "City Museum." From

The Malta Kiosk in Yıldız Park was constructed during the reign of Abdülaziz.

A view of Yıldız Palace.

here, one passes through a second large gate into another courtyard, where Sultan Abdülhamid resided. Once inside, one sees the Küçük Mabeyn, which was constructed by Abdülhamid II in 1900. This building is where Sultan Abdülhamid received word that he had been deposed. It is also where Sultan Vahideddin met with Mustafa Kemal just prior to his departure for Samsun in May 1919.

The Harem Gate is situated between the Çit Pavilion and the Küçük Mabeyn. From this gate, one passes into a courtyard that is encircled by a 10-meter-high wall. This is where the theater and the pavilions of the sultans, crown princes and the sultans' womenfolk are located. Foreign symphony orchestras and theater groups used to perform for royal audiences at the theater in the third courtyard. The ceiling of this theater is decorated with yellow stars against a blue background. The loggias facing the stage belonged to the sultan, whereas those on the top floor belonged

Door with mother-of-pearl inlays which opens into (below) the dining hall of the Şale Pavilion. This structure was built during the reign of Sultan Abdülhamid II in honor of the visit of Kaiser Wilhelm II in 1889.

Interior view of the dining hall of the Şale Pavilion (opposite).

to the crown princes. The palace also had a museum. Next to the mosque is a building called the Silah Pavilion. This is here where the palace arms were on display. Today these arms are on exhibit at the Military Museum in Harbiye. Fond of flowers and insects, Sultan Abdülhamid established an insect and aviary museum. Yıldız Palace also had a rich library, which has since been incorporated into the library at Istanbul University. The inner garden is exquisite and meticulously cared for. Caiques once plied the waters of a 240,000-m2 pool, adding a distinct beauty to the garden. The most important structure here is that of the "Cihannüma" (Observation) Pavilion, which possesses an extremely alluring view. The outer garden, where the palace womenfolk promenaded, is today's Yıldız Park. This is where the Şale, Malta and Çadır Pavilions are located. The large gate found next to the Yıldız Palace Theater opens into the Şale Pavilion.

There is a pool, which was constructed by Sultan Abdülaziz, in front of the Çadır Paviliion. It was here in 1881 that Mithat Pasha and his associates were put on trial for the assassination of Sultan Abdülaziz. Abdülaziz also built the two-storey Malta Pavilion, which has a magnificent view. On the top floor, there is a hall and rooms opening into the hall, while on the bottom floor, there is a pool. Though Sultan Abdülaziz had this pavilion built, he chose not to use it very much. Abdülhamid had Yıldız Park connected to Yıldız Palace, which led to the pavilion being used, in particular, by those in the Harem. The pavilion underwent major renovation in 1979.

No longer extant is the carpentry workshop, the repair shop and tailor shop of Abdülhamid II, who was known for his carpentry skills. The Yıldız Porcelain Factory, which produced porcelain exclusively for the palace, is still standing.

Yıldız Palace came to constitute a small city, with 12,000 people residing within its confines. A mosque was constructed in 1886 and a Clock Tower, in 1891. The best maintained section of the palace is the Şale Pavilion. Though it is called a pavilion, it is actually the size of a large palace. The Şale Pavilion was completed in 1889, in time to host the second visit of Kaiser Wilhelm II. Its name is derived from the mountain villas in France called "chalets." The Şale Pavilion, which has three floors including a basement, is comprised of a Harem and men's quarters. The most important halls in the Şale Pavilion are those in the Harem, the Mother-of-Pearl Hall as well as the Sultan's Official Hall, the floor of which is covered by a 406-m2 carpet. Possessing a splendid appearance with parquet floors, porcelain stoves and chandeliers, the Chalet Pavilion is administered by the Department of National Palaces and is open to the public as a museum.

Pavilions and Summer Palaces

The pavilions and summer palaces used by the sultans from time to time to hunt and relax added a distinct beauty to Istanbul.

The Ottoman Sultans had several palaces, such as Topkapı, Dolmabahçe and Beylerbeyi, where they resided and administered the state. Besides these, they also had pavilions and summer palaces built, which they used temporarily or for going on the occasional hunt. Summer palaces are those described as slightly smaller than palaces and were built for sultans. Pavilions, on the other hand, were larger than residences but not as large as palaces. Pavilions situated along the shore are called "yalıs" or "waterside mansions." Though sultans commissioned pavilions and waterside mansions, they were mostly built and resided in by grand viziers, generals and statesmen. There are several pavilions found within the palaces of Topkapı, Beylerbeyi and Yıldız. They will be discussed, but for now, let's simply describe some of the places that are still around which were constructed as single units. As it is, most of these are open to the public as museums. Besides those in Topkapı Palace, there are only three surviving pavilions. The first of these is Çinili Pavilion, which dates back to 1472. This pavilion is found on the grounds of the Istanbul Museum of Archaeological and is utilized as the Tile and Porcelain Museum. The Alay Pavilion, which is located on the edge of Gülhane Park over the light rail line, has four storeys, windows and is capped with a conical-shaped roof. Dating back to Mehmed the Conqueror, it was renovated during the 19th century in the Empiric style. It is called the "Alay" ("Procession") Pavilion, as sultans would watch religious processions, merchant and diplomatic processions as well as army parades from here.

The Sepetçiler Summer Palace is located on the seaside and was constructed by Sultan İbrahim in 1643. Renovated during the period of Mahmud I, it was constructed for the sultan and those of the Harem to watch naval ceremonies. Restored in recent years, it is currently used as the International Press Center.

Küçüksu Summer Palace

Situated in Göksu on the shore of the Bosphorus, the Küçüksu Summer Palace is attractive for its beautiful stone masonry. Today's summer palace is found in place of previous buildings. Attracting attention during the period of Mahmud I as an excursion spot, Divitdar Emin Pasha had a pavilion built in 1752, which he presented to the sultan. This summer palace was expanded in 1792 by Sultan Selim III, who had a fountain with rich Rococo reliefs made there as well. After commissioning the architect Nikoğos Balyan to construct

the Dolmabahçe Palace, he had him erect a summer palace here on a plot of land 15 meters x 27 meters in dimension. This palace, which was constructed by pounding pilings into the seabed and positioning blocks of stone on top of them, has three storeys, including the basement. The basement is where the pantries, kitchen and servants' rooms are located. There are four rooms placed around the stairway anteroom on the other two floors. The parquet, hearths,

Exterior and interior views of Küçüksu Summer Palace built during the reign of Sultan Abdülmecid in 1857. With its striking architectural style, Küçüksu is one of the most beautiful structures along the Bosphorus.

ceiling and wall decorations are all strikingly beautiful. On the sea façade outside, one sees a double set of baroque marble stairs. Between these stairs are reliefs of exuberant acanthus and hearts. The stone masonry on the outer walls consists of some fine examples of craftsmanship. This summer palace is administered by the Department of National Palaces as a museum and serves as a tourist attraction.

Aynalı Kavak Pavilion

The Shipyard Shore Palace, whose foundation was laid during the period of Sultan Ahmed I, was used until the end of the 18th century. The only part of it that remains is the Aynalı Kavak Summer Palace. The sultans would watch naval and circumcision ceremonies held on the Golden Horn from the Shipyard Shore Palace. Starting from the second half of the 18th century, it began to be neglected. Sultan Selim III had a large section of it torn down in an effort to modernize the shipyard, giving the land to the shipyard. Selim III expanded his Sultan's Chambers here and began utilizing it in 1791. It is said that he composed music and played with musicians here. The summer palace appeared to be two-storeys from the side facing the sea and a single-storey from the side facing the land. It receives plenty of light thanks to the wide rectangular windows. Sultan Selim III had the interior décor furnished in the Rococo style. Yesarizade's "Eulogy to Enderunlu Vasıf," which he wrote in calligraphy, is found here. The Submission Room is next to the Council Apartment. They are decorated in the Rococo style. A eulogy to the sultan that the Sheikh Galib wrote is above the windows in the room. The Mother-of-Pearl Room is behind the Submission Room. It derives its name from the mother-of-pearl inlaid work. Musical instruments are also displayed on the bottom floor. Located within a wide garden in Hasköy, the Aynalı Kavak Summer Palace is administered by the Department of National Palaces as a museum serving as a tourist attraction.

Ihlamur Pavilion

Situated in Beşiktaş, Sultan Abdülmecid commissioned Nikoğos Balyan to construct the Ihlamur Summer Palace as a place of rest having an archery range and hunting lodge. It was built between 1849-55. There are actually two pavilions, one of which is the Ceremony Pavilion and the other, the Retinue Pavilion, with the former being more decorated than the later. These pavilions have two rooms surrounding an anteroom. The two pavilions are located in an extensive garden. Both of the pavilions were built with two floors added to a basement. One goes from the basement to the floor above via two sets of

Situated in Emirgan Park, the Sarı Pavilion was commissioned by the Egyptian Khedive İsmail Pasha in the 19th century.

curved symmetrical staircases. While the interior and exterior of the Ceremony Pavilion originally was decorated in elegant Empiric style, it was redecorated in a Baroque style with exaggerated ornamentation during the reign of Sultan Abdülaziz. There are enormous statues on pedastals inside niches on the sides and under the entry arch. The exaggerated decoration of the pavilion is apparent from the windows, stairs and balustrades, heavy garlands, columns and grid balconies. The interior is decorated with gold leaf stucco borders and baroque reliefs. The Ihlamur Summer Palace was recently restored and is currently administered by the Department of National Palaces as a museum serving as a tourist attraction.

Maslak Summer Palaces

The first summer palaces that were built during the period of Mahmud II gained importance during the period of Sultan Abdülhamid II, who used it while he was Crown Prince. The group of Maslak Pavilions is made up of the following: Kasr-ı Hümayun, Mabeyn-i Hümayun, Limonluk, Çadır Pavilion and Pasha Apartments. The Kasr-ı Hümayun has two floors, the bottom of which is made from stone while the top is made of wood. Mabeyn-i Hümayun is to the northwest of this structure. It is an elegant single-floor stucture made of stone. The Limonluk is adjacent to this building. The Kasr-ı Hümayun is in a spot that dominates the woods on the northwestern side where the Çadır Pavilion is found. The octagonal-shaped Çadır Pavilion displays some of the finest examples of wooden decoration. The General's Apartments were built as a single-storey stone building. The Ihlamur Summer Palace was recently restored and is currently administered by the Department of National Palaces.

The Beykoz Summer Palace

The Egyptian Khedive Mehmed Ali Pasha commissioned the architects Nikoğos and Sarkis Balyan to build the Beykoz Summer Palace next to the Sultan's Quay in Beykoz between 1855-66. This neo-classical style summer palace was to be presented to Sultan Abdülmecid but he passed away just prior to its completion, so Said Pasha presented it to Abdülaziz instead, who

Khedive Summer Palace was built by the order of Abbas Hilmi Pasha in 1907. Recently restored, this venue is currently operated by the Istanbul Greater Municipality as a tourist attraction.

had recently ascended to the throne. Established over a wide terrace, this stone structure is covered with marble. Surrounded by trees, the gardens of the palace extend all the way down to the sea. The palace halls are wide and have lofty decorated ceilings, whereas the upper floor is reached via a wide staircase.

The Khedive Summer Palace

Egyptian Khedive Abbas Hilmi Pasha commissioned the Italian architect Delfa Seminoti to construct this summer palace in the extensive woodlands of Çubuklu in 1907. With two main storeys and a service attic, this stone structure has a commanding view of the Bosphorus. The curved dining hall on the lower floor opens out into a garden with a veranda having 24 columns. The floor above this was transformed into a penthouse suite belonging to the Khedive. There are also six bedrooms on the side overlooking the courtyard. The floor terrace with its stairway on this side has a panoramic view on three sides. The tower belonging to the Khedive Suite with a private elevator gives the structure an intriguing appearance. Renovation of the building was recently completed and today the Istanbul Greater Municipality operates the building as a tourist attraction.

In addition to these, the Khedives had some pavilions such as those situated within the Emirgan Woods constructed as well. Sultan Abdülaziz allocated the Emirgan Woods to Egyptian Khedive İsmail Pasha. The Khedive had two ponds and three wooden pavilions – "Yellow," "Pink" and "White," constructed on the site during the latter half of the 19th century. These are currently operated by the municipality as tourist attractions. Among the other structures that the other Egyptian Khedives had constructed in Istanbul, are the Abbas Halim Pasha pavilions on Heybeliada (1897), and the Bebek Khediva Summer Palace, which was constructed at the start of the 20th century. The Italian architect d'Aronco was commissioned to construct the palace in Bebek by the mother of Egyptian Khedive Abbas Hilmi Pasha, Khediva Emine. It is currently used as the Egyptian Consulate General.

Let us briefly mention a few pavilions not previously covered. Sultan Abdülmecid commissioned the Balyans in 1851 to construct the Tophane Summer Palace in Tophane. Nikoğos Balyan built the Adile Sultan Summer Palace in Validebağı, Üsküdar in 1853. He also built the Hunting Lodge of Abdülaziz on the grounds of the palace garden. Abdülaziz commissioned Sarkis Balyan to build a Hunting Lodge in Ayazağa while he was still the Crown Prince. Sultan Abdülaziz commissioned Sarkis Balyan to construct the Kalender Summer Palace in Tarabya was in 1862-63; it is currently utilized as the Presidential Pavilion. Situated on the grounds of a 20-acre garden, the Yusuf İzzeddin Efendi Pavilion was constructed at the bottom of Büyük Çamlıca Hill at the end of the 19th century. This three-storey wooden pavilion

was constructed in the neo-classical style for the son of Sultan Abdülaziz, Crown Prince Yusuf İzzeddin Efendi. The Men's Quarters Apartment is all that remains of a pavilion that was built for Crown Prince Abdülmecid Efendi in Bağlarbaşı in 1901. There is also the Crown Prince Vahideddin Efendi Pavilions situated within a 50-acre plot of land above Çengelköy. Sultan Abdülhamid allocated this pavilion to the crown prince. These palaces and pavilions make up some of the important historical structures in Istanbul.

Sultan Abdülmecid commissioned Nikoğos Balyan to build the Ihlamur Summer Palace (1849-55), which was used as a hunting and leisure mansion.

Aynalı Kavak Summer Palace, where Sultan Selim III studied music.

The Museums of Istanbul

The works of art in Istanbul wich has been the capital of three empires are exhibited in various museums.

The many works brought from beyond Turkey's frontiers, from such places as Egypt, Mesopotamia, Palestine and the Arabian Peninsula, are exhibited in three museums under the auspices of the Istanbul Archaeological Museum. They are 1) the Museum of the Ancient Orient, 2) the Museum of Classical Works, where one can see famous sarcophagi such as that of Alexander the Great, 3) and the Çinili Pavilion, with its famous Ottoman ceramic tiles and porcelain. Apart from these important museums, there is the imposing Byzantine Hagia Sophia Church, which is also open to visitors as a museum, and the Church of Hagia Eirene, which is also open as a monumental museum.

There are two museums in Edirnekapı – the Chora, and the Fethiye, both of which are world renown for their Byzantine mosaics and frescoes. Situated behind the Sultan Ahmed Mosque in the Arasta Bazaar, the Topkapı Palace Mosaic Museum exhibits some truly amazing Byzantine mosaics. Among other fabulous Ottoman and Seljuk works of art, one can see the finest examples of Seljuk-Ottoman carpets as well as exemplary Ottoman wood craftsmanship in the Museum of Turkish and Islamic Art. Situated just opposite the Sultan Ahmed Mosque, the Columns and Obelisks in the Hippodrome are seen in front of this museum. Topkapı Palace is testimony to the splendor of the Ottomans. Constructed after this palace, Dolmabahçe Palace continues to enchant visitors. Besides these, there are palaces from the late-Ottoman period, such as Beylerbeyi and Yıldız, both of which are open to the public. Apart from these palaces, there are also Yıldız Şale Pavilion, Aynalı Kavak, Ihlamur, Küçüksu and Maslak Summer Palaces, which are administered by the General Directorate of National Palaces. The Khedive Summer Palace and the pavilions in the Emirgan Woods are open to the public and are administered by the Istanbul Greater Municipality. Also worth a visit is the Şerifler Yalısı in Emirgan, which is a mansion administered by the Ministry of Culture. The Military Museum in Harbiye is worthy of attention because of its paintings and the military works remaining from the Ottoman Era. In addition to other works on display at the Naval Museum in Beşiktaş, one must see the splendid caiques that were once used by the Ottoman sultans. Right next to this museum, the Painting and Sculpture Museum, which is located inside the Dolmabahçe Palace Crown Prince Apartments, houses the paintings of many famous artists. In addition, there is also the Aviation Museum located in Yeşilköy, behind the airport. It houses the world's only existing example of a Polish P.Z.L. P-24 pursuit aircraft.

Located in Hisarüstü, there is the house of the famous poet, Tevfik Fikret, which is known as the Aşiyan Museum and is operated by the municipality. Other museums in Istanbul include the Atatürk Museum in Şişli, as well as the Fire Department Museum in Fatih, where obsolete fire fighting

The detail from the flank of a 14th-century minber. The areas between the geometrical designs contain carved embellishments. Museum of Turkish and Islamic Art.

Dating back 6000 B.C. a human-shaped vessel exhibited at Sadberk Hanım Museum.

Mother-of-pearl ceiling designs of a pavilion from the Sultan's caiguie. 16th-17th century. Naval Museum.

equipment is on display. Constructed under the orders of Sultan Mehmed III's Head Palace Servant, Gazanfer Ağa, the Gazanfer Ağa Medrese in Saraçhane is situated beneath the Bozdoğan Aqueduct. Today, it houses the Caricature and Humor Museum. The famous Byzantine Yerebatan Cistern is open to the public as a museum. So is the Carpet Museum, which is located below the Sultan Ahmed Mosque. Operated by the General Directorate of Foundations, there are many examples of priceless historical carpets, kilims and straight-woven ground cloths. The medrese in Fatih, constructed by

Grand Vizier Hüseyin Pasha in 1697, is utilized today as the Museum of Turkish Art and Architecture, which houses monograms and inscriptions, tile coverings, wooden architectural pieces and lighting tools.

The Turkish Foundation of Calligraphic Arts Museum is housed in what used to be the medrese of the complex constructed by Bayezid II in 1507. Here one can see such works of Ottoman sultans as Korans, pamphlets, manuscripts, signboards and calligraphy. The building constructed by Ottoman Foreign Minister Saffet Pasha along Divanyolu Caddesi in 1856

currently houses the Press and Media Museum. Not far from here, on the same avenue, is the Health Museum. Located on Yüksek Kaldırım, just south of Tünel, the Galata Mevlevi Lodge continues to serve as a museum called Council of State Literature. ("Divan Edebiyatı"). The Feshane and Weaving Factory was re-organized and converted into the Museum of Industrial Structures. Named after the wife of the late-Vehbi Koç,Sadberk Hanım, this museum was opened after the restoration of Azaryan Yalısı in Sarıyer. It is one of the museums that should be visited because of the very old Seljuk and Ottoman monuments on exhibit there. Some shoreline structures in Hasköy, which were once used as the Ottoman Empire's Shipyard and Iron Foundry, were recently opened to the public as the Rahmi M. Koç Industrial Museum. This is truly a world-class museum that has antique motor vehicles, steam engines, an interactive section, railroad cars, maritime engines and boats, and so on. Apart from these, there are also such collections in Istanbul as Şişe Cam Fabrikası, and Yapı Kredi Bankası Vedat - Nedim Tör in Galatasaray.

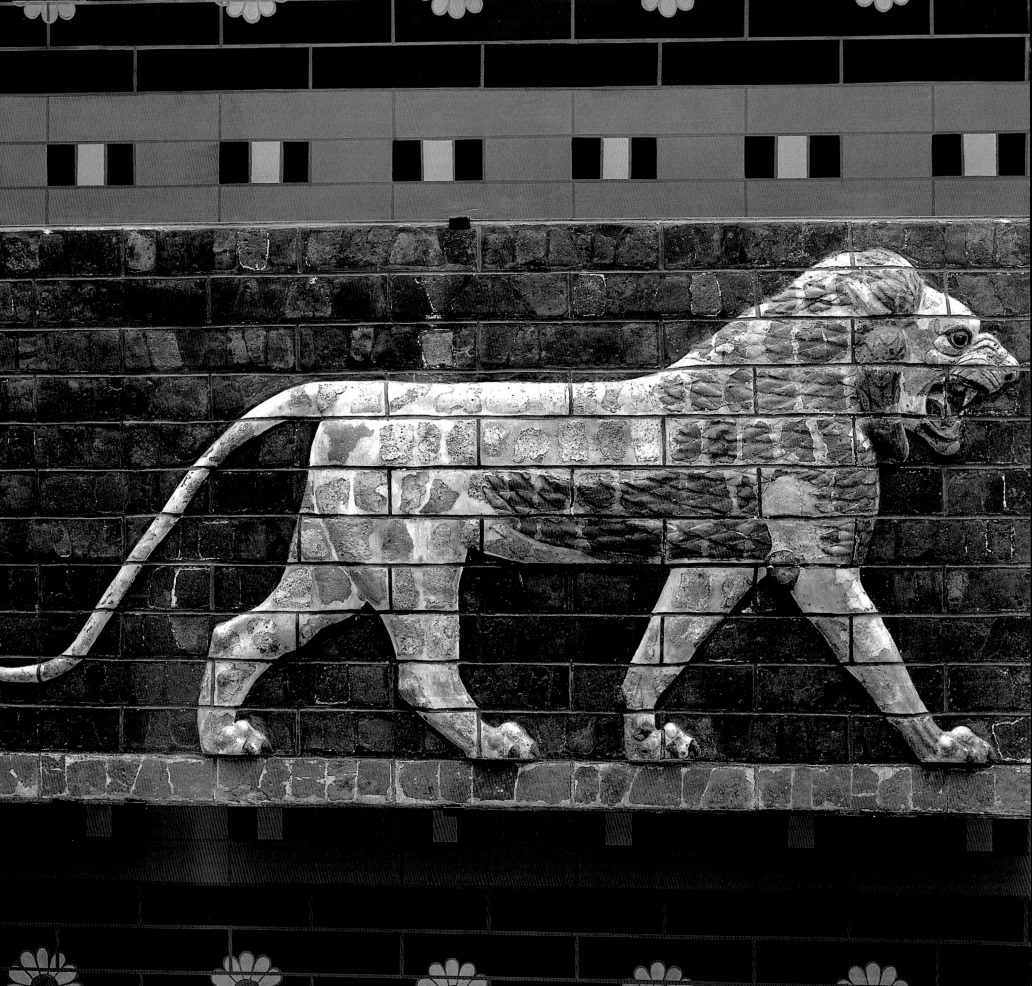

Istanbul Archaeological Museums

Istanbul archeological museums are incredibly rich with their works of art from the Ottoman period.

The three museums collectively known as the "Istanbul Archaeological Museums" are considered to be among the most important museums in the world. Founded as the Imperial Museum during the Ottoman period, the collection includes a number of artifacts from various parts of the Ottoman Empire and Mesopotamia, such as the Tomb of Alexander the Great, the Tomb of the Weeping Maidens, and the Lycian Tomb, found in 1891 at Sayda, in Syria. Originally, the museum collection was exhibited in the Çinili Pavilion, a wing of the Topkapı Museum, but that building is now in use as the Museum of Tile and Ceramics. It houses items that date as far back as the period of Mehmed II. As the collection grew, the present building was erected (1892-1908) to which a wing has been added in recent years. Stylistically speaking, the late-19th-century museum building was inspired by the Tomb of the Weeping Maidens. The museum collection includes 60,000 archaeological findings of various kinds, nearly 800,000 coins and medallions, and nearly 75,000 cuneiform tablets, making it one of the greatest collections in the world. The collection can be seen in three separate sections: in the Museum of the Ancient Orient, which is situated opposite the main building; in the Classical section housed in the main building; as well as in the Çinili Pavilion. In the Museum of the Ancient Orient, the first hall houses Egyptian artifacts, including tombs and mummies. Halls III and IV display work from Mesopotamia, including findings from Aleppo, Ninevah, the periods of Early Sumerian, classical and Late Sumerian, and the Gudea statues.

In the section containing works of the Assyrian period are the statues of Puzur Ishtar, governor of Mari, his son and Salmanasar III, and reliefs of winged spirits from the walls of the palace of King Tiglat Pileser at Nemrut. Other parts of the museum display seals and hieroglyphic tablets from Mesopotamia, and works of the Urartu and Phrygian periods.

The Hittite period in Anatolia (2000-1200 B.C.) is well represented, and the works on display include those of the Hittite Imperial period, and of the later Hittite city-states (dating after 1200 B.C.). Among the most notable works of the period are vessels of various kinds, bronze axes and a hieroglyphic tablet inscribed with the text of the famous Kadesh Treaty. Late-Hittite works of note include the Zincirli reliefs, the Maraş findings, as

well as the famous Babylonian reliefs, which are decorated with bull, dragon and lion figures in brickwork. They were originally part of the walls of the ceremonial pathway and the Ishtar Gate at Babylon.

The classical section of the museum was rearranged and opened to visitors in 1992. The triangular pediment of the Classical Section is supported by four pillars and is reached by white marble stairs. These stairs lead to a

Reliefs of a lion (opposite) and a bull (below). Made from glazed bricks, these were found on the walls of the ceremonial route leading to the Ishtar Gate in Babylon. 16th century B.C. Museum of Ancient Orient Works, Istanbul Archaelogical Museum.

hallway where the statue of the god Bes of the Roman period stands. In the galleries on both sides of this hallway, masterpieces of the world are on exhibit. In the halls on the right hand side are ancient statues.

The works in the first gallery are of the Archaic period. Works dating from the period of Persian dominance of Anatolia (546-333 B.C.) are in the second gallery, whereas Attic tomb stelae and reliefs of the 6th-5th centuries B.C. are in the third gallery. Works of the Hellenistic period (330-30 B.C.) adorn the hall in the following gallery.

Beautiful busts and a statue of Alexander the Great, whose reign initiated the period, are in this hall. One of these busts, found in Pergamon, draws attention because of the hair in the form of a lion's mane. Based on a portrait made by Lysippus in the 4th century B.C., this type of hair is peculiar to Alexander. This statue was made in a Pergamon sculpture workshop in the 2nd century B.C. Also in this hall is a statue of Marsyas, a work from the Roman period copied from the style of similar statues from the 3rd century B.C. According to mythology, Apollo punished Marsyas for daring to enter into a music contest with him by flogging his backside. This statue depicts Marsyas tied upside-down from a tree for punishment.

The most remarkable statues in this hall are those of Zeus, and a large divine statue found at the Temple of Hera in Pergamon most probably belonged to Pergamon King Attalos II (2nd century B.C.). Statues found in the Magnesia of Meander (today's Menderes River) and the Tralles (Aydin) are on exhibit in the fifth gallery. Across the hall is the Statue of the famous Ephebos, a young athlete. This statue, which was found in Tralles and belongs to the Early-Roman period, depicts a child athlete of about 12 years old at rest, exhausted from athletic activity. The boy wears a "pelerine" thrown over his short garments. On the right hand side of the door is the statue of Apollo, goddess heads, and a statue of a half-naked Nymph. On the left hand side, is a statue of a woman named Balbia (1st century B.C.), a statue of Athena, as well as statues of a number of anonymous dignitaries. On the left side of the passageway, there is a striking statue of a woman, found at Tralles and used as a pillar. In the style of examples encountered with the Nereids Monument in Xanthos near Fethiye, and at the monument

The world-renown Tomb of Alexander the Great. Measuring 3.18 meters in length, 1.67 meters in width, and 2.12 meters in height, this tomb really belonged to the Phoenician King Abdalonymus, but was called the Tomb of Alexander due to the depictions of Alexander chiseled into its sides. One side shows Alexander and the Greeks fighting against the Persians while the side pictured here depicts a lion hunt.

A 5th century B.C. Lycian tomb. Found in Sidon, Lebanon together with those of the Weeping Maidens and Alexander the Great, the "Satrap Sacrophagus" is also known as the "Lycian Sarcophagus" as it strongly resembles those of Lycia. One side depicts a lion hunt with two chariots, while the other side shows a boar hunt. The Battle of the Centaurs is portrayed on the narrow ends, and griffon and female sphinx acroters are shown on the lid.

of Limyra near Finike, these statues have been used in place of pillars in various locations. Examples of Roman sculpture art are displayed in the next hall. In the center of the hall is a bust of the poetess Sappho, sculpted in the Roman period. On the right are statues of Aphrodite and Kybele. On the wall are the relief made in honor of Euripides, author of Greek tragedies and a relief of the Muses playing lyres. To the left of the hall are examples of Roman portrait art. Here are the busts of Emperors Augustus, Tiberius, and Claudius, and the statues of Nero and Hadrian. In addition, the statue and the bust of Marcus Aurelius, the bust of Empress Faustina and busts of anonymous citizens adorn the hall. On the right hand side of the Aphrodisias Hall named for Prof. Kenan Erim, who conducted excavations for many years at Aphrodisias before he passed away in 1990, statues of Roman judges and the statue of a woman are on exhibit. Aphrodisias is near the provincial district of Karacasu in the province of Aydin in Western

Anatolia. When Attalos III, King of Pergamon bequeathed his territory to Rome in 133 B.C., sculptors here migrated to Aphrodisias, then the capital of the Carian region, and created marvelous works from marble obtained from rich marble quarries here. Statues that emerged from this Aphrodisias School of Sculpture were exported to Greece and Rome. Reliefs illustrating the war between the gods and giants are depicted on the walls of this hall. Works that have been uncovered in excavations at Aphrodisias are on display in the local museum whereas those found in Ephesus are on exhibit in the center of this hall. On the floor is a statue of the River God Oceanus, and next to it, the statue of Polemaeanus, the Prefect of Asia Minor, which was found in the Celsus Library of Ephesus. Artifacts found in Miletus, and, on the opposite wall, statues found in the Faustina Baths, are displayed on the left hand side of the hall. These statues from Faustina are of a Muse playing the flute, of Melpomene, and of Apollo playing the lyre. Next to the

works found in Anatolia are works found within the former borders of the Ottoman Empire. The busts of Poseidon and Artemis, statues of Zeus and the Goddess of Good Fortune Tyche are among the works displayed in this hall. In the gallery, on the left hand side of the entrance, is an exhibit of sarcophagi, each more beautiful than the next, including that of belonging to King Tabnit of Sidon, which was sculpted from basalt. From the inscription on the sarcophagus, it has been concluded that it once belonged to General Peneftah, who lived during the time of the 26th dynasty of Egypt, and was later re-used for King Tabnit of Sayda. Surrounding this sarcophagus are Egyptian and Greek sarcophagi. Situated behind these is a magnificent 5th-century B.C. Lycian sarcophagus, which was found in the necropolis of the King of Sidon. Called the Lycian Sarcophagus due to its resemblence to the sarcophagi of the Lycian region, it was found at Sidon by Osman Hamdi in 1877 and subsequently brought to Istanbul. One side

depicts a lion hunt and two chariots, each drawn by four horses, while the other side is an illustration of a boar hunt. On the narrow surfaces are carvings of the fight of Centaur and Lapith and a scene of a struggle over a deer between two Centaurs. Also brought from Sidon is another late-5th-century sarcophagus behind this, depicting the life of a satrap of Persia. Made from white marble and bearing beautiful reliefs, the so called Sarcophagus of Alexander the Great, did not in fact belong to Alexander, but carries his name due to the war and hunt scenes which decorate it. Measuring 2.12 meters high, 3.18 meters long, and 1.67 meters wide, this sarcophagus is carved with the following images; Alexander's battle against the Greeks is depicted on the narrow surfaces; on the left end is an illustration of Alexander; while scenes of lion and deer hunts cover the other end. The wounded lion in the center of the hunting scene is illustrated in the act of biting. The cavalier to the left of the lion is

Tomb of the Weeping Maidens. The reliefs on this sarcophagus, which was built for Straton I, King of Sidon, portray 18 female figures separated by columns. Each figure is depicted in a different state of grief, hence the name. The form of the sarcophagus is similar to that of a temple. Traces of polychrome paintwork can still be seen on the stonework (350 B.C.).

Alexander himself, wearing the royal symbol on his hand. This 4th-century B.C. sarcophagus is covered with beautifully painted, delicate stonework. Behind this sarcophagus is that of the Weeping Maidens. Made for a Sidonian in 350 B.C., there are 18 separately carved women mourning on this sarcophagus. Two identical funeral processions are depicted on the top cover. Some of the halls in this section of the museum are in the process of being restructured. On the upper floor of the newly opened section of the museum is an exhibition of Anatolian Civilizations. The "Through The Ages" exhibit is also on display. On the left side of the second floor are artifacts from the ancient city of Troy. Located 30 kilometers from Çanakkale, Troy was razed and rebuilt nine times. As the site of the first archaeological excavation in Anatolia, Troy was the subject of one of Homer's legendary works. The city of Troy was continuously inhabited from 3500 B.C to 300 A.D., making it possible to trace its cultural evolution through the ages. First excavated Heinrich Schliemann in 1870, the story of

these excavations and the tremendously colorful personality of Schliemann has made Troy an even more interesting and important site to visit. The works on exhibit here are those found during the excavations conducted by Schliemann and Dörpfeld, whereas the gold decorative objects from Level II Troy and double-handled ceramic pots peculiar to Troy are seen in the first display case. Schliemann found these objects near the ramped gate of Troy in 1873 and thought that they belonged to the Treasury of King Priam of VI Level Troy. However, it was later proven during subsequent excavations that these works belonged to Level II Troy between 2500-2200 B.C. The Troy beneath the second layer started in the third millennium B.C. and terminated quite suddenly with heavy destruction around 2500 B.C. Again, in this hall, ceramics uncovered from Levels III, IV and V (2200-1800 B.C.) of Troy works, as well as works belonging to Level VI and Level VII Troy, just prior to the major war (1800-1275 B.C.). One can also see artifacts displayed from the works from Levels VIII and IX, the latter of which was the period when Troy was under Roman domination. Moreover, the head of Zeus uncovered in the Troy excavations is displayed next to these exhibits. A reproduction of the Temple of Athena, which was located in an ancient city behind Troy, called Assos, conforms exactly to its original. Dating back to 530 B.C., this was the oldest Doric-style temple in western Anatolia. After the Troy exhibits, Anatolian works from throughout the ages are exhibited in chronological order in the opposite cases. Palaeolithic, Neolithic and Chalcolithic period works uncovered at sites located on the outskirts of Istanbul, such as Yarımburgaz, Fikirtepe and Pendik, are also displayed in this gallery. Moreover, the cultures of Kumtepe, Karaağaçtepe, Babaköy and Yortan, which produced the first Bronze Age works in the third millennium B.C. in Western Anatolia, as well as works found in Bozhöyük, are also on display. Ceramics and bronze works from the Early Bronze Age are seen side-by-side in these showcases.

Nymph Statue. 1st century B.C. This Late-Hellenistic-period work was uncovered at the Tralles, in modern-day Aydın. (lower left).

Caryatid. This was the name given to columns sculpted in the shape of a woman (left). Roman era.

Statue of Apollo playing the lyre, which was uncovered in Miletus (Roman period; 2nd century A.D.).

Findings of Boğazköy and Kültepe dating to the Middle Bronze Age (1900-1500 B.C.) can be viewed here as well. Numerous cuneiform tablets uncovered at Boğazköy and Kültepe, which contain historical, religious and legal matters, as well as private letters, are on display in the same section. Works of the Anatolian Iron Age (1200-546 B.C.) are found in the succeeding display cases. Works of the Urartu civilization, which thrived in Eastern Anatolia between the 8th-6th centuries B.C., are displayed separately from the works of Phrygian civilization, which existed in Central Anatolia during the same period. After examining the large vessels found in Kargamış and Boğazköy and pots and ceramics found in the Phrygian city of Yazılıkaya (City of Midas), let us proceed to the upper floor to look at the works displayed there. Works that were brought from beyond Anatolia, such as Palestine, Cyprus and Syria, are on display here. The section displaying Byzantine artworks that were uncovered in excavations in the Istanbul area is on the museum's lower floor.

Museum of Turkish and Islamic Arts

*This museum which contains works of art extending from the
early period of Islam the 20th century, is the first of its kind in Turkey.*

The Museum of Turkish and Islamic Art is not only the first museum in Turkey devoted to the display of Islamic art, it is one of the few museums in the world to have an extensive collection of Islamic art covering all periods and types of art.

For many years, the collection of art was displayed in the Soup Kitchen of the Süleymaniye Complex. But because of its expanding size and the lack of modern facilities, the need for a new museum building grew. It was with the restoration of the 16th-century İbrahim Pasha Palace, located on the grounds of the Byzantine Hippodrome, that the museum found its new home in 1983.

While it is not clear just when the palace, which was made with stone and brick in spite of the fact that wood was generally used in Turkish civilian architecture was built, it is known that it was repaired by Sultan Süleyman the Magnificent and given to the Grand Vezier İbrahim Pasha as a gift. İbrahim Pasha had married the daughter of the Sultan, Hatice Sultan, and settled in the palace. After his death, the palace, which became known by his name, continued to be used up until the present. A number of miniatures from 1528 that contain scenes of celebrations picture the building exactly as it is today. On them, for example, can be seen the balcony where the sultan and his entourage would sit, the Divanhane, as well as the painted columns and latticework of the building.

The Museum of Turkish and Islamic Art contains a great variety of works ranging from the earliest period of Islam right up to the 20th century. For example, those of the Umayyad, Abbasid and Fatimid period are some of the earliest found at the museum. Following the death of the Prophet Muhammed, the Prophet Osman became chosen as the Caliph. His clan, known as the Omayyads, subsequently grew in size. They became the first dynasty based on inheritance of political power from father to son. Pages of the Koran, written with Kufic letters, that were brought from the Umayyad Mosque in Damascus, are among the important documents reflecting the art of that period

The Abbasids, who were descendents of the uncle of the Prophet Muhammed, established a dynasty that ruled between 749-1258. They played an important role in art during the time of the Caliph Harun el Reşid. The pieces of art on display at the Museum, which were brought from archeological digs in Samarra, are examples reflecting the art of that period.

The Fatimids, who were of the Shiite sect of Islam, created a philosophy and understanding of art in North Africa, where they established their rule, that was different from that of the countries of Eastern Islam. Establishing Cairo as their capital, they rule other areas. The pages from the Koran, painted and wooden works, and the ceramic and ivory works found at the Museum are symbols of Fatimid art.

A gold necklace, belt buckle and hairpins from the Ottoman period are exhibited at the Museum of Turkish Islamic Arts.

A silver ball. A 16th-century silver ball covered with floral designs inlaid with turquoise and other colored gems. Museum of Turkish and Islamic Arts.

The Great Seljuk State exercised hegemony over Asia between 1037-1194. This state, which had accepted Islam, also founded the Anatolian Seljuk State, which was subservient to them. It is possible to find tiles, ceramic and metallic works from this period at the Museum.

Having accepted Islam, the Great Seljuk State undertook to act as the protector of the Caliph. In order to do this, it was necessary to dominate Anatolia. When the Byzantines were defeated by the Great Seljuk Sultan Alparslan at Malazkirt in 1071, the Turks overran Anatolia. Wherever the Turkish cavalry got the upper hand, it established what have come to be called the "early emirates." One of the first of these was the Artuks, who established their emirates in the region of southern Anatolia. Drums, candleholders, and mirrors of the Artuks, who built the first mosques and medreses in Anatolia, as well as the doorknocker of the Ulu Mosque in Cizre are on display at the Museum.

After the period of the early emirates, the Seljuks continued to advance in Anatolia under the leadership of Kutalmışoğlu Süleyman. In 1096, they established the Anatolian Seljuk State, with Konya as its capital. They subsequently assumed sovereignty over all of Anatolia. The Anatolian Seljuks, who were first subject to the Great Seljuk State, continued to exercise sovereignty independently even after the latter collapsed. They bequeathed the Turkish inheritance upon all of Anatolia by extensively building such edifices as mosques, medreses, caravanserais and tombs all over Anatolia. Metal and wooden works, and especially carpets, left by them are worth seeing.

Being defeated by the Mongols in 1243, the Seljuks became subject to the Anatolian Mongol State. But with its collapse, the İlhanid State, established by the son of Cengiz, Hülagu, came to dominate Anatolia. When the Anatolian Seljuk State collapsed in 1308, the previously established emirates began declaring their independence from place to place, which ushered in the Anatolian Emirates Period. The fact that the Karamanoğuls, one of these emirates, continued the traditions of the Seljuks, is important. The window shutters of the Karamanoğlu İbrahim Bey Soup Kitchen, a wooden

Window shutters from the Karamanoğlu İbrahim Bey Soup Kitchen. This 173x92 cm work is thought to be older than the Soup Kitchen, which was built in 1432. It is currently on display at the Museum of Turkish and Islamic Art.

A detail of a window shutter. This early 14th–century window shutter, which was brought from the Tomb of Sadreddin Konevi in Konya, is found in the Museum of Turkish and Islamic Arts. In the upper part of the carved shutter is an inscription panel. The panel in the middle contains multiple-level designs. It has been decorated with floral embellishments combining flowers, buds, and hatayi- and rumi-style motifs.

A detail of a carpet belonging to the Seljuk period. Measuring 333x243 cm, it was brought from the Tomb of Alaeddin Keykubad. Konya; 13th century.

A 16th-century carpet measuring 218x160 cm. Brought from Sivrihisar, Eskişehir.

sarcophagus and wooden minber wings are among the major works of the Karamanoğuls on display at the Museum. Another emirate that declared its independence was the Ottomans. Having been established in 1299, it increasing grew to a point where it had begun to roam the European continent. However, when Yıldırım Bayezid defeated Timur in 1402, there began a 10-year period of chaos in Anatolia. Süleyman Çelebi, Yıldırım's son, once again established the state. There are works on display at the Museum from the Yıldırım period. The Ottomans, reestablishing their sovereignty over Anatolia, took Istanbul, thereby breathing life into the Ottoman Empire, which came to exercise its sovereignty over three continents. There are many works from the Ottoman period on display at the Museum. These include carpets from Uşak, Gördes, Pergamon, and Ladik, tiles, metal candlesticks, silver oil pots and hangers. Moreover, in addition to such manuscripts as edicts and Kurans, there are Koran protectors and Koran reading tables there, too.

Each of the many sections of the Museum of Turkish and Islamic Art is so rich as to be able to form a separate museum all by itself. In the manuscript section of the Museum, there is a manuscript collection spanning the whole of Islam, from the Early Islamic Period to the Ottomans. In addition to these, there are nearly 3000 unsurpassed works produced by the Ottoman Sultans themselves, which include deeds of trust of pious foundations, edicts and acquittals.

In the carpet section of the Museum, there are 1700 historical carpets. This is why the Museum has been called the "carpet museum." In addition to famous examples from the Seljuk period, all groups of carpets, extending till the Ottoman period, are represented. These include the large-sized Uşak carpets, for example, as well as the prayer rug from the Edirne Selimiye Mosque. Carpets from such famous carpet centers as Pergamon, Ladik and Gördes are on display at the Museum.

Metal works exhibited at the Museum are important from the point of view of metal working of the Middle Ages. Among the metal works found at the Museum are the Artuknid drums, the doorknockers from the Cizre Ulu Mosque, and candlesticks from the Artuknid and Seljuk periods.

The wooden forms of art at the Museum are extremely interesting. Those from the Seljuk Emirate Period are particularly exquisite. Door and window shutters, sarcophaguses and Koran reading tables are among the works on display. Works of genius reflecting superior workworking craftsmanship include Koran reading tables belonging to the Seljuk Period, window shutters of the Karaman İbrahim Pasha Mosque, from the emirates period, and the sarcophagus brought from the Mahmud Hayrani Tomb. Furthermore, the side-wings of wooden minbers of mosques can be seen at the Museum. Koran protectors and Koran reading tables with mother-of-pearl inlays belonging to the Ottoman period are example of the superb Ottoman art of woodworking.

The tiles and bas-reliefs of Seljuk and Ottoman edifices that are no longer standing make up a completely separate section of the Museum. The tiles from the palace in Samarra, which was the capital of the Abbasids, tiles from Seljuk palaces, and tiles from the Ottoman period on which there are designs of the Kabe are particularly fascinating.

The Ethnographic section of The Museum of Turkish and Islamic Art is significant because it displays examples of Ottoman social life.

Inns and Bazaars

The Grand Bazaar develops not only the eyes but also ideas.
Edmondo de Amicis

Spaced roughly a day's distance apart from each other, inns were constructed to develop the trade routes of the Seljuks in Anatolia. Inns continued to function as such throughout the Ottoman Empire. The Ottomans altered the previous layout of lining up rooms around a courtyard, and built inns according to their own tastes. While the Seljuks constructed their inns with ashlar blocks, the Ottomans utilized bricks and stone. Also, the Ottomans preferred simple gates as opposed to the Seljuks, who built splendid victory gates.

A second courtyard was added to inns that were constructed in Istanbul after the city's conquest. They implemented features that differed from the inns of the Seljuk, such as stables in the basement and mescids in the courtyard. There aren't many examples from the 15th-16th centuries. Inns constructed in the 17th century were organized according to the layout of the land and roads, as we begin to see a more crowded city. Meanwhile, a third courtyard was added which separated the stables from living quarters, with the stables being introduced into this third courtyard.

Three-storey inns that were mainly for guests appear in the 18th century. In the 19th century, these were transformed into an integral part of the city's commercial life. By then, inns were also starting to appear in arcades, which were initially built in Beyoğlu, then on down into Karaköy.

Istanbul's historical inns and caravanserai were for the most part situated inside complexes that were constructed as per orders of the sultan. Though the caravanserai in the Fatih Complex no longer exists, those seen today in the Crown Prince Complex, the Süleymaniye Complex as well as the Atik Valide Complex in Toptaşı, Üsküdar, built by Nurbanu Valide Sultan, all give us a fair idea about the classic Ottoman caravanserai. Constructed by Sultan Mehmed II's Grand Vizier, Mahmud Pasha, the oldest inn still intact in Istanbul is the Kürkçü Inn, near the Grand Bazaar. The two-storey inn has two courtyards, with stores and warehouses on the bottom floor and offices and lodgings on the upper floor.

The courtyard is surrounded with a vaulted gallery. The Galata vaulted bazaar in the Perşembe Pazarı-Galata district also dates back to the period of Sultan Mehmed II. With its four façades and nine domes, the structure has four pillars in the center that support the arches. The nine parts that emerge are covered with hoopless domes. The shops around the historic district of Perşembe Pazarı are no longer in business.

Grand Vizier Rüstem Pasha commissioned Mimar Sinan to construct the Kurşunlu Inn on the northern shore of the Golden Horn in the 16th century. This inn possesses two stories and a courtyard. The Büyük Valide Inn was constructed on the Eminönü-Çakmakçılar Yokuşu by Murad II's mother

Aerial view of the Grand Bazaar, the oldest and largest covered market in town.

There are shops selling copper souvenirs in the Grand Bazaar. One of them is seen in the photograph.

289

Kösem Sultan in the mid-17th century. This structure, which had two floors and three courtyards, is in ruins and has been greatly altered. Constructed by Köprülü Fazıl Ahmed Pasha in Çemberlitaş in the second half of the 17th century, the two-storey Vezir Inn was expanded with some additional wings and so is quite different from its original state. Constructed by Damat İbrahim Pasha in the 18th century, the two-storey Çukur Inn in Nuruosmaniye has a courtyard as well as a basement. One of the inns that is still intact is the Hasan Pasha Inn, located in Beyazıt on Aksaray Caddesi. It was constructed in 1770 by the architect Mustafa Çelebi on the orders of Seis Hasan Pasha. The two-storey inn has a courtyard, but does not have any stables or warehouses, a clear indication that it was built as a lodging inn. The inn has lost its original state because of the road construction and subsequent restoration work, which transformed it into an unrecognizable state. The Büyük Yeni Inn, which has three storeys and a courtyard, and is located on Çakmakçılar Yokuşu, was constructed by Sultan III during the second half of the 18th century. Also built during the 18th century is the Safevi Inn, which is one of the inns of the Grand Bazaar.

There are also some so-called "foundation" inns in Istanbul, the first of which is on the corner of Sultanhamam. Built by the architect Kemaleddin between 1911-18, this seven-storey inn has 50 rooms, including the basement. The Second Foundation Inn is also in Sultanhamam. The Third Foundation Inn, also built by Kemaleddin, has six stories, and is located in Beyoğlu at the intersection of Kuloğlu Sokağı and Turnacı Sokağı. Located in Bahçekapı, the construction of the Fourth Foundation Inn was begun in 1912 by Kemaleddin as well, but the various wars kept it from being completed until the year 1926.

The Fifth Foundation Inn was built in Vefa to accommodate students of the Teacher's School, but was opened in 1923 as the Yüksek Muallim School.

Both the Narmanlı Inn in Beyoğlu and the Değirmen Inn in Eminönü are 19th-century buildings. The Rumeli, Anadolu and Africa Inns in Beyoğlu were all built by the Court Chamberlain of Abdülhamid II, Ragıp Pasha, at the end of the 19th century. Istanbul is home to such other inns as the Abet Inn in Karaköy, the Fransız Inn in Tophane, the Nordstem Inn in Karaköy, the Metro Inn, the Liman Inn in Sirkeci, and the Karaköy Palas in Karaköy. There are also a number of arcades situated next to these inns.

There are arcades in Beyoğlu such as Hacopula Pasaj (1850), Çiçek Pasajı

Egyptian Bazaar. The mosque courtyard and the entrance of the bazaar are seen from one of minarets of the Yeni Mosque.
An aerial view of the Grand Bazaar, which is the size of a town.

(1874), Halep Pasajı (1883) and Aynalı Pasaj (1870). Other historical arcades constructed in the 19th century are those of Tünel Pasajı, Fresko Pasajı in Beyoğlu-Tepebaşı and Aznavur Pasajı in Galatasaray. Now, let's mention something separately about the most famous bazaars in Istanbul, the Grand Bazaar and the Egyptian Bazaar.

The Egyptian Bazaar

The Egyptian Bazaar is the second most important bazaar in Istanbul. The bazaar is within the Yeni Mosque Complex and was designed in 1597 as a source of income for the mosque. The construction of the complex began in 1603 by the mother of Mehmed III, Safiye Sultan. It was halted because of her son's death and the fact that she was no longer the Dowager Sultan. Construction on the site was to be postponed for 59 years, until the mother of Mehmed IV, Hatice Turhan Sultan completed the mosque and bazaar in 1663.

The L-shaped Egyptian Bazaar is illuminated by 88 upper windows. It is called the Egyptian Bazaar because it sold goods from Egypt. The Bazaar has four main gates, two small gates and 86 shops. The two-storey bazaar was built with the main gates at either end and the lower floor vaulted. The rooms on the top floor, which were once used as commercial courts, are accessed via a flight of stairs. While cases between merchants were handled in one room, cases between the public and merchants were tried in the other room. In the early days, the bazaar was allocated to the cotton dealers and herbalists, but today the bazaar is better known for its spice shops. The Egyptian Bazaar burned down in 1691 but it reopened after restoration. It suffered heavy damage in a second fire that struck in 1940. Again, it was reopened after being restored in 1943.

The Grand Bazaar

We can certainly say that one of the most magnificent bazaars in Istanbul is the Grand Bazaar. The foundation of this great bazaar, which extended from Beyazıt to Nuruosmaniye, was laid after the conquest of Constantinople. While establishing the Grand Bazaar, Mehmed II first laid the foundations for the Eski Bedesten and then did the same for the Sandal Bedesten. The sultan had inns and shops built on streets for the wealthy class; then he had them covered. The Grand Bazaar consequently assumed its initial shape, which has survived until today, with several alterations.

Receiving light from the top windows, the upper part of the streets is covered

A view of the Egyptian Bazaar, which was designed as a source of income for Yeni Mosque. This market became a place that mostly sells spices.

with arches and roofs. Each street was turned into a trade center with quilt-makers, armchair and slipper-makers. There are 4,400 shops, and 40 inns with 2,200 rooms situated on more than 50 streets. With its workplaces, mosque, 10 separate mescids, 19 fountains and a hamam, the Grand Bazaar has the appearance of a city. When the Grand Bazaar was first constructed, there were four gates situated in the Eski Bedesten's four façades. The "Sahaflar," "Takkeciler," "Zenneciler" and "Kuyumcular" Gates opened out into main avenues in the immediate vicinity called Çadırcılar, Yorgancılar, Fesciler, Kalpakçılar, Keseciler, Takkeciler and Nuruosmaniye, with a number of side streets merging into them.

The most important streets inside the 50 streets in the bazaar have such names as Kavaflar, Basmacılar, Sandal Bedesteni and Ağa Sokağı. The bazaar was badly damaged during fires that struck in 1546 as well as in 1660, 1695, 1701 and 1750. The Grand Bazaar was also badly damaged during the earthquakes of 1766, 1791, 1826 and 1894. The inns, in particular, were rendered useless. Moreover, subsequent to the 1894 earthquake, two gates with the monogram of Sultan Abdülhamid II embossed above them were built on the two corners of Kalpakçılar Caddesi, which joins Beyazıt and Nuruosmaniye. Hit by two more fires, one in 1943 and the other in 1954, it has since lost much of its old atmosphere. However, despite this, it is continues to be a center where Turkish-jewelry making, carpet-weaving, embroidery and various handicrafts are displayed. It started off with the Eski Bedesten as a foundation in the central area. Later, with the construction of the Sandal Bedesten, it took on the form it has today, albeit with even further expansion. Representing the nucleus of the bazaar, the Eski Bedesten is surrounded with 1.5-meter thick walls and a roof covered with 15 domes. It was established over an area measuring 1,336 m2. Its four gates open onto avenues named Keseciler, Takkeciler, Sahaflar and Kuyumcular. A second covered market, situated to the east, is called Sandal Bedesten.

This covered market is on the side of the Nuruosmaniye Mosque and has a layout similar to that of the Eski Bedesten. In the past, the covered market had four gates but now it has two opening onto Nuruosmaniye Caddesi. The Inner gate opens onto Sandal Bedesten Sokağı. Measuring 40 meters x 32 meters, the Sandal Bedesten is supported by 20 domes and 12 elephantine pillars. Today, the municipality operates it as an auction house. It was called Sandal Bedesten in the past because valuable fabric called "sandal" was sold there.

Grand Bazaar. Housing a labyrinth of streets lined with hundreds of shops, a vast range of touristic items such as leather, Turkish carpets and gold jewelry are sold here.

Waterside Mansions by the Bosphorus

Many happy and sad events were experienced in the waterside mansions constructed like pearls along both sides of the Bosphorus.

here are many waterside mansions, which have attractive architecture and décor, that were built during the Ottoman period. The word "yalı" means "shore" in Greek, but in Turkish it is expressed as a "house on the shore." Let's talk about some of the more important remaining residences. One of the oldest on the Anatolian side of the Bosphorus is the Amcazade Hüseyin Pasha Yalısı. Constructed in 1699, it is unfortunate that only the pool and its "T"-shaped antechamber remain. Its construction was ordered by one of the grand viziers of Mustafa II, Amcazade Hüseyin Pasha. Painted a bright red color, this waterside mansion represents a mature example of Turkish decorative art. The gold leaf ceiling decorations and the engravings on the walls are priceless and are unique heirlooms of history. The recently restored waterside mansion looks as if it is about to slide into the water. The Count Ostrorog Yalısı in Kandilli dates back to 1850 and is one of the most important waterside mansions along the Bosphorus. It was purchased from the Ottoman Foreign Minister Server Pasha by Polish ex-patriate, Lord Leon Valerien Ostrorog, while he was the law advisor to the Ottoman Empire at the turn of the 20th century. This residence, painted in bright red, has always been associated with his name. It later passed into the hands of the Count's wife, who was originally from Czechoslovakia. The famous Turcophile, Pierre Loti also stayed here for a long time as a guest. There is yet another beautiful waterside mansion in Kandilli. It is called the Kıbrıslı Mehmed Emin Pasha Yalısı. Complemented by the extensive woods in the back, this residence has the longest façade of any building along the Bosphorus. It looks just marvelous when looked at from the sea. Mehmed Emin Pasha from Cyprus, who worked in embassies and in governor's offices, was also a grand vizier and the Commodore of the Ottoman Navy. There is a fountain in the center of a grand ballroom of the residence, which was constructed in the 1840s. The columns of the mansion are fashioned from wood. The dome-fitted ceiling is decorated with pictures. At first, the owner of the mansion, Emin Pasha married an English woman, but as they had no children, he married a second time to a woman named Aliye Hanım. The children from his second wife organized literary meetings here, which is why this residence was on everyone's lips. A waterside mansion named the Ethem Pertev Bey Yalısı (1860) was constructed in a neo-classical style and has exquisite woodwork. It, along with the nearby Nazım Pasha Yalıs,

make up two of the most important works of the period. Another yalı that must be mentioned is the striking Efendi Yalısı (1853). The neo-classical style Rukiye Sultan Yalısı, which is otherwise known as the Vecihi Pasha Yalısı, lies in the gulf between Kanlıca and Anadolu Hisarı. There are many such historical waterside mansions between the gulf and Anadolu Hisarı, such as the Hekimbaşı Salih Efendi Yalısı. This residence painted in bright red

Preceding Overleaf: While the Istanbul Bosphorus divides Asia from Europe, the Bosphorus and Fatih Sultan Mehmed Bridges connect the two continents. The Bosphorus Bridge is seen in the foreground.

Map of the Bosphorus Straits of Istanbul.

Waterside mansions in Kanlıca (below).

Istanbul is one of the most beautiful cities on earth with historical mansions on both sides of the Bosphorus, suspension bridges connecting two continents and greenery surrounding the blue waters of the straits. The Fatih Sultan Mehmed Bridge is seen with Rumeli Hisarı in the background.

belonged to Palace Physician Salih Efendi. He lived here until 1895. He used to grow medicinal plants in the garden behind the yalı. Another residence is the Marki Necip Yalısı, also known today as the Demirören Yalısı. The first owner was a French Marquis who later took the Turkish name "Necip Pasha." The Amcazade Yalısı and Zarifi Mustafa Pasha Yalısı, which are located in this area, are from the 18th century. The Nazif Pasha Yalısı was constructed in Vaniköy in 1870. A little further down the shore from the Nail Pasha Yalısı is

the Koç Yalısı, which was constructed by Sedat Hakkı Eldem. Located next to it is the striking Grand Vizier Mahmud Nedim Pasha Yalısı (1870).

The most well known waterside mansion in Çengelköy is the Sadullah Pasha Yalısı. Sadullah Pasha was the Grand Vizier of both Murad V and Abdülhamid II. Thinking that he was close to Murad V, Abdülhamid II appointed the general the post of ambassador to Vienna to get him away from Istanbul. Whatever the case, the general committed suicide in Vienna. The bright red painted

waterside mansion has two storeys. Its wonderfully decorative walls show the influence of Western styles on the architect. The Fethi Ahmed Pasha Yalısı in Kuzguncuk is also an historical waterside mansion. Having served as the Minister in both the War and Commerce Departments, Fethi Ahmed Pasha was the first person to establish a museum in Turkey. He married the sister of Abdülmecid, Aliye Sultan. Constructed in 1812, this waterside residence is known as the Pembe Yalısı, or the Mocanlar Yalısı, because the Mocans were

his grandchildren. There are many other waterside mansions like these on the Anatolian side. These include the 18th-century Çürüksulu Yalısı Salacak, the Edip Efendi Yalısı (1760) in Kandilli, the Abdüllah Yalısı (1815) in Çengelköy, the mid-19th century Recai Ekrem Bey Yalısı in Vaniköy, the 19th-century Ethem İbrahim Pasha Yalısı in Çubuklu as well as the Dehreli İsmail Pasha Yalısı (1890) in Beylerbeyi. Many also dot the European side of the Bosphorus. The most famous of these is the Şerifler Yalısı in Emirgan. The coastal road passes in front of this residence, which was constructed in 1872. Today, the only part that still exists of this historical waterside mansion is the Selamlık Pavilion, along with its pool. Illuminated by 20 windows, the dazzling ceiling décor of this residence, along with its 19th-century-influenced wall ornamentation, is a sight to be seen. It is named "Şerifler Yalısı" for it was once the summer residence of the Sheriff of Mecca.

The waterside mansion where the Egyptian Consulate is housed was constructed as a summer residence by the Khedive's family. It was named the Valide Pasha Yalısı after the very ambitious mother of the Khedive. Apart from this, the 18th-century Yılanlı Yalısı (Mansion with Snakes) is situated next to the Aşiyan Tea Garden in Rumeli Hisarı. Despite the name, of course there are

Ethem Pertev Pasha Yalısı. Situated in Kanlıca, it was built by Saraylı Fatma Hanım in 1860. As it has some fancy woodwork, it is also referred to as the "Süslü Yalı."

Afif Pasha Yalısı. Situated between İstinye to Yeniköy, this Eclectic-style waterside mansion was built by the architect Vallaury for Ahmed Afif Pasha in 1910.

Sadullah Pasha Yalısı. Located in Çengelköy, this Baroque-style mansion on the Bosphorus was built in 1783. It was bought by Esat Pasha in 1851. As his son Sadullah Pasha started to live there, it has always been remembered by his name.

no snakes on the premises. It got its name from an incident where Sultan Mahmud II was admiring the residence while passing in front of it in his caique, and the person next to him, thinking of its owner, said, "My Lord, that residence is infested with snakes." The name has remained since then. The first waterside mansion in Yeniköy is that of the Firdevs-Nuri Baras Yalısı. Next door is the Atıf Pasha Yalısı, which is attractive for its fancy décor and architecture. Atif Pasha was the Head of the Quartermaster General's Department. It is said that he bought it from Ferendiz Hanım, the daughter of Reşid Pasha. The Atif Pasha Yalısı was constructed by the Vallaury on behalf of Ahmed Atif Pasha. After this residence comes that of Crown Prince Burhaneddin Efendi. This delightful palace was constructed using both timber and concrete. It is particularly striking because of the large balcony it has in the middle. Yeniköy resembles a city of waterside mansions. After the Beyazciyan Yalısı and Karateodo Pasha Yalısı, there is the Said Halim Pasha Yalısı, which was recently destroyed in a fire. Said Halim Pasha was the grandson of Mehmed Ali Pasha, who served the Ottoman Empire as Grand Vizier between 1913-17. He was murdered in Italy shortly after his arrival in the country. The Said Halim Pasha Yalısı is currently undergoing restoration after the devastating blaze. The waterside mansions of Faik Bey and Bekir Bey are situated right next to the quay. A little further down the road from here, one sees the Ali Rıza Pasha Yalısı, the Hamapolas Yalısı, which features Venetian-style architecture, while the Kalkavanlar Yalısı is situated next door. A number of foreign embassies in Istanbul constructed their summer

mansions here along the shore, giving Yeniköy a distinct ambiance. The first such residence seen in Yeniköy was the neo-classical style Austrian Embassy, which was built in 1898. It was bought from a rich Armenian named Mığırdıç Cezayırliyan who was a relative of Mustafa Reşid Pasha. He lost all his wealth after the death of Mustafa Reşid Pasha and sold his residence to the Austrian Embassy. After Yeniköy comes Tarabya, where there are several waterside mansions as well. Particularly striking is the Huber Pavilion, which currently serves as the summerhouse of the President of Turkey. This place belonged to Herr Huber, who was the Krupp representative during the Ottoman period. The Finance Minister, Necmeddin Molla bought the Huber Yalısı later only to sell it to Egyptian Princess Kadriye. This residence was donated to a charitable institution when the Princess returned to Egypt, whereby it

Zarif Mustafa Pasha Yalısı. Located in Anadolu Hisarı, this neo-classical waterside mansion was built in the late 17th century. It was named after Zarif Mustafa Pasha, who purchased it in 1848.

Count Ostrorog Yalısı. Originally built in the 19th century, this neo-Classical-style mansion house was bought in 1904 by Polish Count Ostrorog, who worked for the Turkish Ministry of Foreign Affairs.

Situated on Köybaşı Caddesi in Yeniköy, the Faik and Bekir Bey waterside mansions were built in the Eclectic style between 1890-95.

(Backpage) A view form Kanlıca, on the Anatolian side. Forests surround the waterside mansions like green cloth.

Two interior views of the Şerifler Yalısı. Located in Emirgan, it remains a bit inland as the shoreline has since been filled in with other structures. Constructed in the 18th century, it later became a summer residence of the Sheriff of Mecca, Abdullah Pasha.

became the summer pavilion of the President of Turkey in 1980. There is another whitewashed waterside mansion situated in the Tarabya Bay, which is particularly spectacular. During the period of Sultan Abdülaziz, Crown Prince Abdülhamid had his pavilion built on the grounds of this building, which used to belong to the German Embassy. Abdülaziz did not like the architectural style of this wooden structure and had it razed to the ground. Then, when Abdülhamid II ascended to the throne, he granted the land, which was his personal property, to the Germans who later reconstructed the building as their embassy. Sailing past Tarabya Bay, one comes to the Italian Embassy in Kireçburnu. D'Aronco constructed the existing waterside mansion

in the early 20th century, next to a previously constructed building. The French Embassy can be seen a bit further down the way. This was the waterside mansion of Alexander Ipslante, whose family was once very influential in Istanbul. When it was discovered that he was spying against the Ottoman Empire, all his possessions were seized during the reign of Selim III, with this residence being donated to the French by Sultan Selim III. The English Embassy was constructed just beyond this mansion, but was subsequently destroyed in a fire. After Kireçburnu comes Büyükdere, where one can also see an abundance of waterside mansions. The first that comes into sight is the Azaryanlar Yalısı, which is currently the home of the Sadberk

Hanım Museum. Together with the adjacent building, it was recently acquired by the Koç family and converted into a museum. A little further down the road is the Kocataş Yalısı, whose first owner was Abraham Pasha. While we have come this far, let us say something about Abraham Pasha, who owned a wooded area in Beykoz. While he was the Chief Doorkeeper of the Egyptian Khedive, İsmail Pasha, he also used to take care of the Khedive's financial business in Istanbul. In carrying out his duties, he was so highly regarded as to have befriended Sultan Abdülaziz, who promoted him to the rank of Pasha. In return, to express how grateful he was, he presented the sultan with a backgammon set inlaid with ivory, emerald and tortoise-shell. Sultan Abdülaziz is said to have hosted some serious backgammon tournaments, most of which he lost. Abraham Pasha is said to have earned his wealth from beating the sultan in backgammon matches over and over again. In addition to this waterside mansion, the pasha is said to have owned much of the land from Beykoz to Riva. He also had a reputation for being quite a playboy during the period of Abdülhamid II. One day, he fell off his horse and died, whereupon Abdülhamid II nationalized all of his property. Famous for its many varieties of trees, the Abraham Pasha Woods is maintained today by the Beykoz Municipality. Well, there you have it; the owner of the Kocataş Yalısı was none other than our dashing man-about-town, Abraham Pasha.

Hekimbaşı Salih Efendi Yalısı. Located between Anadolu Hisarı and Kanlıca, this waterside residence was built as a harem and "selamlık" in the second half of the 18th century. The residence was named after a previous owner Salih Efendi, who was a physician during the sultanate of Mahmud II. Only the harem, with its three sections, is still extant.

Amcazade Yalısı. Situated in Anadolu Hisarı, this waterside mansion was built by the order of the Grand Vizier Köprülü Hüseyin Pasha in 1699. It is the oldest residence still standing on the Bosphorus. Also known as the Köprülü Yalısı, only the "divanhane" of the mansion's "selamlık" section is still extant.

(Backpage) A view of Tarabya, one of the beautiful bays on the Bosphorus.

305

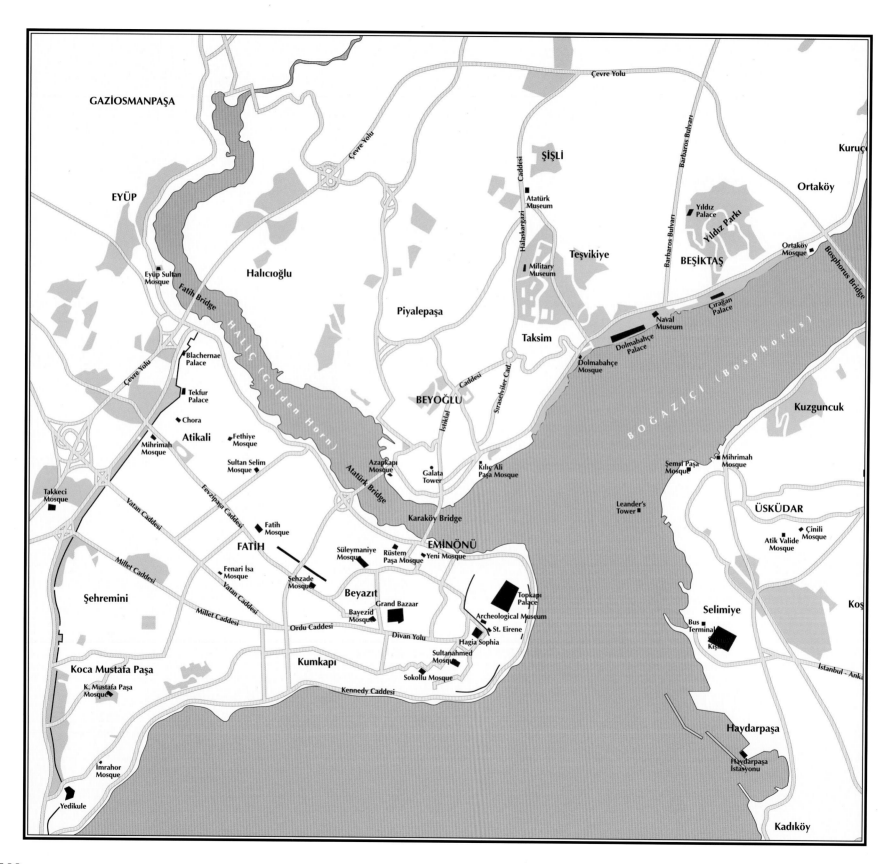

GAZİOSMANPAŞA

ŞİŞLİ

Kuruçe

Ortaköy

EYÜP

Atatürk
Museum

Teşvikiye

BEŞİKTAŞ

Yıldız
Palace

Yıldız Parkı

Ortaköy
Mosque

Bosphorus Bridge

Eyüp Sultan
Mosque

Halıcıoğlu

Military
Museum

Çırağan
Palace

Fatih Bridge

Piyalepaşa

Naval
Museum

Taksim

HALİÇ (Golden Horn)

Dolmabahçe
Palace

Blachernae
Palace

BOĞAZİÇİ (Bosphorus)

Çevre Yolu

Dolmabahçe
Mosque

Tekfur
Palace

BEYOĞLU

Kuzguncuk

Chora

Atikali

Fethiye
Mosque

Mihrimah
Mosque

Azapkapı
Mosque

Şemşi Paşa
Mosque

Mihrimah
Mosque

Sultan Selim
Mosque

Kılıç Ali
Paşa Mosque

Galata
Tower

ÜSKÜDAR

Takkeci
Mosque

Atatürk Bridge

Leander's
Tower

Çinili
Mosque

Atik Valide
Mosque

Koş

Vatan Caddesi

Fevzipaşa Caddesi

Fatih
Mosque

Karaköy Bridge

FATİH

Süleymaniye
Mosque

Rüstem
Paşa Mosque

EMİNÖNÜ

Yeni Mosque

Selimiye

Fenari İsa
Mosque

Şehzade
Mosque

Bus
Terminal

Millet Caddesi

Beyazıt

Grand Bazaar

Topkapı
Palace

Kış

Şehremini

Vatan Caddesi

Bayezid
Mosque

Archeological Museum

St. Eirene

İstanbul - Anka

Millet Caddesi

Ordu Caddesi

Divan Yolu

Hagia Sophia

Kumkapı

Sultanahmed
Mosque

Koca Mustafa Paşa

Sokollu Mosque

K. Mustafa Paşa
Mosque

Kennedy Caddesi

Haydarpaşa

İmrahor
Mosque

Haydarpaşa
İstasyonu

Yedikule

Kadıköy

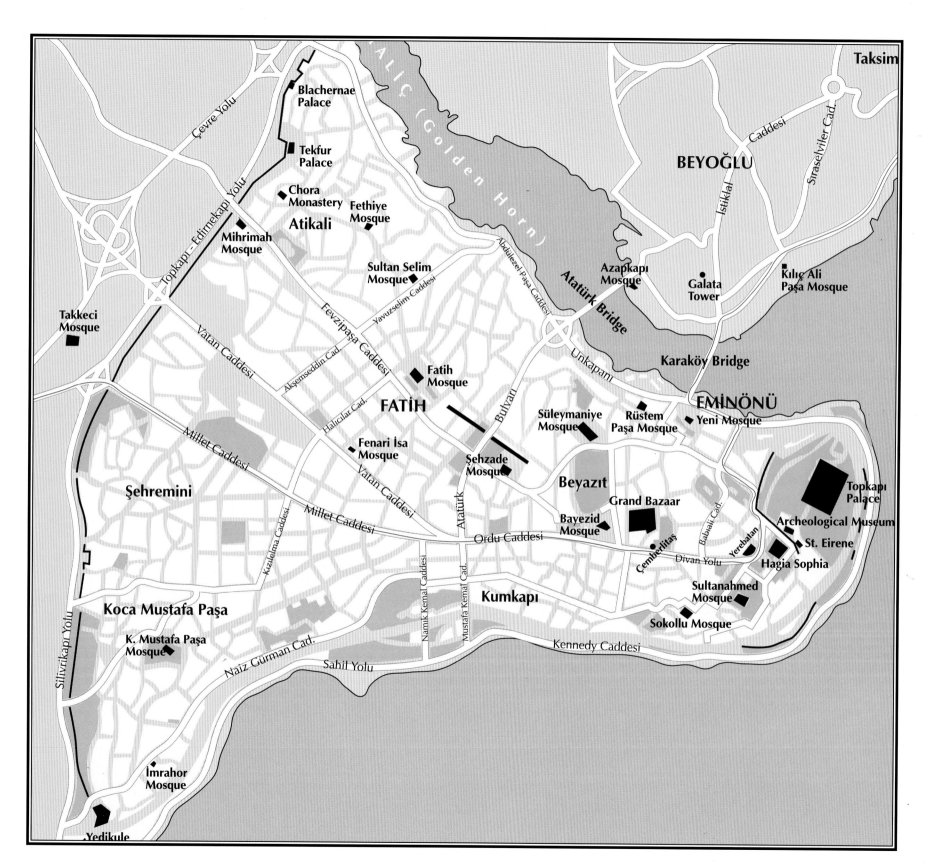

HALİÇ (Golden Horn)

Taksim

BEYOĞLU

Blachernae
Palace

Tekfur
Palace

Çevre Yolu

Chora
Monastery

Fethiye
Mosque

Atikali

Mihrimah
Mosque

Topkapı - Edirnekapı Yolu

Sultan Selim
Mosque

Abdülezel Paşa Caddesi

Azapkapı
Mosque

Atatürk Bridge

Galata
Tower

Kılıç Ali
Paşa Mosque

İstiklal

Sıraselviler Cad.

Caddesi

Takkeci
Mosque

Vatan Caddesi

Fevzipaşa Caddesi

Yavuzselim Caddesi

Aksemseddin Cad.

Fatih
Mosque

FATİH

Unkapanı

Karaköy Bridge

EMİNÖNÜ

Haliclar Cad.

Bulvarı

Süleymaniye
Mosque

Rüstem
Paşa Mosque

Yeni Mosque

Fenari İsa
Mosque

Vatan Caddesi

Şehzade
Mosque

Beyazıt

Grand Bazaar

Topkapı
Palace

Millet Caddesi

Şehremini

Millet Caddesi

Kızılelma Caddesi

Bayezid
Mosque

Babıali Cad.

Archeological Museum

St. Eirene

Ordu Caddesi

Atatürk

Çemberlitaş

Divan Yolu

Yerebatan

Hagia Sophia

Silivrikapı Yolu

Koca Mustafa Paşa

Namık Kemal Caddesi

Mustafa Kemal Cad.

Kumkapı

Sultanahmed
Mosque

Sokollu Mosque

K. Mustafa Paşa
Mosque

Naiz Gürman Cad.

Sahil Yolu

Kennedy Caddesi

İmrahor
Mosque

Yedikule

Roman Emperors

1. Julius Caesar (59-44 B.C.)
2. Augustus (27 B.C.-14 A.D.)
3. Tiberus (A.D. 14-37)
4. Caligula (37-41)
5. Claudius (41-54)
6. Nero (54-68)
7. Galba, Otho, Vitellius (68-69)
8. Vespasian (69-79)
9. Titus (79-81)
10. Domitian (81-96)
11. Nerva (96-98)
12. Traian (98-117)
13. Hadrian (117-38)
14. Antoninus Pius (138-61)
15. Marcus Aurelius (161-80)
16. Commodus (180-92)
17. Septimius Severus (193-211)
18. Caracalla (211-17)
19. Elagabalus (217-22)
20. Alexander Severus (222-35)
21. Maximus Thrax (235-38)
22. Gordian III (238-44)
23. Philippus Arabs (244-49)
24. Decius (249-51)
25. Valerian (253-60)
26. Gallien (260-68)
27. Claudius II Goticus (268-70)
28. Aurelianus (270-75)
29. Probus (276-82)
30. Diocletian (284-305)
31. Constantine I (305-06)
32. Constantine the Great (306-37)
33. Constantius II (337-61)
34. Iulian (361-63)
35. Jovian (363-64)
36. Valens (364-78)
37. Theodosius (378-95)

Byzantine Emperors

7. Arcadius (395-408)
8. Theodosius II (408-50)
9. Marcian (450-57)
10. Leo I (457-74)
11. Leo II (474)
12. Zeno (474-75)
13. Basiliscus (475-76)
14. Zeno (re-crowned) (476-91)
15. Anastasius I (491-518)
16. Justin I (518-27)
17. Justinian I (527-65)
18. Justin II (565-78)
19. Tiberius I Constantine (578-82)
20. Maurice (582-602)
21. Phocas (602-10)
22. Heraclius (610-41)
23. Constantine III and Heraclonas (641)
24. Heraclonas (641)
25. Constans II (641-68)
26. Constantine IV (668-85)
27. Justinian II (685-95)
28. Leontius (695-98)
29. Tiberius II (698-705)
30. Justinian II (re-crowned) (705-11)
31. Philippicus (711-13)
32. Anastasius II (713-15)
33. Theodosius III (715-17)
34. Leo III (717-41)
35. Constantine V (741-75)
36. Leo IV (775-80)
37. Constantine VI (780-97)
38. Irene (797-802)
39. Nicephorus I (802-11)
40. Stauracius (811)
41. Michael I Rhangabe (811-13)
42. Leo V (813-20)
43. Michael II (820-29)
44. Theophilus (829-42)
45. Michael III (842-67)
46. Basil I (867-86)
47. Leo VI (886-912)
48. Alexander (912-13)
49. Constantine VII (913-59)
50. Romanus I (920-44)
51. Romanus II (959-63)
52. Nicephorus II Phocas (963-69)
53. John I Tzimisces (969-76)
54. Basil II (976-1025)
55. Constantine VIII (1025-28)
56. Romanus III Argyrus (1028-34)
57. Michael IV (1034-41)
58. Michael V (1041-42)
59. Zoe and Theodora (1042)
60. Constantine IX Monomachus (1042-55)
61. Theodora (re-crowned) (1055-56)
62. Michael VI (1056-57)
63. Isaac I Comnenus (1057-59)
64. Constantine X Dukas (1059-67)
65. Romanus IV Diogenes (1068-71)
66. Michael VII (1071-78)
67. Nicephorus III Botaniates (1078-81)
68. Alexius I Comnenus (1081-1118)
69. John II Comnenus (1118-43)
70. Manuel I Comnenus (1143-80)
71. Alexius II Comnenus (1180-83)
72. Andronicus I Comnenus (1183-85)
73. Isaac II Angelus (1185-95)
74. Alexius III Angelus (1195-1203)
75. Isaac II (re-crowned) and Alexius IV Angelus (1203-04)
76. Alexius V Murtzuphlus (1204)
77. Theodore I Lascaris (1204-22)
78. John III. Dukas Vatatzes (1222-54)
79. Theodore II Lascaris (1254-58)
80. John IV Lascaris (1258-61)
81. Michael VIII Palaeologus (1259-82)
82. Andronicus II Palaeologus (1282-1328)
83. Andronicus III Palaeologus (1328-41)
84. John V Palaeologus (1341-91)
85. John VI Cantacuzenus (1347-54)
86. Andronicus IV Palaeologus (1376-79)
87. John VII Palaeologus (1390)
88. Manuel II Palaeologus (1391-25)
89. John VIII Palaeologus (1425-48)
90. Constantine XI Palaeologus (1449-53)

Ottoman Sultans

1. Osman Gazi (1299-1324)
2. Orhan Gazi (1324-62)
3. Murad I (1362-89)
4. Yıldırım Bayezid (1389-1402)
   Interregnum (1402-13)
5. Çelebi Mehmed (1413-21)
6. Murad II (1421-51)
7. Mehmed II (1451-81)
8. Bayezid II (1481-1512)
9. Selim I (1512-20)
10. Süleyman I (1520-66)
11. Selim II (1566-74)
12. Murad III (1574-95)
13. Mehmed III (1595-1603)
14. Ahmed I (1603-17)
15. Mustafa I (1617-18 and 1622-23)
16. Osman II (1618-22)
17. Murad IV (1623-40)
18. İbrahim (1640-48)
19. Mehmed IV (1648-87)
20. Süleyman II (1687-91)
21. Ahmed II (1691-95)
22. Mustafa II (1695-1703)
23. Ahmed III (1703-30)
24. Mahmud I (1730-54)
25. Osman III (1754-57)
26. Mustafa III (1757-74)
27. Abdülhamid I (1774-89)
28. Selim III (1789-1807)
29. Mustafa IV (1807-08)
30. Mahmud II (1808-39)
31. Abdülmecid (1839-61)
32. Abdülaziz (1861-76)
33. Murad V (1876)
34. Abdülhamid II (1876-1909)
35. Mehmed V Reşad (1909-18)
36. Mehmed Vahideddin VI (1918-22)